W9-AMX-229

Critical Essays on Phillis Wheatley

PS
866
.W5
Z583
1982

Critical Essays on Phillis Wheatley

William H. Robinson

G. K. Hall & Co. • Boston, Massachusetts

Salem Academy and College
Gramley Library
Winston-Salem, N.C. 27108

Copyright © 1982 by William H. Robinson

Library of Congress Cataloging in Publication Data
Main entry under title:

Critical essays on Phillis Wheatley.

(Critical essays on American literature)
Includes bibliographical references and index.
1. Wheatley, Phillis, 1753–1784—Criticism and interpretation—Addresses, essays, lectures.
I. Robinson, William Henry, 1922– II. Series.
PS866.W5Z583 811'.1 81-23757
ISBN 0-8161-8336-8 AACR2

This publication is printed on permanent/durable acid-free paper
MANUFACTURED IN THE UNITED STATES OF AMERICA

CRITICAL ESSAYS ON AMERICAN LITERATURE

This series seeks to publish the most important reprinted criticism on writers and topics in American literature along with, in various volumes, original essays, interviews, bibliographies, letters, manuscript sections, and other materials brought to public attention for the first time. William H. Robinson's present volume is a remarkable contribution to the study of Black American writers. It contains over sixty selections, ranging from the early comments of such contemporaries of Wheatley as George Washington, Benjamin Franklin, and Thomas Jefferson, to the best of modern critical articles, to a section of original essays by Albertha Sistrunk, John C. Shields, Mukhtar Ali Isani, and Henry Louis Gates, Jr. There is also an original poem, "Phillis," by Naomi Long Madgett. In all it is a fitting tribute to the first important Black writer in this country. We are confident that this collection will make a permanent and significant contribution to American literary study.

JAMES NAGEL, GENERAL EDITOR

Northeastern University

ARISE, my soul, on wings enraptur'd, rise
To praise the monarch of the earth and skies,
Whose goodness and beneficence appear
As round its centre moves the rolling year.
Or when the morning glows with rosy charms,
Or the sun slumbers in the ocean's arms:
Of light divine be a rich portion lent
To guide my soul, and favour my intent.
Celestial muse, my arduous flight sustain,
And raise my mind to a seraphic strain!

From "Thoughts on the Works of
Providence" (1773)

CONTENTS

PREFACE

Although Phillis Wheatley (1753?–1784) has been discussed, propagandized, praised, and denigrated for over two hundred years, the appropriate history of her criticism does not earnestly develop as such until quite recent times. Earlier, especially in the eighteenth century but continuing through the nineteenth century, the great bulk of these Wheatley notices, appearing in diaries, letters, newspapers, footnotes, etc., were fragmentary and casual. Rarely did any of these comments reach a page or more in length.

Because, early on, there was not much original research into Wheatley's writings and life, much of this bulk was wearisomely repetitive. Writers seemed never to tire of telling and retelling "the Phillis Wheatley story." Curiously, however, for all of its repetitiveness, the earlier Wheatley critical history managed to engender a perfect welter of bewilderingly contradictory and wrong biographical and bibliographical data. Happily, a few scholars, taking Wheatley more seriously than others, continued to unearth and publish new or little known poems, letters, and biographical information. It was because of the persistence of these scholars that Wheatley criticism finally, in recent times, took the form of full-fledged essay observations.

The history of Wheatley criticism, then, has shaped the format of this book. What is intended here is an illustration of the evolution of this history from its time of brief, often "interpretive" comments, to its present day status of full-length, documented essays. While they are otherwise variously repetitive, many early remarks do have the virtue of displaying some of Wheatley's poems. Efforts have been made editorially to regulate this matter. Verse selections—good and bad—have been retained for the consideration of those readers new to Wheatley. When a verse selection is repeated, it is to show how such a selection can provoke differing reactions by different writers. Early comments are arranged chronologically according to known dates of composition; reprinted essays are arranged according to dates of publication; original essays are arranged according to dates of receipt. An abbreviated chronology of the highlights in Wheatley's life is included.

For assistance in assembling this book, I am indebted beyond the costs of permission fees to several colleagues and cooperative publishers. I am especially grateful to scholars who wrote pieces for this collection. As in the past, I owe much to the often extraordinary help by staff members of the Massachusetts Historical Society, the American Antiquarian Society, the Medford (Massachusetts) Historical Society, the Newport Historical Society, the Rhode Island Historical Society, and the libraries of Harvard, Brown, Duke, and other universities, including Cambridge and the University of London. Thanks are hereby tendered, again, to considerate administrative persons at Rhode Island College for generous Faculty Research Grant monies and for teaching load concessions. Thanks are also due to Dr. Henry Louis Gates, Jr., one of the driving forces at Yale University who are arranging for the publications of important Afro-American literary information. My editor, Dr. James Nagel, already knows how very much I am obligated to him. Whatever success this book might enjoy must be shared among these and other persons, including D. C. J. R. Whatever errors are found are, of course, my own.

INTRODUCTION

On Being Young, Gifted, and Black

William H. Robinson, Jr.

Since October of 1770, when she published her much reprinted eulogy on the death of the celebrated Reverend George Whitefield, English Methodist evangelist, the name of Phillis Wheatley, African-born, Boston-educated slave poet, has been nationally and internationally known. Her name has appeared in a variety of publications—newspapers, broadsides, pamphlets, magazines, biographical dictionaries, historical and general reference works; and in the letters and writings of such prominent Americans as Benjamin Rush, Benjamin Franklin, John Paul Jones, Thomas Jefferson, George Washington, and others. Her name was familiar to Thomas Clarkson, the English abolitionist. Another English abolitionist, Granville Sharp, personally escorted her on a 1773 summer tourist trek of London sights. Wheatley's name was known to several English peers: the countess of Huntingdon (Selina Hastings), the earl of Dartmouth (William Legge), Lord Lyttelton, Lord Lincoln (Henry Fiennes), and others. She was known also to ranking French personalities. Voltaire, atypically, praised her poetry as "tres-bons vers anglais";[1] the zealous Jacobin, Henri Grégoire, wrote an early biographical sketch;[2] the German zoologist, Johan F. Blumenbach, wrote favorably of her poems.[3] In 1949, Leone Piccioni discussed her work in his native Italian. Writing in Spanish, Venezuelan born Mulatto, Francisco de Miranda recorded his impressions of her in his diary for 1783–1784.[4] Phillis Wheatley is mentioned in a recent book written in Dutch.[5] Her collected volume of poems was commended by a Scots critic.[6] A Ghanaian cleric edited a 1905 book that devoted a chapter to Phillis Wheatley.[7] Of course, Wheatley's name is most especially treasured among her fellow Afro-Americans, who, with some notable recent exceptions, point to her with pride.

To be sure, Wheatley's name did not achieve international fame without concomitant controversy. As a young, gifted, and black woman, Phillis has, quite innocently, provoked veritable schools of criticism—by racists, abolitionists, militant black Americans, and, encouragingly, steadfast scholars. With the exception of most scholarly studies, however, each of these groups has often put forward contradictory and wrong claims about the life and work of this slave poet of colonial Boston.

Racists writings are, whatever else, predictably predictable, but, judging from some of the comments of most other kinds of critics, it seems clear that many of them too were indifferent to the hard facts of Wheatley's peculiar situation. These writers are not much concerned with establishment of the social, political, literary, and psychological tensions that tightly surrounded Phillis every day of her life; or with documenting the surprising bulk of verse and letters that she composed, revised, published, or left in manuscript; or with gleaning supportable revelations of her personality. Instead, many of these writers have been more interested in citing her as an example of their own respective notions of black inferiority or black equality.

Readers's tastes being so widely varied, it is understandable that their aesthetic regard for Wheatley's writings would vary accordingly; that is as it should be. But the empirical matter of biographical and bibliographical data has also varied, often inexplicably. That is decidedly not as it should be. The array of these critics's remarks—disparate and antagonistic—has led to some confusion. There is, for example, disagreement over such easily verifiable matters as the time she arrived in Boston from Africa; the time she left Boston for a brief visit to London; the time of her manumission; the time of the publication of her volume of poems; the time of her death—to mention only some of the many areas of presently confused Wheatley information.

Almost from the beginning of Wheatley commentary she has been the victim of gross misdatings. No less an authority than John Wheatley, her master, wrote a thumbnail biographical sketch of her that began with "Phillis was brought from Africa to America in the year 1761 between Seven and Eight years of age. . . ." This sketch is prefaced to one, but not all of the original London editions, and almost every subsequent American reprinted edition of *Poems on Various Subjects, Religious and Moral.* Nevertheless, there are those who have written that "Phillis was brought to this country in a slave ship in the early days of 1792";[8] or that she was sold into slavery in 1760;[9] or that she was sold in the Boston slave market of 1759;[10] or that she was purchased in 1770.[11]

As was clear from many notices published in more than a half dozen New England newspapers, Phillis Wheatley left Boston for London on May 8, 1771. Beginning as early as September 16 of the same year, almost as many newspapers also reported her return to Boston. Yet, over the years, the dates of Wheatley's departure from and return to Boston have been otherwise reported. In 1865 William Wells Brown wrote that Phillis sailed for England "at the age of twenty-one years" (i.e., in 1775 by his reckoning of her chronology).[12] *Appleton's Cyclopedia of American Biography* of 1889 said she visited England in 1774. In 1859 Rufus Griswold, historian, claimed that she left Boston in 1772 and returned from London in 1773. Another writer insisted that she visited London in 1771 or 1772, and returned to Boston in 1775.[13] She arrived in London in

1773, where she achieved eminence and remained until 1777, when she returned to Boston, said another.[14]

In her colorful but not always accurate book, *Old Boston Days and Ways* (1909), Mary Crawford was confident that when Phillis left Boston, she was under the protection of Nathaniel, the son of her master, and Nathaniel's wife; but Nathaniel did not marry Mary Enderby of London's Thames Street until November of 1773, by which time Phillis had been back in Boston for a month.

The bottom lines on the title page of the original London editions of Wheatley's poems explain that the book was printed "for A[rchibald] Bell, Bookseller, Aldgate; and sold by Messrs Cox and Berry, King-Street, Boston, M DCC LXXIII." Reprinted editions include the same publication date. But this has not stood in the way of several writers who have assigned other publication dates. In 1794, only ten years after Wheatley had died, James Angell, the most prominent publisher of Baltimore, wrote that her volume was published in 1772.[15] This date was repeated by several later writers, including the French abolitionist Henri Grégoire, who said in 1808, "En 1772, à dix-neuf ans, Phillis Wheatley publia un petit volume de poésies. . . ." It must be noted that Grégoire was wholly dependent upon "M. Giraud consul de France à Boston" for his information. As Giraud claimed that he personally knew Phillis's husband, John Peters, his information would seem to be reliable. The fact is, however, that Giraud relayed to Grégoire several points of misinformation. Grégoire's misdatings were picked up by his English translator, D. B. Warden, in 1810. Curiously, both Grégoire and Warden cite a footnote that spells out both the place and publication date of the book of poems—"London, 1773." In 1833, black historian George B. Williams indicated that Wheatley published a "first volume" in 1770 in Boston. This notion was repeated by writers in 1900 who said "Phillis's poems were first published in Boston in 1770. But her admiring friends prevailed upon her to bring out a second and better edition in London in 1773."[16] Another historian held that the volume appeared in 1774.[17] As late as 1976, still another historian believed that 1770 was the year of publication.[18]

The confused dating of Wheatley's manumission is less intolerable than other biographical confusions because only quite recently has authoritative documentation become publicly available. The absence of such confirmation, however, can hardly explain by itself the array of dates that has been put forth. Following information conveyed to him in a letter from Boston, Grégoire supposed that "son maitre l'affranchit en 1775." D. N. Shurtleff reckoned that Wheatley was freed after March of 1778, when her master, John Wheatley, died.[19] "Phillis was emancipated by her master at the age of twenty-one years," (i.e., in 1775) said William Wells Brown. In 1884, a reviewer of a reprinted edition reported that, before she left Boston for London in 1773, "her master emancipated her, thus gracefully putting a finishing stroke to generous treatment of years."[20] In 1964, another manumission date was introduced: ". . . 1772, the year that Mrs. Susanna Wheatley freed her."[21]

Still other dates for the time of Wheatley's freedom have been suggested, but certainty was revealed only recently. In 1974, Kenneth Silverman published four newly unearthed manuscript letters written by Wheatley to the millionaire Christian philanthropist of London, John Thornton. In the last of these letters, dated from Boston on October 30, 1774, she mentioned that her master had freed her "about 3 months before the death of my dear mistress & at her desire, as well as his own humanity."[22] She continued by asserting that even if her master had not freed her, she would willingly submit to servitude, as long as she could be free in Christ. Now if it were true that she had indeed been freed at the time she reported to Thornton, that would mean that, since Mrs. Susanna Wheatley had died on March 3, 1774, Phillis Wheatley had been a free woman from about December, 1773, or January, 1774. But in writing, Phillis may really have been anxious to convey an emphasis on Christian preoccupation, thereby appearing properly deferential to Thornton's enormous prestige and influence. She was very much aware of his well-known and strict Calvinist strictures, for he had written her a letter warning her about the unchristian folly of heeding the worldly acclaim of her touted poetic genius.

The truth is that Phillis Wheatley had been freed, but not "about 3 months before the death of my dear mistress." Indeed, she was a free person for almost six months before the death of her mistress. In a letter dated "Boston, Oct. 18, 1773," newly released from a private collection, Wheatley had written to Colonel David Wooster of New Haven that she had been freed "since my return to America" (i.e., since between, at least September 16 and October 18, 1773). Moreover, as this letter reveals, she was freed not only by the desire of her mistress, nor merely at the humanity of her master. The letter reads: "Since my return to America my Master has at the desire of my friends in England given me my freedom." She goes on in the letter to rehearse several details of the terms of her manumission. She would be continuously concerned with sales of her volume, as noted in her letters to her black friend Obour Tanner, a domestic living in nearby Newport, Rhode Island; but in the letter to Wooster, she is especially solicitous of receiving funds from his sales of her volume in New Haven, "as I am now upon my own footing and whatever I get by this is entirely mine. It is the Chief I have to depend upon. . . ."[23] Also, while the sincere and profound and lifelong Christian piety of Phillis Wheatley is not to be questioned for a moment, it seems nevertheless true that she was not as indifferent about remaining in slavery as she indicated to Thornton in this letter. As much is perfectly clear from a genteel sarcastic antislavery, protest letter she wrote and published in several New England papers in the spring of 1774; [24] and from a poem she wrote on

Wooster's death and mailed to his widow on July 15, 1778. In this eulogy, she writes:

> . . . But how, presumptuous shall we hope to find
> Divine acceptance with th'Almighty mind—
> While yet (O deed ungenerous!) they disgrace
> And hold in bondage Afric's blameless race?[25]

When one is young, gifted, and black, and determined to survive, one is sometimes called upon to wear different faces in different places for the same reasons.

According to the accounts of some writers, Phillis Wheatley has died over a half dozen different times, although her obituary, noting her death in Boston on December 5, 1784, was published several times in New England periodicals. Yet, following his informant, Grégoire wrote ". . . elle perit de chagrin en 1787." D. B. Warden translated this as ". . . in 1780 she died of a broken heart." Warden's date was copied by several later commentators, including Abigail Mott in 1828 and F. Freeman in 1837. Rufus Griswold said she died in 1794. In 1863, Mrs. William Beecher of Brookfield, Massachusetts, gave copies of seven Wheatley manuscript letters to the Massachusetts Historical Society. In an accompanying letter explaining how the letters came into her possession, Mrs. Beecher declared that Phillis "lived some twelve or fifteen years after her marriage and died in 1794 or 5, a little more than forty years of age."[26] Phillis Wheatley died in 1796, wrote John Daniels, who referred readers curious to know more about the poet to a book by William Wells Brown, who, in turn, said she died in 1780. In 1967, a social historian averred that she died in 1782,[27] while, in 1974, another writer reported 1786 as Wheatley's death date.[28]

A 1964 notice claimed that Wheatley died in childbirth,[29] while, four years later, another source said she was survived by her third child.[30] The 1834 memoir of Wheatley said, "A grand niece of Phillis's benefactress, passing up Court-Street, met the funeral of an adult and a child: a bystander informed her they were bearing Phillis Wheatley to that silent mansion. . . ." There are other areas of variously dated Wheatley biography and bibliography—one Hannibal Wheatley managed to confuse his own genealogy by claiming the wrong set of Wheatleys as his forebears who, he said, owned Phillis.

Mistakes of another kind were made by a succession of writers who were more preoccupied with Phillis's race and color than with her actual work and life. Thomas Jefferson wrote that "implacable barriers" between whites and blacks could probably never end without the extermination of one or the other race. Jefferson also wrote that blacks prefer whites to their own kind as uniformly as "Ouran-outans" prefer to mate with black women over females of their own species. Jefferson doubted that a black could be found anywhere who was capable of tracing and comprehending the investigations of Euclid. Having written these and similar statements in his *Notes on Virginia* (1784), it was predictable, perhaps incumbent upon him to dismiss the otherwise anomolous "Phyllis Whately, [*sic*]." (Jefferson's library contained a copy of Wheatley's poems in which her name is spelled correctly.) Wheatley's poems, he wrote, are "below the dignity of criticism."

Against the approval and recommendation of Wheatley's poetry in a pamphlet published by Benjamin Rush in 1773, Richard Nisbet, in a pamphlet of later that year, argued that blacks were inferior; and that all Rush had done to refute that belief was no more than to "give a single example of a negro girl writing a few silly poems. . . ." *The Antheneum Journal and Foreign Literature, Science and Arts* for 1835 seemed pleased to inform its readers that all of Wheatley's learning had not made her an uppity black: to her credit, "she remained as humble as before." Critic James Parton, in an 1878 essay, leveled a salvo of racist charges against Wheatley—and all blacks—when, commending Jefferson's evaluation of Wheatley, he went on to add that, from Jefferson's time to his own, "we cannot yet name one negro of pure blood who has taken the first, the second, the third, or the tenth rank in business, politics, art, literature, scholarship, science or philosophy. To the present hour, the negro has contributed nothing to the intellectual resources of man. . . ."[31]

Twenty years later, the popular literary historian, Moses Coit Tyler, found it academically curious that Wheatley's name should have survived as it did. "A glance at what she wrote will show there is no adequate basis for such tradition," he wrote, patronizing her poems and dismissing her letters as "pious and almost infantile platitudes expressed in extremely stilted English."[32] William J. Long expressed open dismay in 1913 at not finding what he expected in Wheatley's verses. Knowing that she was African born, he expected her to recall poetically "the wild, free life of the tribe—chant of victory, wail of defeat, leaping flames, gloom of forest, cries of wild beasts. . . ." Looking for the outbursts of a stock African, he found only the polite poems of Afro-American Phillis Wheatley.

Despite the fact that other, concerned camps of abolitionists and some modern militant black American writers have cited and appropriated Wheatley for their own purposes, she has nevertheless managed to survive to accrue a respectable reputation, thanks largely to the work of persistent scholars.

A member of the French antislavery organization, Amis des Noirs, Jean de Marsillac found it useful in his book, *Le More-Lack* (1789), to praise Wheatley's work as distinguished for its gentle, humane sentiments. It was clearly the abolitionary stance of Henri Grégoire, another member of Amis des Noirs, that prompted him to write a sympathetic biographical sketch of Wheatley, and prose renderings of several of her poems from English to French. Like-minded was the English abolitionist, Thomas Clarkson, who also quoted Wheatley's poems in his prize-winning *Essay on the Slavery and Commerce of the Human Species, Particularly the African* (1786). Two days after Wilberforce moved his first motion against the English slave trade in the House of Commons, the July 14, 1789, issue of the London daily newspaper, *The Diary,* reprinted Wheatley's poem "An Hymn to Humanity," and in its May 16 issue of the same year, it reprinted her poem to the earl of Dartmouth.[33]

American abolitionists long made special use of the black poetess of Boston. Plagued by a chilling guilt at having once been a successful dealer in black slaves, Thomas Branagan confessed all in an expiatory volume in 1804, citing Wheatley flatteringly if defensively. William Lloyd Garrison's *Liberator* came into being expressly to battle American slavery; it was thus no surprise to note that its issues through 1832 reprinted almost all of the poems from her 1773 volume. Nor was it surprising that it encouraged its readers to purchase the 1834 and 1835 reprinted editions. For years, the newspaper listed Wheatley's book among its antislavery publications, always, of course, in behalf of the cause. The October 27, 1837, issue, for instance, advertised the anonymous *Memoir of Phillis Wheatley* (1834; by Margaretta Matilda Odell) as revealing "what the irrepressible aspirations of a slave accomplished." This same issue reminds its readers of the value of purchasing the book of poems, "it will be well to have them always at hand, that we may have some conception of the amount of genius which slavery is murdering. . . ."

Among American blacks there has been a sustained interest in Phillis Wheatley from the beginning. Her poems must assuredly have been read with pride by some of the literate blacks in contemporary New England, New York, and Philadelphia. Long Island–born slave, versifier Jupiter Hammon acknowledged his Boston counterpart in his wearying broadside, "Address to Miss Phillis Wheatly [*sic*] Ethiopian poetess, in Boston, who came from Africa at eight years of age and soon became acquainted with the Gospel of Jesus Christ" (1778). Wheatley's lifelong black friend, Obour Tanner, gladly served as agent and bookseller, drawing from the literate blacks and whites of her Newport, Rhode Island home. Incidentally, the number of literate colonial blacks is surprising. For instance, Obour Tanner was only one of seventeen Newport blacks who subscribed to the Reverend Samuel Hopkins's two-volume abstract work, *System of Doctrines* (1793). Hopkins, on the other hand, is on record as having purchased a copy of Wheatley's book when it cost "3s. 4d. L.M. Bound" (i.e., 3 shillings, 4 pence, legal money) despite the known fact that he did not like any kind of poetry instead of the more usual price of 2s. 6d.

The 1801 reprinting of Wheatley's volume concludes with several pages of subscribers's names, including those of such prominent blacks as James Forten, and the reverends Richard Allen and Absalom Jones, all of Philadelphia. John B. Russwurm, publisher (1827–29) of the first black American newspaper, *Freedom's Journal,* printed several references to the Boston slave poet. The well-known fugitive slave minister, the Reverend James W. Pennington, sometimes of Connecticut, wrote of Wheatley in his introduction to *Prose and Poetry,* a small—and dull—collection of essays and verses by Ann Plato, as though his readers were as familiar with Phillis as he was. (What Pennington may not have realized is that Ann Plato of Hartford had appropriated without acknowledgment several lines of Wheatley's verse.) "The Committee of Colored Gentlemen" of Boston published an 1844 history of blacks and Indians, and took care to feature remarks on Wheatley and her work.[34] Robert T. Greener, the first black to graduate from Harvard College (1870), published a survey article in the *National Quarterly Review* (1880) that professed incredulity at the little that supposedly informed whites knew about black American life, even about a black as otherwise widely known as Phillis Wheatley.

Some blacks have contributed new or little known Wheatley information. Besides compiling an early bibliography of Wheatley, bibliophile Arthur A. Schomburg has also collected several gift books that Wheatley received while she was in London. These books are today in the famous Schomburg Collection in Harlem, New York. Thomas Oxley published an unknown Wheatley letter,[35] and T. T. Fletcher discovered three manuscript poems in 1933; regrettably, he did not publish them—as Robert Kuncio would do in 1970.[36] Historian Benjamin Quarles reprinted a little known Wheatley letter that was first published in 1839 by the poet John Greenleaf Whittier.[37] In his *Negro in the American Revolution* (1961), Quarles reminded his readers that American naval hero John Paul Jones submitted some of his verses to "the Celebrated Phillis, the African Favorite of the Muses and Apollo. . . ." Quarles also pointed out that Benjamin Franklin had written of his summer, 1773, visit with Phillis while the two of them were in London. In 1972, federal archivist Dr. Sarah D. Jackson published three newly unearthed Wheatley manuscript letters addressed to the countess of Huntingdon in London and Wales, and two other manuscript letters from Mrs. Susanna Wheatley to the countess. Until the appearance of these letters, every Wheatley critic, following earlier comments, had believed that Phillis had been greeted and feted personally by the countess in London. These letters make it clear, however, that Phillis Wheatley never saw her ladyship at all.[38]

To be sure, not all black criticism has been uniformly favorable. In the tumultuous 1960s and shortly thereafter, there appeared a group of black American writers who were impatient with what they regarded as Wheatley's utter lack of relevance to the struggles of black America. Leroi Jones jeered at her work as "ludicrous departures from the huge black voices that splintered southern nights."[39] Another writer lamented that, unlike Freneau, Phillis failed to use her poetic gifts to call a new black nation into being.[40] Another writer found that, unsure of her own identity and personality, Wheatley was too derivative of Alexander Pope; she should have sung an African song.[41]

African born, Wheatley has modern African critics who are no less favorable. Africanist Edward W. Blyden announced his open contempt for her work when he delivered a speech as president of Liberia College in 1881.[42] South African-born critic Ezekiel Mphalele has self-consciously confessed embarrassment at having to mention her work at all.[43] Ghanaian poet and novelist Kofi Awoonor noticed only that Wheatley's style was "tediously sententious.[44]

Other black Americans have countered such charges. Even without resort to a consideration of Wheatley's various contexts, Arthur P. Davis has found that the text of her poetry is clearly and markedly race conscious.[45] Roseann Bell recognized in 1979 that Wheatley can be fairly evaluated only in terms of contemporary colonial realities.[46] This insight was shared by Gloria T. Hull in the same year in a piece that suggested that there is much more to Phillis Wheatley than her critics have hitherto seen or cared to see.[47]

Happily, other scholars were among Wheatley's readers. After the Civil War, after the *de jure* abolition of domestic and foreign slave trading, sundry literary caretakers kept Wheatley's name alive in several ways. Even before this time, in 1863–64, the *Proceedings of the Massachusetts Historical Society* devoted many of its pages to the continuous printing of Wheatlyana. In this year, for instance, were published a newly found Wheatley manuscript poem; a facsimile of her handwriting; two biographical sketches; seven Wheatley letters from manuscript; an account of American reprintings of the 1773 volume through 1863; and documentation of Phillis's husband practicing law in Boston courtrooms. Indeed, the Massachusetts Historical Society has remained a steadfast printer of Wheatley information ever since. In 1864 a member of that Society, Charles Deane, reprinted the seven Wheatley letters separately at his own expense.

Charles F. Heartman published the first collected edition of the poems and letters, and also a partial bibliography in 1915. The 1773 edition of Wheatley's poetry has been reprinted almost two dozen times in America. Historian Carl Bridenbaugh set the traditional date of Wheatley's long supposed first published poem of 1770 back three years earlier in "The First Published Poem of Phillis Wheatley," in the December, 1969, issue of the *New England Quarterly*. This periodical has also published other important Wheatley information, including five recently "discovered" manuscript poems, edited by Robert C. Kuncio in June of 1970. In 1975, Robert Twombly was the first of several to reprint an important, hitherto unknown antislavery protest letter written by Wheatley and published in several New England newspapers in the spring of 1774. Since 1976, Mukhtar Ali Isani has published more than a half dozen Wheatley articles, including two new letters, a poem, and several variants of poems from the 1773 volume. In 1966, Julian Mason showed that Wheatley had written a grand total of eighty-seven titles of poems; he reprinted fifty-four of these, including eight variants of poems from the 1773 volume. He also published and reprinted nine letters. Today, it is known that she wrote titles for at least 145 poems, including over two dozen variants from the 1773 volume alone, and almost two dozen miscellaneous poems. Also extant are nearly two dozen notes and letters written by Phillis. Not all of the poems she is known to have written have been published; some of them have been surely lost. But Wheatley scholarship is an ongoing affair, and more of her poems and letters may yet turn up.

While it is useful to note how often and how deliberately this black poet has been overlooked in discussions of American literature, a survey of her confused critical history makes it clear that, all things considered, Phillis Wheatley has enjoyed a good share of selected representation. She is referred to in several eighteenth-century diaries, books, and letters. Her volume was listed in the 1790 *New Select Catalogue of Benjamin Guild's Circulating Library*, along with *The Iliad*, *The Odyssey*, Samuel Johnson's *Lives of the English Poets*, the works of Shakespeare, and other prominent authors. Three of her titles were cited in Samuel Kettell's pioneering anthology, *Specimens* [*sic*] *of American Poetry* (1829). She has been represented in anthologies edited by Rufus Griswold in 1856 and 1859; by Caroline May in 1868; by Edward Steadman and Ellen Hutchins in 1888; and by others throughout the later nineteenth century. In this century, it is not unusual for selections of her work to appear in American literature textbooks.

Thanks to sound and persistent Wheatley scholarship, her name and fame are becoming more widely known and valued. She has been the subject of several recent doctoral dissertations.[48] In one place, it was advertised that an authentic Wheatley letter, signed by her, could be purchased for $900.[49] and that a copy of her original London volume would cost $665. Elsewhere it is noted that in 1979, a copy of Wheatley's London volume could be purchased for $1,000.[50] An edition including all her known poems (and variants) and letters is forthcoming.

Being young, gifted, and black may indeed have its peculiarly vexing problems; but, as with Phillis Wheatley, it may also sometimes yield its unique satisfactions, however long delayed.

Notes

1. E. D. Seeber, "Phillis Wheatley," *Journal of Negro History*, 24, No. 3 (July, 1939), 259–62.

2. *De La Littérature Des Nègres ou Recherches sur leurs facultés intellectuelles, leurs qualités morales et leur littérature* (Paris: Maradan, 1808), pp. 26–63.

3. Thomas Bendyshe, ed. and trans., *The Anthropological Treatises of Johann Friedrich Blumenbach, Late Professor of Gottingen and Court Physician to the King of Britain* (London: Longman & Green, Longman, 1865), p. 310.

4. William S. Robertson, ed., *The Diary of Francisco De Miranda; Tour of the United States; 1783–1784; The Spanish Text* (New York: Hispanic Society of America, 1928), p. 119.

5. J. W. Nordholt Schulte, *The People That Walk in Darkness;* Van Loghum Salterus, *Het Volk dat in duesternis wandelt,* trans. M. B. Wijjngaarden (London: Burke, 1960), pp. 30, 202.

6. John Nichol, *American Literature An Historical Sketch 1620–1880* (Edinburgh: Adam and Charles Black, 1882), pp. 86–87.

7. S. B. Attoh Ahuma, ed., *Memorial of West African Celebrities* (Liverpool: D. Marples, 1905), pp. 332–48.

8. Garland Penn et al., eds., *The College of Life* (Boston: Bay State, 1900), pp. 20, 103–05.

9. Richard Wright, Introd., *Black Metropolis,* by St. Claire Drake and Horace Cayton (New York: Harcourt, Brace, 1945), p. xxxiii.

10. Barbara Wetherman, *We Were There: The Story of the Working Woman in America* (New York: Pantheon, 1977), pp. 36–37, 47.

11. Katherine Lee Bates, *American Literature* (New York: Macmillan, 1898), pp. 78–79, 81.

12. *The Black Man, His Antecedents, His Genius, and His Achievements* (Boston: Robert F. Wallcut, 1865; rpt. Miami: Mnemosyne, 1969), p. 140.

13. John Daniels, *In Freedom's Birthplace, A Study of the Boston Negro* (Boston: Houghton Mifflin, 1914; rpt. New York: Negro Universities Press, 1968), pp. 19–21.

14. Edward Scobie, *Black Brittania: A History of Blacks in Britain* (Chicago: Johnson, 1972), pp. 88–89.

15. Silvio Bedini, *The Life of Benjamin Banneker* (New York, Charles Scribner's, 1972), p. 322.

16. Penn, pp. 103–05.

17. John C. Cromwell, *The Negro in American History* (Washington, D.C.: American Negro Academy, 1914; rpt. New York: Johnson Reprint, 1968), pp. 77–85.

18. Page Smith, *A New Age for A New Beginning,* 2 vols. (New York: McGraw-Hill, 1976), I, 1802.

19. *Boston Daily Advertiser,* December 21, 1863, p. 3.

20. John B. Slattery, "Phillis Wheatley, the Negro Poetess," *Catholic World,* 39 (July, 1884), 484–98.

21. Russell Adams et al., *Great Negroes Past and Present* (Chicago: Afro-Am. Publishing, 1964), pp. 117–18.

22. "Four New Letters by Phillis Wheatley," *Early American Literature,* 7, No. 3 (Winter, 1974), 257–71.

23. Hugh Upham Clark Papers, United States Federal Archives, Washington, D.C.

24. *Massachusetts Gazette and Boston Post Boy and Advertiser,* March 21, 1774, p. 3, and in several other New England newspapers throughout March and April of 1774.

25. Clark Papers.

26. *Proceedings of the Massachusetts Historical Society for 1863–1864* (Boston: By the Society, 1864), pp. 270n.–273n.

27. C. Eric Lincoln, *The Negro Pilgrimage in America* (New York: Bantam Books, 1967), p. 13.

Salem Academy and College
Gramley Library
Winston-Salem, N.C. 27108

28. Carole A. Parks, "Phillis Wheatley Comes Home," *Black World*, 23 (February, 1974), 92–97.

29. Adams, p. 118.

30. Anonymous, *American Black Heroes in World History* (New York: Bantam Books, 1968), p. 69.

31. James Parton, "Antipathy to the Negro," *North American Review*, 127 (November–December, 1878), 488.

32. Moses Coit Tyler, *The Literary History of the American Revolution 1763–1783*, 2 vols. (New York: Putnam's, 1897), I, 186–87.

33. Folarin Shyllon, *Black People in Britain 1555–1832* (London: Oxford University Press, 1977), pp. 195–99.

34. R. B. Lewis, *Light and Truth* (Boston: Benjamin R. Roberts, 1844), pp. 330–33.

35. "Survey of Negro Literature," *Messenger, World's Greatest Negro Monthly*, 60, No. 2 (February, 1927), 37–39.

36. "Book Department," *Pittsburgh Courier*, June 30, 1933; Robert C. Kuncio, "Some Unpublished Poems of Phillis Wheatley," *New England Quarterly*, 43, No. 2 (June, 1970), 287–97.

37. "A Phillis Wheatley Letter," *Journal of Negro History*, 34, No. 4 (October, 1949), 462–66.

38. Sarah D. Jackson, "Letters of Phillis Wheatley and Susanna Wheatley," *Journal of Negro History*, 57, No. 2 (April, 1972), 211–15.

39. "The Myth of a Negro Literature," in *Home* (New York: William B. Morrow, 1966), pp. 105–06.

40. Addison Gayle, "The Function of Black Literature at the Present Time," in *The Black Aesthetic* (New York: Doubleday, 1971), p. 409.

41. Nathaniel Huggins, *The Harlem Renaissance* (New York: Oxford Univ. Press, 1971), p. 232.

42. Christopher Fyfe, ed., *Christianity, Islam and the Negro Race: Edward W. Blyden* (Edinburgh: Univ. Press, 1967), p. 83.

43. "From the Black American World," pt. 4, "Images of Africa in Afro-American Literature," *Okike, An African Journal of New Writing*, No. 10 (May, 1976), pp. 98–99.

44. *Breast of the Earth* (New York: Doubleday, 1975), p. 148.

45. "Personal Elements in the Poetry of Phillis Wheatley," *Phylon*, 13, No. 2 (2nd quarter, 1953), 191–98.

46. *Sturdy Black Bridges: Visions of Black Women in Literature* (New York: Doubleday, 1979), pp. 70–72.

47. "Afro-American Women Poets: A Bio-Critical Survey," in *Shakespeare's Sisters—Feminist Essays on Women Poets*, ed. Sandra M. Gilbert and Susan Gubar (Bloomington: Indiana Univ. Press, 1979), pp. 165–82.

48. Recent doctoral dissertations include Kenneth R. Holder, "Some Linguistic Aspects of the Heroic Couplet in the Poetry of Phillis Wheatley," Diss. North Texas State Univ. 1973; and John C. Shields, "Phillis Wheatley's Poetics of Ascent," Diss. Univ. of Tennessee 1978.

49. Charles Hamilton, *The Book of Autographs* (New York: Simon & Schuster, 1978), pp. 130–31.

50. *Catalogue of Sale Books* (Bristol, R.I.: Current Company, n.d.), p. 5.

CHRONOLOGY OF IMPORTANT DATES

1761 Phillis arrives from Africa as a 7- or 8-year-old slave, and is purchased by pious, well-to-do Mrs. Susanna Wheatley of Boston.

1765 Tutored at home in English, Latin, and the Bible, Phillis writes a letter to her friend, Reverend Samson Occum, converted Mohegan Indian Christian minister then abroad lecturing for funds to help create what is today Dartmouth College.

1767 Phillis publishes her first poem, "On Messrs. Hussey and Coffin," in *Newport* (R.I.) *Mercury*, December 21.

1770 Phillis publishes her elegy on the death of popular English evangelist, George Whitefield.
Phillis writes a letter covering a poem to countess of Huntingdon in London.

1772 Phillis publishes solicitations for subscribers to projected volume of twenty-eight poems, which Bostonians reject.
Phillis writes a letter covering a poem to Lord Dartmouth.

1773 To recuperate from her chronically poor health, Phillis sails to London, where she visits and is visited by members of the peerage, prominent divines, and other celebrities.
By her dying mistress in Boston Phillis is called home; she is not in London when her volume *Poems on Various Subjects, Religious and Moral* is published there in September.
A few weeks after her return to Boston from London in mid-September, Phillis is manumitted.

1774 Throughout March and April Phillis's subtle and sarcastic anti-slavery letter is reprinted in a dozen New England newspapers.

1776 Phillis's poem to George Washington is composed in Providence, R.I., October 26, is printed in the *Virginia Gazette*, March 20, and in the *Pennsylvania Magazine* in April.

1778 Phillis marries John Peters, an ambitious black free man; they live in his home on fashionable Queen (today's Court) Street.

1779 Beginning October 30, Phillis advertises proposals for a volume of her poems and letters for six weeks. Again, her proposals are rejected.

1783 July 28, John Peters petitions Boston authorities for a license to retail liquor from his shop near the Boston end of the Charlestown Bridge.

1784 After publishing her last three poems, Phillis dies on December 5, and is buried, with the last of three short-lived infants, in an unknown grave.

SELECTED EARLY COMMENTS

On Messrs. Hussey and Coffin

Phillis Wheatley*

To the Printer. Please to insert the following lines, composed by a Negro girl (belonging to one Mr. Wheatley of Boston) on the following Occasion, viz. Messrs. Hussey and Coffin, as undermentioned, belonging to Nantucket, being bound from thence to Boston, narrowly escaped being cast away on Cape Cod, in one of the late Storms;[1] *upon their Arrival, being at Mr. Wheatley's and while at Dinner, told of their narrow escape, this Negro girl at the same Time 'tending Table, heard the Relations, from which she composed the following Verses.*

On Messrs. Hussey and Coffin.

Did Fear and Danger so perplex your Mind,
As made you fearful of the whistling wind?
Was it not Boreas[2] knit his angry Brow
Against you? or did Consideration bow?
To lend you Aid, did not his Winds combine?
To stop your Passage with a churlish Line,
Did haughty Eolus[3] with Contempt look down
With aspect windy, and a study'd Frown?
Regard them not;—the Great Supreme, the Wise,
Intends for something hidden from our Eyes.
Suppose the groundless Gulph[4] had snatch'd away
Hussey and Coffin to the raging Sea;
Where wou'd they go? where wou'd be their abode?
With the supreme and independent God,
Or made their Beds down in the Shades below,
Where neither Pleasure nor Content can stow.
To Heaven their Souls with eager Raptures soar,
Enjoy the Bliss of him they wou'd adore.
Had the soft gliding Streams of Grace been near,
Some favourite Hope their fainting hearts to cheer,
Doubtless the Fear of Danger far had fled:
No more repeated Victory crown their Heads.

*Reprinted from the *Newport* (Rhode Island) *Mercury*, December 21, 1767, p. 3. This is the first known published poem by Phillis.

Had I the Tongue of a Seraphim,[5] *how would I exalt thy Praise; thy Name as Incense to the Heavens should fly, and the Remembrance of thy Goodness to the shoreless Oceans of Beatitude!—Then should the Earth flow with seraphick Ardour.*

Blest Soul, which sees the Day while Light doth shine,
To guide his Steps to trace the Mark divine.
Phillis Wheatley.

Notes

1. In the *Providence Gazette and Country Journal*, October 10, 1767, p. 3: "Boston, October 5. Capt. Coffin, in a schooner, loaded with oil, was cast ashore in the storm mentioned in our last on the back of Cape Cod, but the vessell has since been got off and arrived here yesterday. . . . The oldest Seamen say they never experienced a more terrible gale."
2. Boreas: The north wind.
3. Eolus (or Aelus): king of the four winds in Greek mythology.
4. Gulph: Gulf, Cape Cod Bay.
5. Seraphim: angel(s).

[Advertisement of Phillis Wheatley's Condolatory Address]

Anonymous*

This Day was published, price seven Coppers, (Embellished with a plate, representing the posture in which the Rev. Mr. Whitfield [*sic*] lay before and after his interment at Newbury-Port.) An Elegiac POEM, on the Death of that celebrated Divine, and eminent servant of Jesus Christ, the reverend and learned GEORGE WHITEFIELD, Chaplain to the Right Hon. the Countess of Huntingdon, &c. who made his exit from this transitory state, to dwell in the celestial realms of bliss, on Lord's day, 30th of September, 1770, when he was seized with a fit of the Asthma, at Newbury-Port, near Boston, New England. In which is a condolatory Address to his truly noble benefactress the worthy and pious Lady Huntingdon; and the Orphan children in Georgia, who with many thousands, are left, by the death of this great man, to lament the loss of a father, friend and benefactor. by PHILLIS, A Servant girl of seventeen years of age, belonging to Mr. J. Wheatly [*sic*], of Boston:—She has been but nine years in this country from Africa. Sold by Ezekiel Russell, in Queen-street, and John Boyles, in Marlborough-street.

*Reprinted from *Massachusetts Spy*, October 9–11, 1770, p. 1. Variously worded, this advertisement was widely reprinted in Boston, New York, and Philadelphia newspapers through October, 1770. The poem itself, which established Wheatley's international reputation, was reprinted almost a dozen times in broadside or pamphlet form, and exists in at least three variant texts.

[A young Afric damsels virgin tongue]

Jane Dunlap*

Another [i.e., another poem]

Shall his[1] due praises be so loudly sung
By a young Afric damsels virgin tongue?
And I be silent! and no mention make
of his blest name, who did so often speak. . . .

Notes

1. The Reverend George Whitefield. This slim twenty-three-page volume of twenty-two sorry but sincere verses has not been much noted in compilations of early American volumes of verses. One of the many registrations of Whitefield's considerable evangelical impact on eighteenth-century Boston, the volume is also the first to acknowledge Phillis Wheatley as a poet.

[First Proposals for Phillis Wheatley's Volume of Poems]

[Ezekiel Russell?]*

PROPOSALS
For Printing by Subscription

A collection of POEMS, wrote at several times, and upon various occasions, by PHILLIS, a Negro Girl, from the Strength of her own Genius, it being but a few years since she came to this Town an uncultivated Barbarian from *Africa.* The Poems having been seen and read by the best judges, who think them well worthy of the Publick View; and upon critical examination, they find that the declared Author was capable of writing them. The Order in which they were penned, together with the Occasion, are as follows:[1] On the Death of the Rev. Dr. *Sewell,* when sick, 1765;—On Virtue, 1766;—On two Friends who were cast away, do* [i.e., ditto; i.e., 1766];—To the University of Cambridge, 1767;*[2]—An Address to the Atheist, do;—An Address to the Deist, do:—On America, do;—On the King, do;*—On Friendship, do; Thoughts on being brought from Africa to America, do;*—On the Nuptials of Mr. *Spence* to Miss *Hooper,* do. On the Hon. Commodore Hood, on his pardoning a

*Reprinted from Jane Dunlap, *Poems, Upon several Sermons, Preached by the Rev'd, and Renowned, George Whitefield, while in Boston* (Boston, 1771), p. 4.

*Reprinted from *Boston Censor,* February 29, 1772, p. 2. Repeated in the same newspaper for March 14 and April 11, 1772, the proposals were rejected.

Deserter, 1769;—On the Death of the Reverend Dr. *Sewell*, do;*—On the Death of Master *Seider*, who was killed by *Ebenezer Richardson*, 1770;*—On the Death of the Rev. *George Whitefield*, do;*—On the Death of a young Miss, aged 5 years, do;*—On the Arrival of the Ships of War, and landing of the Troops, do;—On the Affray in King-Street, on the Evening of the 5th of March:—On the Death of a Young Gentleman;—To Samuel Quincy, Esq; a Panegyrick;—To a Lady on her coming to America for her Health;*—To Mrs. Leonard, on the Death of her Husband;*—To Mrs. Boylston and Children, on the Death of her Son and their Brother;*—To a Gentleman and Lady on the Death of their Son, aged 9 Months.*—To a Lady on her remarkable Deliverance in a Hurricane.*—To *James Sullivan*, Esq. and Lady on the Death of her Brother and Sister, and a Child *Avis*, aged 12 Months.*—*Goliab* [*sic*, i.e., Goliath] of Gath.*—On the Death of Dr. *Samuel Marshall.* *It is supposed they will make one small Octavo Volume, and will contain about 200 Pages. They will be printed on Demy Paper, and beautiful Types. The Price to Subscribers, handsomely bound and lettered, will be Four Shillings—Stitched in blue, Three Shillings. It is hoped Encouragement will be given to this Publication, as a reward to a very uncommon Genius, at present a Slave. The Work will be put to the Press as soon as three Hundred Copies are subscribed for, and shall be published with all Speed. Subscriptions are taken in by E. Russell, in Marlborough Street.

Notes

1. Only the first sixteen titles are dated.

2. Asterisked titles were revised, as were presumably their respective texts, and included in Wheatley's *Poems on Various Subjects, Religious and Moral*, published in London in September, 1773.

[". . . a very Extraordinary female Slave . . ."]

Thomas Wooldridge*

. . . While in Boston, I heard of a very Extraordinary female Slave, who had made some verses on our mutually Dear deceased friend;[1] I visited her Mistress, and found by conversing with the African, that she was no Imposter; I asked if she could write on any Subject; she said Yes: we had just heard of your Lordships Appointment;[2] I gave her your name, which she was acquainted with. She immediately wrote a rough Copy of the inclosed address & letter,[3] which I promised to convey or deliver. I was

*Printed from the manuscript with permission of the earl of Dartmouth, whose papers are housed in the County Record Office, Stafford, England. Wooldridge writes to the earl of Dartmouth from "New York, November 24, 1772."

astonish'd, and could hardly believe my own Eyes. I was present while she wrote, and can attest that it is her own production; she shew'd me her letter to Lady Huntingdon, which I daresay your Lordship has seen;[4] I send you an account signed by her master of her Importation, Education &c they are all wrote in her own hand.[5] Pardon the account I have given you of this poor untutor'd slave, when possibly your precious time may be very ill bestowed in reading my scrawls. . . .

Notes

1. The Reverend George Whitefield (1714–70), chaplain to the countess of Huntingdon and spiritual leader to the earl of Dartmouth and others in evangelical reform action in England and colonial America.

2. Dartmouth was appointed secretary of state for the colonies in August, 1772.

3. The manuscript poem, and the covering letter dated "Boston N.E. Oct. 10, 1772," were delivered and are today among Lord Dartmouth's papers in the County Record Office, Stafford, England.

4. Phillis mailed a nonextant manuscript eulogy on the death of the Reverend George Whitefield to the countess, and a covering letter dated "Oct.r 25th 1770."

5. Dated "Boston New England Oct. 12.th 1772," bearing Nathaniel Wheatley's signature, this biographical "account" was written in Phillis's hand. The sketch of 112 words was expanded into 152 words and bore the name of John Wheatley, Nathaniel's father, and the date of "*Boston, Nov. 14,* 1772," and was part of the prefatory matter to one of the original London editions of Wheatley's *Poems*; it also prefaced several American reprintings of the *Poems*.

["An accomplished mistress of her pen . . ."]

"L"*

To the Author of the London Magazine. *Boston, in New England, Jan. 1, 1772.*

SIR,

As your Magazine is a proper repository for anything valuable or curious, I hope you will excuse the communicating the following by one of your subscribers. L. There is in this town a young *Negro woman*, who left her country at ten years of age, and has been in this eight years. She is a compleat sempstress, an accomplished mistress of her pen, and discovers a most surprising genius. Some of her productions have seen the light, among which is a poem on the death of the Rev. Mr. George

*Reprinted from *Massachusetts Gazette*, March 1, 1773, p. 1. The identity of "L" is unknown, as is that of "MISS A—M—," the dedicatee of the poem, which first appeared in this fifty-eight line version in the *London Magazine*, 41 (March, 1772), 134–35. It was reprinted in the *London Annual Register for 1772* (London: J. Dodsley, 1795), pp. 214–15; and in the *Salem Essex Gazette*, March 16–23, 1773, p. 1. It was revised, shortened to fifty lines, and included in the 1773 edition of the *Poems*.

Whitefield.—The following was occasioned by her being in company with some young ladies of family, when one of them said she did not remember, among all the political[1] pieces she had seen, ever to have met with a poem upon RECOLLECTION. The *African* (so let me call her, for so in fact she is) took the hint, went home to her master's, and soon sent what follows.

"MADAM,

"Agreeable to your proposing *Recollection* as a subject proper for me to write upon, I enclose these few thoughts upon it; and, as you was the first person who mentioned it, I thought none more proper to dedicate it to; and, if it meets with your approbation, the poem is honoured, and the authoress satisfied. I am, Madam, Your very humble servant

PHILLIS.

RECOLLECTION

To Miss A—M—, humbly inscribed by the Authoress.

MNEME,[2] begin; inspire, ye sacred Nine?
Your vent'rous *Afric* in the deep design.
Do ye rekindle the celestial fire,
Ye god-like powers! the glowing thoughts inspire,
Immortal Pow'r! I trace thy sacred spring,
Assist my strains, while I *thy* glories sing.
By *thee*, past acts of many thousand years,
Rang'd in due order, to the mind appears;
The *long-forgot* thy gentle hand conveys,
Returns, and soft upon the fancy plays.
Calm, in the visions of the night he pours
Th'exhaustless treasures of his secret stores.
Swift from above he wings his downy flight
Thro' *Phoebe*'s realm,[3] fair regent of the night.
Thence to the raptur'd poet gives his aid,
Dwells in his heart, or hovers round his head;
To give instructions to the lab'ring mind,
Diffusing light celestial and refin'd.
Still he pursues, unwearied in the race,
And wraps his senses in the pleasing maze.
The Heav'nly Phantom *points*[4] the actions done
In the past worlds, and tribes beneath the sun.
He, from his throne in ev'ry human breast,
Has *vice* condemn'd, and ev'ry *virtue* bless'd.
Sweet are the sounds in which thy words we hear,
Coelestial musick to the ravish'd ear.
We hear thy voice, resounding o'er the plains,
Excelling Maro's[5] sweet Menellian strains.
But awful *Thou*! to that perfidious race,
Who scorn thy warnings, nor the good embrace;

By *Thee* unveil'd, the horrid crime appears,
Thy mighty hand redoubled fury bears;
The time mis-spent augments their hell of woes,
While through each breast the dire contagion flows.
Now turn and leave the rude ungrateful scene,
And paint fair Virtue in immortal green.
For ever flourish in the glowing veins,
For ever flourish in poetick strains.
Be *Thy* employ to guide my early days,
And *Thine* the tribute of my youthful lays.
Now **eighteen years* their destin'd course have run,
In due succession, round the central sun;
How did each folly unregarded pass!
But sure 'tis graven on eternal brass!
To *recollect*, inglorious I return;
Tis mine past follies and past crimes[6] to mourn.
The *virtue*, ah! unequal to the *vice*,
Will scarce afford small reason to rejoice.
Such, *recollection*! is thy pow'r, high thron'd
In ev'ry breast of mortals, ever own'd.
The wretch, who dar'd the vengeance of the skies,
At last awakes with horror and surprise.
By *Thee* alarm'd, he sees impending fate,
He howls in anguish, and repents too late.
But oft *thy* kindness moves with timely fear
The furious rebel in his mad career.
Thrice bless'd the man, who in *thy* sacred shrine
Improves the REFUGE from the wrath divine.

Notes

1. In other printings: "poetical."
2. Mneme: Mnemosyne, goddess of memory in mythology.
3. Phoebe's realm: The sky, Phoebus Apollo being the god of the sky.
4. That is, "paints."
5. Maro: Publius Vergilius Maro, or Vergil, Latin author of the *Aeneid*, one of Wheatley's favorite poems.
6. "past crimes": an instance of Wheatley's pious hyperbole.

*Her age.

["A Free Negro Girl of singular genius . . ."]

Benjamin Rush*

There is now in the town of Boston a Free Negro Girl, about 18 years of age, who has been but 9 years in the country, whose singular genius and accomplishments are such as not only do honor to her sex, but to human nature. Several of her poems have been printed, and read with pleasure by the public.

[Announcement of London Proposals of Wheatley's Poems]

[Mrs. Susanna Wheatley?]*

Proposals[1] for printing *in London* by Subscription, A volume of Poems, Dedicated by permission to the Right Hon. the Countess of Huntingdon Written by Phillis, a Negro Servant to Mr. Wheatley, of Boston in New England. Terms of Subscription.

I. The Book to be neatly printed in 12 mo. on a new Type and a fine paper adorned with an elegant Frontispiece, representing the Author.

II. That the Price to Subscribers shall be Two Shillings Sewed, or Two Shillings and six-pence neatly bound.

II, [*sic*]That every Subscriber deposit One Shilling at the
* * Time of Subscribing; and the Remainders to be paid
* on the Delivery of the Book.

Subscriptions are received by Cox and Berry in *Boston*.

Notes

1. Stung into resolve by Bostonian rejection of her beloved protegee's 1772 proposals to publish a volume of poems in Boston, and perhaps excited by a rumored expectation of greater remuneration for a London-published edition, Mrs. Susanna Wheatley arranged by mail with the wealthy and influential countess of Huntingdon to have Phillis's poems published abroad. Thus, Mrs. Wheatley may have run this advertisement-proposal notice in a pique of unchristian retaliation; the notice can easily be read as an announcement to fellow Bostonians that, despite their rejection of the 1772 proposals, Phillis Wheatley's volume would indeed be published, in London, and dedicated by permission to the countess of Huntingdon.

*Reprinted from Benjamin Rush, *An Address to the Inhabitants of the British Settlements in America Upon Slave Keeping* (Philadelphia: John Dunlap, 1773), p. 2n.

*Reprinted from *Boston Post Boy*, April 16, 1773, p. 3. Reprinted in the same newspaper for April 19 and 22, and in the *Boston Weekly Newsletter*, April 16, 1773, p. 3.

["Phillis, the extraordinary negro girl" in London]

[Mrs. Susanna Wheatley?]*

To the Printer *of the* London Chronicle. SIR, *Boston, New England*, May 10. You have no doubt heard of Phillis the extraordinary negro girl here, who has by her own application, unassisted by others, cultivated her natural talents for poetry in such a manner as to write several pieces which (all circumstances considered) have great merit. This girl, who is a servant to Mr. John Wheatley of this place, sailed last Saturday for London, under the protection of Mr. Nathaniel Wheatley;[1] since which the following little piece of her's has been published here:[2]

FAREWELL TO AMERICA.
Addressed to Mrs. Susanna W——. By
Phillis Wheatley.

Adieu New England's smiling meads,
Adieu the flow'ry plain,
I leave thy opening charms O spring!
To try the azure reign.

In vain for me the flow'rets rise
And show their gaudy pride,
While here beneath the Northern skies
I mourn for health deny'd.

Thee, charming Maid! while I pursue
In thy luxuriant reign,
And sigh and languish, thee to view,
Thy pleasures to regain.

Susanna mourns, nor can I bear
To see the christal show'r
Fast falling—the indulgent tear
In sad departure's hour.

Not unregarding lo! I see
Thy soul with grief oppres'd;
Ah! curb the rising groan for me,
Nor sighs disturb thy breast.

*Reprinted from *London Chronicle*, July 1–3, 1773, p. 3. Unsigned, the headnote was likely written by Mrs. Susanna Wheatley, Phillis's mistress, who exerted herself for her prodigy as long as her failing health allowed. This verse was revised and shortened by eight lines, and included in Wheatley's 1773 volume of *Poems*.

In vain the feather'd songsters sing;
In vain the garden blooms,
And in the bosom of the spring,
Breathes out her sweet perfumes.

While for Britannia's distant shore,
We sweep the liquid plain,
Till Aura[3] to the arms restore
Of this beloved domain.

Lo! Health appears! Celestial Dame,
Complacent and serene,
With Hebe's[4] mantle o'er her frame,
With soul-delighting mein.

Deep in a vale where London lies,
With mighty vapours crown'd,
Which cloud Aurora's thousand dyes,
And veil her charms around.

Why Phoebus! moves thy car so slow,
So slow the rising ray;
Nor gives the mantled town to view,
Thee glorious King of day!

But late from Orient skies, behold!
He shines benignly bright,
He decks his native plain with gold,
With chearing rays of light.

For thee, Britannia, I resign
New England's smiling face,
To view again her charms divine,
One short reluctant space.

But thou temptation! hence, away,
With all thy hated train
Of ills—nor tempt my mind astray.
From Virtue's sacred strain.

Most happy! who with sword and shield
Is screen'd from dire alarms,
And fell temptation, on the field,
Of fatal power disarms.

But cease thy lays, my lute forbear
Nor frown my gentle muse,
To see the secret falling tears,
Nor pitying look refute.

Notes

1. Phillis Wheatley's departure from Boston on May 8, 1773, for a medically recommended voyage to London in hopes of recovering her chronically poor health—asthma and a suspicion of tuberculosis—was widely noted by many newspapers throughout and beyond New England. She was variously described as "ingenious negro poet," "extraordinary Negro genius," "the celebrated young negro poetess" in the *Boston Evening Post*, May 3, 10; *Providence Gazette and Country Journal*, May 8, 10; *Salem Essex Gazette*, May 11; *Pennsylvania Packet and General Advertiser*, May 13; *Connecticut Courant*, May 25; *Massachusetts Spy*, May 27; *New York Gazette and Weekly Mercury*, May 27; and others.

2. Variously punctuated and spelled, "Farewell to America" was published in at least a half dozen New England newspapers throughout May, 1773.

3. Aura, i.e., Aurora, who in Greek mythology announced the coming of the sun of a new day.

4. Hebe, goddess of youth.

["I went to see the black poetess . . ."]

Benjamin Franklin*

. . . Upon your recommendation I went to see the black poetess and offered her any services I could do her. Before I left the house I understood her master was there, and had sent her to me, but did not come into the room himself, and I thought was not pleased with the visit.[1] I should perhaps have inquired first for him; but I had heard nothing of him, and I have heard nothing since of her.

London, 7 July, 1773.

Notes

1. In a letter from Boston on October 17, 1773, Jonathan Williams wrote to Franklin, informing him that both Mr. and Mrs. Wheatley had urged him to mention Phillis in his letters, "but as it turned out I am sorry I did." *The Papers of Benjamin Franklin*, ed. William Willcox, 20 vol. (New Haven: Yale Univ. Press, 1976), xx, 445.

*Reprinted from *The Works of Benjamin Franklin*, ed. John Bigelow, 12 vols. (New York: G. P. Putnam's, 1904), vi, 172–73. Franklin is writing to Jonathan Williams, Sr., his nephew-in-law in Boston.

[". . . one of the greatest instances of pure, unassisted Genius, that the world ever produced"]

Archibald Bell*

Dedicated, by Permission, to the Right Hon. the Countess of Huntingdon. This day, Sept. 11, will be published, Price Two Shillings, sewed, or Two Shillings and sixpence neatly bound, adorned with an elegant engraved like-ness of the Author. A Volume of POEMS, ON VARIOUS SUBJECTS: RELIGIOUS AND MORAL. By PHILLIS WHEATLEY, Negro Servant to Mr. John Wheatley, of Boston, London: Printed for A. Bell, Bookseller, Aldgate; and at Boston, for Messrs. Cox and Berry, in King-Street.[1] To the Public. The Book here proposed for publication displays perhaps one of the greatest instances of pure, unassisted Genius, that the world ever produced. The Author is a native of Africa, and left not that dark part of the habitable system, till she was eight years old. She is now no more than nineteen, and many of the Poems were penned before she arrived at near that age.

They were wrote upon a variety of interesting subjects, and in a stile rather to have been expected from those who, a native genius, have had the happiness of a liberal education, than from one born in the wilds of Africa.

The writer while in England a few weeks since, was conversed with by many of the principal Nobility and Gentry of this Country, who have been signally distinguished for their learning and abilities, among whom was the Earl of Dartmouth, the late Lord Lyttelton, and others who unanimously expressed their approbation of her genius, and their amazement at the gifts with which infinite Wisdom has furnished her.

But the Publisher means not, in this advertisement, to deliver any peculiar eulogiums on the present publication; he rather desires to submit the striking beauties of its contents to the unabashed candour of the impartial public.

As it has been repeatedly suggested to him, by persons, who have seen the manuscripts, that numbers would be ready to suspect they were not really the writings of Phillis, he has procured the following attestation, from the most respectable characters in Boston, that none might have the least ground for disputing their original.

[The Attestation]

We, whose Names are under-written, do assure the World, that the Poems specified in the following Page† were (as we verily believe) written

*Reprinted from *Morning Post and Advertiser* [London], September 3, 1773, p. 3.

†The words "following page" allude to the Contents of the Manuscript copy, which are wrote at the Back of the above Attestation.

by Phillis, a young Negro girl, who was but a few years since, brought an uncultivated Barbarian from Africa, and has ever since been, and now is, under the Disadvantage of serving as a Slave in a Family in this Town. She has been examined by some of the best Judges, and is thought qualified to write them. Boston. Octo. 8, 1772.[2]

His Excellency, Thomas Hutchinson, Governor; the Hon. Andrew Oliver, Lieutenant-Governor; the Hon. Thomas Hubbard, John Erving, James Pitts, Harrison Gray, and James Bowdoin; John Hancock, John Green [*sic.*, i.e., Joseph Green], and Richard Carey, Esqr.; The Rev. Charles Chauncy, D.D., Mather Byles, D.D., Ed. Pemberton, D.D. Andrew Eliot, D.D., Samuel Cooper, D.D., Samuel Mather, John Moorhead; and Mr. John Wheatley, her Master.

N.B. The original Attestation, signed by the above Gentlemen, may be seen, by applying to Archibald Bell, as above.

Notes

1. An obscure London bookseller and publisher, Archibald Bell had received the countess of Huntingdon's approval of the Wheatley manuscript as early as December, 1772, or January, 1773. He spent the next months arranging for the attestation from Boston ascertaining that Phillis was the authentic author of the poems. Bell then displayed proposals for the London publication of the volume in the *Morning Post and Daily Advertiser*, August 6, 9, 11, 12, 16, 1773. When the book finally appeared, he kept promotional notices of its availability in several London newspapers (e.g., the *London Chronicle*, September 9–14, and October 16; *Lloyd's Evening Post and British Chronicle,* September 10–15; the *Public Advertiser*, September 13, 18; and others).

2. One London printing of *Poems* did not include this attestation; in the edition of the *Poems* that did print the attestation, this date was not mentioned.

[Notice of London publication of Wheatley's *Poems*]

Anonymous*

This piece [i.e., Wheatley's poem, "On Recollection"] is taken from a small collection of Poems on Various Subjects, just published, written by PHILLIS WHEATLEY, a negro of Boston, who was brought from Africa in 1761, and is now only in the twenty-first year of her age. A Testimony in favour of the poems, as the genuine productions of this young person, is signed by the Governour, the Lieutenant-Governour, seven clergymen, and others eminent for station and literature, and also by her master; and in this it is said, disgraceful as it may be to all that have signed it that 'this poor girl was brought an *uncultivated barbarian* from Africa, and has *ever since been*, and now is—a SLAVE!' Youth, innocence, and piety,

*Reprinted from *Gentleman's Magazine and Historical Chronicle*, 43 (September, 1773), 456.

united with genius, have not yet been able to restore her to the condition and character with which she was invested by the Great Author of her being. So powerful is custom in rendering the heart insensible to the rights of nature, and the claims of excellence!

[A London Review of Wheatley's *Poems on Various Subjects*]

Anonymous*

If we believed, with the ancient mythologists, that genius is the offspring of the sun, we should rather wonder that the sable race have not yet been more distinguished by it, than express our surprize at a single instance. The experience of the world, however, has left to this part of mythology but little probability for its support; and indeed, it appears to be wrong in its first principles. A proximity to the sun, far from heightening the powers of the mind, appears to enfeeble them, in proportion as it enervates the faculties of the body. Thus we find the topical regions remarkable for nothing but the sloth and languor of their inhabitants, their lascivious dispositions and deadness to invention. The country that gave birth to Alexander and Aristotle, the conqueror of the world, and the greater conqueror of nature, was Macedonia, naturally a cold and ungenial region. Homer and Hesiod breathed the cool and temperate air of the Meles, and the poets and heroes of Greece and Rome had no very intimate commerce with the sun.

The poems written by this young negro bear no endemial marks of solar fire or spirit. They are merely imitative; and, indeed, most of these people have a turn for imitation, though they have little or none for invention.

The following short account of the Author is prefixed to the poems.

> Phillis was brought from Africa to America, in the Year 1761, between Seven and Eight Years of Age. Without any Assistance from School Education, and by only what she was taught in the Family, she, in Sixteen Months Time from her Arrival, attained the English Language, to which she was an utter Stranger before, to such a Degree, as to read any, the most difficult parts of the Sacred Parts of the Sacred Writings, to the great Astonishment of all who heard her.
>
> As to her Writing, her own Curiosity led her to it; and this she learnt in so short a Time, that in the Year 1765, she wrote a Letter to the Rev. Mr. Occom, the Indian Minister, while in England.
>
> She has a great inclination to learn the Latin Tongue, and has made

*Reprinted from *London Monthly Review; or, Literary Journal from June, 1773 to January, 1774*, 49 (October, 1774), 457–59.

some Progress in it. This Relation is given by her Master who bought her, and with whom she now lives.

John Wheatley.

Boston, Nov. 14, 1772.

She has written many good lines, and now and then one of superior character has dropped from her pen; as in the Epistle to Maecenas,

'The lengthening line moves languishing along.'

And in the 'Thoughts on the Works of Providence;'

'Or the sun slumbers in the ocean's arms.'

In her verses to the Earl of Dartmouth, on his being appointed Secretary of State for the American department, she speaks of her own situation and country, which she seldom does in any other part of her poems. After bespeaking his Lordship's favourable sentiments in behalf of American liberty, she asks,

'Should you, my Lord, while you peruse my song,
Wonder from whence my love of Freedom sprung,
Whence flow these wishes for the common good,
By feeling hearts alone best understood,
I, young in life, by seeming cruel fate
Was snatch'd from Afric's fancy'd happy seat:
What pangs excruciating must molest,
What sorrows labour in my parent's breast?
Steel'd was that soul and by no misery mov'd
That from a father seiz'd his babe belov'd:
Such, such my case. And can I then but pray
Others may never feel tyrannic sway?

We are much concerned to find that this ingenious young woman is yet a slave. The people of Boston boast themselves chiefly on their principles of liberty. One such act as the purchase of her freedom, would, in our opinion, have done more honour than hanging a thousand trees with ribbons and emblems.

["A negro girl writing a few silly poems . . ."]

Richard Nisbet*

. . . A few instances may be found, of African negroes possessing virtues and becoming ingenious; but still, what I have said, with regard to their general character, I dare say, most people acquainted with them, will agree to.[1]

["That ingenious African *Phillis Wheatly* [*sic*] of Boston"]

Philip V. Fithian*

[March 5, 1774] I was reading in the Evening to *Bob* in the Monthly Review the remarks on the writings of Phillis Wheatly of Boston; at which he seem'd in astonishment; sometimes wanting to see her, then to know if She knew grammer [*sic*], Latin &c. at last he expressed himself in a manner very unusual for a Boy of his turn, & suddenly exclaimed, Good God! I wish I was in Heaven!—

Like *Bob* I am at once fill'd with pleasure & surprise, when I see the remarks of the Reviewers confirmed as to the Writings of that ingenious African *Phillis Wheatly* of Boston; her verses seem to discover that She is tolerably well acquainted with *Poetry, Learning,* & *Religion.*

In the Universal Magazine for September 1773 are the following Lines on her being brought from *Africa* to *America* by herself:

Twas mercy brought me from my Pagan land,
Taught my benighted soul to understand
That there's a God, that there's a Saviour too:
Once I redemption neither sought nor knew.
Some view our race with scornful eye,
"Their colour is a diabolic die."
Remember, Christians, Negroes, black as Cain,
May be refin'd, and join th'angelic train.

*Reprinted from Richard Nisbet, *Slavery Not Forbidden by Scripture* (Philadelphia: John Dunlap, 1773), p. 23n. The "Author of the Address" referred to in Nisbet's footnote is Benjamin Rush, for whom see above.

1. The Author of the Address gives a single example of a negro girl writing a few silly poems, to prove that the blacks are not deficient to us in understanding.

*Reprinted from *Philip Vickers Fithian: Journal and Letters 1767–1774*, ed. John R. Williams (Princeton: University Library, 1900), pp. 117–19.

["a Negro woman who writes very good English verse . . ."]

Voltaire*

. . . le génie, qui est rare partout, se trouve aussi en tout climat. Fontenelle avait tort de dire qu'il n'y aurait jamais de poëtes chez les Nègres: il y a actuellement une Négresse qui fait de très-bons vers anglais.[1] L'impératrice de Russie, qui est l'antipode des Négresses, écrit en prose aussi bien que son chamberlain en vers, et tous deux m'éntonnent également. . . .

[Genius, which is rare everywhere, can be found in all parts of the earth. Fontenelle was wrong to say that there would never be poets among Negroes; there is presently a Negro woman who writes very good English verse.[1] The Empress of Russia, who is diametrically different from Negro women, writes in prose as well as her chamberlain in verse, and both astonish me equally.

[A letter and a poem to George Washington]

Phillis Wheatley*

Messrs Dixon and Hunter, *Pray insert the enclosed letter and verses, written by the famous* PHILLIS WHEATLEY *the* African *Poetess in your next gazette.*

SIR,

I have taken the freedom to address your Excellency in the enclosed poem, and entreat it to your acceptance, though I am not insensible of its inaccuracies. Your being appointed by the Grand Continental Congress to be Generalissimo of the armies of North America, together with the fame of your virtues, excite sensations not easy to suppress. Your generosity, therefore, I presume, will pardon the attempt. Wishing your Excellency all possible success in the great cause you are so generously engaged in, I am your Excellency's Most obedient humble servant,

PHILLIS WHEATLEY.[1]

*Reprinted from Voltaire, *Oeuvres Completes*, ed. Louis Moland, 52 vols. (Paris: Garnier, 1882–85), XLVIII, 594–95.

1. Elle s'appelait Phillis Wheatley, et est morte in 1787. Elle habitait Boston, mais ses oeuvres avaient été imprimées en Angleterre sous ce titre: Poems on Various Subjects religious and moral, Londres, 1773.

[1]She is named Phillis Wheatley and died in 1787. She lived in Boston, but her works were published in England under the title Poems on Various Subjects religious and moral, London, 1773.]

*Reprinted from *Virginia Gazette* March 20, 1776, p. 1.

His Excellency General Washington

Celestial choir enthron'd in realms of light,
Columbia's scene of glorious toil I write.
While freedom's cause her anxious breast alarms
She flashes dreadful in refulgent arms.
See mother earth her offspring's fate bemoan,
And nations gaze at scenes before unknown!
See the bright beams of heaven's revolving light
Involv'd in sorrows and the veils of night!
The goddess comes, she moves divinely fair
Olive and laurel bind her golden hair:
Wherever shines this native of the skies
Unnumber'd charms and recent graces rise.
Muse! how propitious, while my pen relates
How pour her armies through a thousand gates:
As when Eolus heaven's fair face deforms,
Enwrap'd in tempest, and a night of storms;
Astonish'd ocean feels the wild uproar,
The refluent surges beat the sounding shore;
Or thick as leaves in autumn's golden reign,
Such, and so many, moves the warrior train.
In bright array they seek the work of war,
Where high unfurl'd the ensign waves in air.
Shall I to Washington their praise recite?
Enough thou know'st them in the fields of fight,
Thee, first in place[2] and honours—we demand
The grace and glory of thy martial band.
Fam'd for thy valour, for thy virtues more,
Hear every tongue thy guardian aid implore!
One century scarce perform's its destin'd round,
When Gallic powers Columbia's fury found;
And so may you, whoever dares disgrace
The land of freedom's heaven defended race!
Fix'd are the eyes of nations on the scales,
For in their hopes Columbia's arm prevails.
Anon Britannia droops the pensive head,
While round increase the rising hills of dead.
Ah! cruel blindness to Columbia's state!
Lament thy thirst of boundless power too late.
Proceed, great chief, with virtue on thy side,
Thy every action let the goddess guide.
A crown, a mansion, and a throne that shine,
With gold unfading, Washington! be thine.

Notes

1. This letter and poem were likely given to the printers of the *Virginia Gazette* by General Washington's adjutant, Colonel Joseph Reed. Another printing of this letter and

poem appeared in the *Pennsylvania Magazine* for April, 1776, when that newspaper was edited by Thomas Paine. Undated in the *Virginia Gazette* printing, the letter in the *Pennsylvania Magazine* printing is dated "Providence, Oct. 26, 1775." See Washington's written response to Wheatley, below, in Jared Sparks.

2. In other printings: "peace."

["With a view of doing justice to her poetical genius"]

George Washington*

Cambridge, February 10, 1776,

. . . I recollect nothing else worthy of giving you[1] the trouble of, unless you can be amused by reading a letter and poem addressed to me by Miss Phillis Wheatley. In searching over a parcel of papers, in order to destroy such as were useless, I brought it to light again. At first, with a view of doing justice to her poetical genius, I had a great mind to publish the poem; but not knowing whether it might not be considered rather as a mark of my own vanity, than as a compliment to her, I laid it aside till I came across it again in the manner just mentioned.

Notes

1. Washington is addressing his adjutant, Joseph Reed, then in Philadelphia. Reed probably mailed the Wheatley poem and covering letter to the *Virginia Gazette*, and a copy to the *Pennsylvania Magazine*, both organs publishing the letter and poem on March 20 and April, 1776, respectively. The original is no longer extant.

["I thank you most sincerely for your polite notice of me"]

George Washington*

Cambridge, February 28, 1776

Miss Phillis,
Your favor of the 26th of October did not reach my hands, till the middle of December. Time enough, you will say, to have given an answer ere

*Reprinted from *The Writings of George Washington: Being His Correspondence, Addresses, Messages, and Other Papers. Official and Private, Selected and Published from the original manuscript with a Life of the Author*, ed. Jared Sparks, 12 vols. (Boston: Hill and Gray, 1833), III, 297–98.

*Reprinted from *The Writings of George Washington*, ed. Jared Sparks, 12 vols. (Boston: Hill and Gray, 1833), III, 297–99n.

this. Granted. But a variety of important occurrences, continually interposing to distract the mind and withdraw the attention, I hope will apologize for the delay, and plead my excuse for the seeming but not real neglect. I thank you most sincerely for your polite notice of me, in the elegant lines you enclosed; and however undeserving I may be of such encomium and panegyric, the style and manner exhibit a striking proof of your poetic talents; in honor of which, and as a tribute justly due to you, I would have published the poem, had I not been apprehensive, that, while I only meant to give the world this new instance of your genius, I might have incurred the imputation of vanity. This, and nothing else, determined me not to give it place in the public prints.

If you should ever come to Cambridge, or near headquarters, I shall be happy to see a person so favored by the Muses, and to whom nature has been so liberal and so beneficient in her dispensations.[1] I am, with great respect, your obedient humble servant.

Notes

1. "Washington invited her to visit with him at Cambridge, which she did a few days before the British evacuated Boston; her master, among others, having left the city by permission, and retired with his family, to Chelsea. She passed half an hour with the Commander-in-Chief, from whom and his officers she received marked attention" (Benson Lossing, *The American Revolution and War of 1812*, 3 vols. [New York: New York Book Concern, 1875], III,556–57).

["Phyllis's [*sic*] poems do credit to nature"]

Ignatius Sancho*

LETTER LVIII

To Mr. F——.

Charles Street, January 27, 1778.

. . . Phyllis's poems do credit to nature—and put art—merely as art—to the blush.—It reflects nothing either to the glory or generosity of her master—if she is still his slave[1]—except he glories in the *low vanity* of having in his wanton power a mind animated by Heaven—a genius superior to himself. The list of splendid, titled, learned names, in confirmation of her being a real authoress, alas! shews how very poor the acquisition of wealth and knowledge are—without generosity—feeling—and humani-

*Reprinted from *Letters of the Late Ignatius Sancho, An African, To which are prefixed Memoirs of his Life*, 3rd ed., ed. Joseph Jekyll (London: J. Nichols, 1784), pp. 158–60.

ty.—These good great folk all knew—and perhaps admired—nay praised Genius in bondage—and then, like the Priests and the Levites in sacred writ, passed by—not one good Samaritan amongst them. . . . Your most humble servant.

IGNATIUS SANCHO.[2]

Notes

1. Phillis Wheatley was manumitted in 1773.

2. Ignatius Sancho (1729–80) was born a slave but grew up in London as an intelligent, articulate butler who eventually married a black woman with whom he struggled to maintain a grocery store and a family in Westminster. He composed stage plays, musical compositions, published on a variety of matters in the London press, and corresponded with David Garrick, Edward Young, the poet, and Laurence Sterne, with whom he was especially friendly. He was an affable, much practiced letter writer, one hundred and fifty odd of his letters being published posthumously in a two-volume edition in 1782.

[". . . one of the strangest creatures . . . perhaps in the whole world"]

Marquis de Barbé-Marbois*

". . . I shall tell you . . . about Phyllis [*sic*], one of the strangest creatures in the country and perhaps in the whole world. Phyllis is a negress, born in Africa, brought to Boston at the age of ten, and sold to a citizen of that city. She learned English with unusual ease, eagerly read and reread the Bible, the only book which had been put in her hands, became steeped in the poetic images of which it is full, and at the age of seventeen published a number of poems in which there is imagination, poetry, and zeal, though no correctness nor order of interest. I read them with some surprise. They are printed and in the front of the book there are certificates of authenticity which leave no doubt that she is its author. . . .

*Reprinted from *Our Revolutionary Forefathers. The Letters of Francois, Marquis de Barbé-Marbois, During His Residence in the United States As Secretary of the French Legation 1779–1785*, ed. and trans. Eugene P. Chase (New York: Duffield, 1929), p. 85. From a letter of August 28, 1779.

[Proposals for a volume of poems and letters]

Phillis Wheatley*

PROPOSALS, For Printing, By Subscription, A VOLUME OF POEMS, And LETTERS, On Various Subjects, Dedicated to the Right Honourable, Benjamin Franklin Esq: One of the Ambassadors of the United States, at the Court of France, by PHILLIS PETERS.[1] *Poems.* Thoughts on the Times. On the Capture of General Lee, to I. B. Esq. To His Excellency General Washington. On the Death of General Wooster. An Address to Dr ———. To Lieut R—— of the Royal Navy. To the same. To T. M. Esq. of Granada. To Sophia of South Carolina. To Mr. A. M'B—— of the Navy. To Lieut R—— D—— of the Navy. Ocean. The choice and advantages of a Friend; to Mr. T—— M——. Farewell to England, 1773. To Mrs. W——ms on Anna Eliza. To Mr. A. McB——d. Epithalamium to Mrs. H——. To P. N. S. & Lady on the death of their infant son. To Mr. El ———y on the death of his Lady. On the death of Lieut. L———ds. To Penelope. To Mr. & Mrs. L—— on the death of their daughter. A Complaint. To Mr. A. I. M. on Virtue. To Dr. L——d and Lady on the death of their son aged 5 years. To Mr. L——g on the death of his son. To Capt. F——r on the death of his granddaughter. To Philandra an Elegy. Niagara. Chloe to Calliope. To Musidora on Florello. To Sir E. L—— Esq. To the Hon. John Montague Esq. Rear Admiral of the Blue. *Letters.*1) To the Right Hon. Wm E. of Dartmouth Secretary of State of N. America. 2) To the Rev. Mr. T. P. Farmington. 3) To Mr. T. W.——— Dartmouth College. 4) To the Hon. T. H. Esq. 5) To Dr. B. Rush, Phila. 6) To the Rev. Dr. Thomas, London. 7) To the Right Hon. Countess of H——. 8) To I. M—— Esq. London. 9) To Mrs. W——e in the County of Surrey. 10) To Mr. T. M. Homerton, near London. 11) To Mrs. S—— W——. 12) To the Rt. Hon. the Countess of H——. 13) To the same.

Messieurs Printers,—The above collection of Poems and Letters was put into my hands by the desire of the Ingenious author in order to be introduced to public View. The subjects are various and curious, and the author a *Female African*, whose lot it was to fall into the hands of a *generous* master and *great* benefactor. The learned and ingenuous as well as those who are pleased with novelty, are invited to incourage the publication, by a generous subscription—the former, that they may fan the sacred fire which is self-enkindled in the breast of this *young* African—The ingenuous that they may by reading this collection have a large play for their imaginations, and be exited [*sic*, i.e., excited] to please and

*Reprinted from *Boston Evening Post and General Advertiser*, October 30, 1779, p. 1. Reprinted verbatim in the same newspaper for November 6, 27, and December 4, 11, 17, 1779.

benefit mankind, by some brilliant production of their own pens.—Those who are *always* in search of some new thing, that they may obtain a sight of this *rara avis in terra*—And every one, that the ingenious author may be encouraged to improve her own mind, benefit and please mankind. CONDITIONS. They will be printed on good Paper and a neat Type; and will Contain about 300 Pages in Octavo. The Price to Subscribers will be *Twelve Pounds*, neatly Bound & Lettered, and *Nine Pounds* sew'd in blue paper one Half to be paid on Subscribing, the other Half on Delivery of the Books. The Work will be put to the Press as soon as a sufficient Number of Encouragers offer.[2] Those who subscribe for Six, will have a Seventh Gratis. Subscriptions are taken by White and Adams, the Publishers, in School-Street, *Boston*.

Notes

1. Phillis Wheatley married John Peters on April 1, 1778, both of them listed as "free Negroes." See *Early History of Boston* (Boston: Municipal Printer, 1902), p. 441, which reprints documents for 1901–02.

2. Bostonians rejected these proposals, and the volume was not published. Several of the poems and letters have been separately printed by various hands.

Elegy on the Death of a Late Celebrated Poetess

Anonymous*

If conscious sense of genius yet remains,
Of lofty verse, and soft poetic strains;
Shall not the muse a grateful tribute rear.
And drop the silent, sympathetic tear?
If aught that glows within the friendly breast,
That weeps at tales of woe, or hearts opprest;
With me your sympathizing tribute pay,
And to her peaceful manes inscribe the lay.
   Ye! who her talents and her virtues knew,
With grief's spontaneous tears her urn bedew,
She too comply'd with nature's sacred tye,
She gently wip'd the sorrow-streaming eye,
As if by heaven inspir'd, did she relate,
The souls grand entrance at the sacred gate!†
And shall the honour, which she oft apply'd,
To other's reliques, be to hers deny'd?

*Reprinted from *Boston Magazine*, December, 1784, pp. 619–20.

†page 488 of this vol. where appears Phillis's last known published poem, "To Mr. and Mrs. ****** on the Death of their Infant. By Phillis Wheatly [*sic*]."

O that the muse, dear spirit! own'd thy art,
To soften grief and captivate the heart,
Then should these lines in numbers soft array'd,
Preserve thy mem'ry from oblivion's shade;
But O! how vain the wish that friendship pays,
Since her own volumes are her greatest praise.
As Orpheus play'd the list'ning herds among,
They own'd the magic of his powerful song;
Mankind no more their savage nature kept,
And foes to music, wonder'd how they wept.
So PHILLIS tun'd her sweet mellifluous lyre;
(Harmonious numbers bid the soul aspire)
While AFRIC's untaught race with transport heard,
They lov'd the poet, and the muse rever'd.
What tho' her outward form did ne'er disclose
The lilly's white, or blushes of the rose;
Shall sensibility regard the skin,
If all be calm, serene, and pure within?
But ah! can beauty, or can genius save?
Genius and beauty moulder in the grave.
The modest graces, and the richest bloom,
The solemn toll soon ushers to the tomb.
Such the sad ruins of the human race,
That reptiles riot on the fairest face!
Hither let pride its sure criterion view;
In vain shall virtue plead, or honour sue;
Hither let luxury and av'rice find,
A cure for the distemper'd canker'd mind.
Tho' now the business of her life is o'er,
Tho' now she breaths and tunes her lyre no more;
Tho' now the body mixes with the clay;
The soul wings upward to immortal day;
Free'd from a world of wo, and scene of cares,
A lyre of gold she tunes, a crown of glory wears.
Seated with angels in that blissful place,
Where she now joins in her Creator's praise,
Where harmony with louder notes is swell'd,
Where her soft numbers only are excell'd.

HORATIO

State Street, Dec. 1784.

[". . . an influence of extraordinary genius"]

Charles Crawford*

The celebrated PHILLIS WHEATLEY may be produced as an influence of extraordinary genius. It would be difficult perhaps to name any living person as being endowed with superiour talents for Poetry. The following lines appear to be faultless [the first 30 lines of the poem follow]:

To A Clergyman on the Death of His Lady

Where contemplation finds her sacred spring,
Where heav'nly music makes the arches ring,
Where virtue reigns unsully'd and divine,
Where wisdom thron'd, and all the graces shine,
There sits thy spouse amidst the radiant throng,
While praise eternal warbles from her tongue;
There choirs angelic shout her welcome round,
With perfect bliss, and peerless glory crown'd.
While thy dear mate, to flesh no more confin'd,
Exults a blest, an heav'n-ascended mind,
Say in thy breast shall floods of sorrow rise?
Say shall its torrents overwhelm thine eyes?
Amid the seats of heav'n a place is free,
And angels open their bright ranks for thee:
For thee they wait, and with expectant eye
Thy spouse leans downward from th'empyreal sky:
"O come away, her longing spirit cries,
"And share with me the raptures of the skies.
"Our bliss divine to mortals is unknown;
"Immortal life and glory are our own.
"There too may the dear pledges of our love
"Arrive, and taste with us the joys above;
"Attune the harp to more than mortal lays,
"And join with us the tribute of their praise
"To him, who dy'd stern justice to atone.
"And make eternal glory all our own.
"He in his death slew ours, and, as he rose,
"He crush'd the dire dominion of our foes;
"Vain were their hopes to put the God to flight,
"Chain us to hell, and bar the gates of light."

*Reprinted from Lord Garnoc, *Observations Upon Slavery by Charles Crawford* (Philadelphia: Joseph Crukshank, 1784), pp. 5–7.

[On the unacceptability of blacks in white America]

Thomas Jefferson*

It will probably be asked, Why not retain and incorporate the blacks into the State, and thus save the expense of supplying by importation of white settlers, the vacancies they will leave? Deep-rooted prejudices entertained by the whites; ten thousand recollections, by the blacks, of the injuries they have sustained; new provocations; the real distinctions which nature has made; and many other circumstances, will divide us into parties, and produce convulsions, which will never end but in the extermination of the one or the other race. To these objections, which are political, may be added others, which are physical and moral.

The first difference which strikes us is that of color. . . . And is this difference of no importance? Is it not the foundation of a greater or less share of beauty in the two races? Are not the fine mixtures of red and white, the expressions of every passion by greater or less suffusions of color in the one, preferable to that eternal monotony, which reigns in the countenances, that immovable veil of black which covers the emotions of the other race? Add to these, flowing hair, a more elegant symmetry of form, their own judgment in favor of the whites, declared by their preference of them, as uniformly as is the preference of the Oran-ootan for the black woman over those of his own species. . . . Besides those of color, figure, and hair, there are other physical distinctions proving a difference of race. They have less hair on the face and body. They secrete less by the kidneys, and more by the glands of the skin, which gives them a very strong and disagreeable odor.

Comparing them by their faculties of memory, reason, and imagination, it appears to me that in memory they are equal to the whites; in reason much inferior, as I think one could scarcely be found capable of tracing and comprehending the investigations of Euclid; and that in imagination they are dull, tasteless, and anomalous. . . . never yet could I find that a black had uttered a thought above the level of plain narration; never saw even an elementary trait of painting or sculpture. . . . In music they are more generally gifted than the whites with accurate ears for tune and time, and they have been found capable of imagining a small catch. . . .

Misery is often the parent of the most affecting touches in poetry. Among the blacks is misery enough, Gods knows, but no poetry. . . . Religion, indeed, has produced a Phyllis Whately;[1] but it could not produce a poet. The compositions published under her name are below the

*Reprinted from *The Writings of Thomas Jefferson*, ed. Albert E. Bergh, 20 vols. (Washington, D.C.: Thomas Jefferson Memorial Association, 1903), II, 192–96.

dignity of criticism. The heroes of the Dunciad are to her, as Hercules to the author of that poem. . . .

Notes

1. Jefferson's library included a copy of Wheatley's *Poems on Various Subjects, Religious and Moral*, in which the poet's name is spelled correctly.

[". . . an African girl, who made no contemptible appearance in this species of composition"]

Thomas Clarkson*

But where . . . impediments have been removed, where they have received an education, and have known and pronounced the language with propriety . . . defects have vanished, and their productions have been less objectionable. For a proof of this, we appeal to the writing of an African girl, who made no contemptible appearance in this species of composition. She was kidnapped when only eight years old, and, in the year, 1761, was transported to America, where she was sold with other slaves. She had no school education there, but receiving some little instruction from the family, with whom she was so fortunate to live, she obtained such a knowledge of the English language within sixteen months from the time of her arrival, as to be able to speak it and read it to the astonishment of those who heard her. She soon afterwards learned to write, and, having a great inclination to learn the Latin tongue, she was indulged by her master, and made a progress. Her poetical works were published with his permission, in the year 1773. They contain thirty-eight pieces on different subjects. We shall beg leave to make a short extract from two or three of them, for the observation of the reader.

From an Hymn to the Evening.

"Fill'd with the praise of him who gives the light,
"And draws the sable curtains of the night,
"Let placid slumbers sooth each weary mind,
"At morn to wake more heav'nly and refin'd;
"More pure and guarded from the snares of sin."

From an Hymn to the Morning.

"Aurora hail! and all the thousand dies,
"That deck thy progress through the vaulted skies!

*Reprinted from Thomas Clarkson, *Essay on the Slavery and Commerce of the Human Species, Particularly the African* (London: J. Phillips, 1786), pp. 171–75.

"The morn awakes, and wide extends her rays,
"On ev'ry leaf the gentle zephyr plays,
"Harmonious lays the feather'd race resume,
"Dart the bright eyes, and shake the painted plume."

From Thoughts on Imagination.

"Now here, now there, the roving *fancy* flies,
"Till some lov'd object strikes her wand'ring eyes,
"Whose silken fetters all the senses bind,
"And soft captivity involves the mind.

"Imagination! who can sing thy force,
"Or who describe the swiftness of thy course?
"Soaring through air to find the bright abode,
"Th'empyreal palace of the thund'ring God,
"We on thy pinions can surpass the wind,
"And leave the rolling universe behind:
"From star to star the mental opticks rove,
"Measure the skies, and range the realms above,
"There in one view we grasp the mighty whole,
"Or with new worlds amaze th'unbounded soul."

Such is the poetry which we produce as a proof of our assertions. How far it has succeeded, the reader may by this time have determined in his own mind. We should therefore only beg leave to accompany it with this observation, that if the author *was designed for slavery*, (as the argument must confess) the greater part of the inhabitants of Britain must lose their claim to freedom.[1]

Notes

1. Thomas Clarkson (1760–1846) has been called the most influential of several outstanding English abolitionists. He spent most of his life and much of his money trying to prove that Africans, when properly educated, could succeed in a Western culture. His famous *Essay* was originally a Latin dissertation "*which was Honoured with the First Prize in the University of Cambridge, for the year 1785*," and went into several editions in English, Swedish, German, French, and Spanish.

[The ample testimony of Phillis Wheatley's *Poems*]

Richard Nisbet*

The Negro's claim to the title of a rational moral agent is clear and incontrovertible from the evidence to support it. . . . The . . . moral natural and ingenious productions of Phillis Wheatley, a slave whose mind was cramped by her condition and whose only tutor was the strength of her own faculties . . . furnished a publick and ample testimony of, at least, as considerable a portion of mental ability, as falls to the lot of mankind in general. . . .

[". . . the charms of an agreeable imagination"]

Jean de Marsillac*

Lisez les lettres d'*Ignatius Sancho*, les Oeuvres de *Phillis Wheatly* [*sic*], les Mémoires d'Andre Brue, &r &r &r l'on verra si les doux sentiments de l'humanité, & les charmes d'une imagination agréable n'ont pas souvent distingué notre plume. . . .

Read the letters of Ignatius Sancho, the works of Phillis Wheatley, the Memoirs of Andre Brue, etc., etc., etc., you will see if the sweet sentiments of humanity, and the charms of an agreeable imagination have not often distinguished our writing. . . .

[Phillis Wheatley as a proof of African capacity]

William Dickinson*

Letter 11, Feb. 17, 1778

. . . I have not room to add, as I intended, extracts from the poems of PHILLIS WHEATLEY, which are so many proofs of African capacity. They

*Reprinted from Richard Nisbet, *The Capacity of Negroes for Religious and Moral Improvement Considered* (London: J. Phillips, 1789), p. 31.

*Reprinted from *Le More-Lack, ou Essai sur les moyens les plus doux & les plus équitables d'abloir la traites & l'esclavages des Nègres d'Afrique, en conservant aux colonies tous les avantages d'une population agricole* (London: Prault, 1789), p. 169.

*Reprinted from William Dickinson, *Letters on Slavery . . . To which are added, Addresses to the Whites, and to the Free Negroes of Barbadoes, and Accounts of some Negroes Eminent for their Virtues and Abilities* (London: J. Phillips, 1789), p. 187n.

were printed in 1773, with an attestation that they were written by her, signed by His Exc. [*sic*] T. Hutchinson, Gov. and the Hon. A. Oliver, Lieut.-Gov. of N. England with nine other gentlemen and seven clergymen. To these I might add a certain respectable gentleman in London,[1] who tells me that he was acquainted with our poetess, while in England, that he corresponded with her after her return to Boston (where she was married to a Mr. Peters, a person of her own colour, who kept a shop) that she was uncommonly ingenious, and that she certainly wrote the poems ascribed to her. . . .

Notes

1. John Thornton (1720–90), was an English millionaire and Christian philanthropist who dispensed several thousands of pounds sterling annually for various charitable causes. For correspondence between Wheatley and Thornton see Kenneth Silverman, "Four New Letters by Phillis Wheatley," *Early American Literature*, 7, No. 3 (Winter, 1974), 257–71.

[On the specimen of Phillis Wheatley's work]

John G. Steadman*

That these people[1] are neither divested of a good ear nor poetical genius, has been frequently proved, when they have had the advantages of a good education. Amongst others, Phillis Wheatley, who was a slave at *Boston* in New England, learned the Latin language, and wrote thirty-eight elegant pieces of poetry on different subjects, which were published in 1773. As a specimen, I cannot refrain here inserting the following extract from that entitled "*Thoughts on Imagination.*"[2]

> Now here, now there, the roving fancy flies,
> Till some lov'd object strikes her wand'ring eyes,
> Whose silken fetters all the senses bind,
> And soft captivity invades[3] the mind.
> Imagination! who can sing thy force?
> Or where describe the swiftness of thy course?
> Soaring through air to find the bright abode,
> Th'imperial palace of the thundering God.
> We on thy pinions can surpass the wind,
> And leave the rolling universe behind.
> From star to star the mental optics rove,
> Measure the skies, and range the realms above;

*Reprinted from John G. Steadman, *Narrative of a five years' expedition against the Revolted Negroes of Surinam, in Guiana, on the Wild Coast of South America: from the year 1772, to 1777*, 2 vols. (London: J. Johnson, 1796), II, 259–60.

> There in one view we grasp the mighty whole,
> Or with new worlds amaze th'unbounded soul.

What can be more beautiful and sublime?

Notes

1. Guyanese blacks, against whom Steadman commanded imperial troops, and for whom he evolved a lasting respect, as he makes clear throughout his profusely illustrated work.
2. "On Imagination" in the 1773 volume.
3. "involves" in the 1773 volume.

[". . . what white person upon this continent has written more beautiful lines"]

Gilbert Imlay*

"Religion has produced a Phyllis [*sic*] Wheatley; but it could not produce a poet," is another of Mr. Jefferson's dogmata. Phyllis was brought from Africa to America between 7 and 8 years of age; and without any assistance from a school education, and before she was 15 years old, wrote many of her poems. This information is attested by her then master, John Wheatley, dated Boston, November 14, 1772. I will transcribe part of her poem on Imagination,[1] and leave you to judge whether it is poetical or not. It will afford you an opportunity, if you have never met with it, of estimating her genius and Mr. Jefferson's judgment; and I think, without any disparagement to him, that, by comparison, Phyllis appears much the superior. Indeed, I should be glad to be informed what white person upon this continent has written more beautiful lines.

Notes

1. Lines 14–32 of "On Imagination" are here transcribed; see the comments by Thomas Clarkson and J. G. Steadman, above.

*Reprinted from Gilbert Imlay, *Topographical Description of the Western Territory of North America: containing a succinct account of its soil, climate, Natural History, population, Agriculture, Manners and Customs*, 3rd ed. (London: J. Debrett, 1797), pp. 229–30.

["Almost all her poetical productions have a religious or moral cast"]

Henri Grégoire*

. . . Jefferson, who appears unwilling to acknowledge the talents of negroes, even those of Phillis Wheatley, pretends that the heroes of the *Dunciad* are divinities, when compared with this African muse. If we were disposed to cavil, we might say, that to an assertion, it is sufficient to oppose a contrary assertion; we might appeal to the judgment of the public, which is manifested by the collection made of the poetry of Phillis Wheatley: but a more direct refutation may be made, by selecting some portions of her works, which will give us some idea of her talents. This has been done by Clarkson, Imlay and others.

It was doubtless her acquaintance with the works of Horace, that induced her to commence like him with an Ode to Macenas, whose protection poets secured by flattery. Their baseness throws a veil over his Augustus, by the same means, buried in oblivion the horrors of the Triumvirate. Phillis in this piece reminds us that Terrence was her compatriot. It is not without merit; but we hasten to subjects more worthy of her muse. Almost all her poetical productions have a religious or moral cast—all breathe a soft and sentimental melancholy. Twelve relate to the death of friends. We are particularly pleased with her odes on the works of Providence, on virtue, humanity, to Neptune [,] to a young painter, of her own color. On seeing his works she vents her grief on the sorrows of her countrymen.

> Remember, Christians, negroes black as Cain
> May be refin'd and join the Angelic train.

The reader will permit us to present to him some of the productions of Phillis.[1]

On the death of J. C. an infant.

> No more the flow'ry scenes of pleasure rise,
> Nor charming prospects greet the mental eyes,
> No more with joy we view that lovely face
> Smiling, disportive, flush'd with ev'ry grace.

*Reprinted from Henri Grégoire, *An Enquiry concerning the Intellectual and Moral Faculties, and Literature of Negroes; followed, with an account of the Life and Works of fifteen Negroes & Mullatoes, Distinguished in Sciences, Literature and the Arts*, trans. Daniel B. Warden (Brooklyn: Thomas Kirk, 1810), pp. 234–46. The original text occurs in Grégoire's *De La Littérature Des Nègres ou Recherches sur leurs facultés intelléctuelles, leurs qualités morales et leur littérature; suivies de Notices sur la vie et les ouvrages des Nègres qui se sont distingués dans les Sciences, les Lettres et les Arts* (Paris: Maradan, 1808), pp. 260–72.

The tear of sorrow flows from ev'ry eye,
Groans answer groans, and sighs to sighs reply;
What sudden pangs shot thro' each aching heart,
When, *Death*, thy messenger dispatch'd his dart!
Thy dread attendants, all destroying *Pow'r*,
Hurried the infant to his mortal hour.
Could'st thou unpitying close those radiant eyes?
Or fail'd his artless beauties to surprize?
Could not his innocence thy stroke controul,
Thy purpose shake, and soften all thy soul?

The blooming babe, with shades of *Death* o'erspread,
No more shall smile, no more shall raise its head;
But like a branch that from the tree is torn,
Falls prostrate, wither'd, languid, and forlorn.
"Where flies my *James*," tis thus I seem to hear
The parent ask, "Some angel tell me where
"He wings his passage thro' the yielding air?"
Me thinks a cherub bending from the skies
Observes the question and serene replies,
"In heav'ns high palaces your babe appears:
"Prepare to meet him, and dismiss your tears."
Shall not th'intelligence your grief restrain,
And turn the mournful to the chearful strain?
Cease your complaints, suspend each rising sigh,
Cease to accuse the Ruler of the sky.
Parents, no more indulge the falling tear:
Let *Faith* to heav'ns refulgent domes repair,
There see your infant like a seraph glow:
What charms celestial in his numbers flow
Melodious, while the soul-enchanting strain
Dwells on his tongue, and fills th'etherial plain?
Enough—forever cease your murm'ring breath;
Not as a foe, but friend converse with *Death*,
Since to the port of happiness unknown
He brought that treasure which you call your own.
The gift of heav'n intrusted to your hand
Chearful resign at the divine command;
Not at your bar must sov'reign *Wisdom* stand.

An hymn to the morning.

Attend my lays, ye ever honour'd nine,
Assist my labours, and my strains refine;
In smoothest numbers pour the notes along,
For bright *Aurora* now demands my song.

Aurora, hail, and all the thousand dies,
Which deck thy progress through the vaulted skies;
The morn awakes, and wide extends her rays,
On ev'ry leaf the gentle zephyr plays;
Harmonious lays the feather'd race resume,
Dart the bright eye, and shake the painted plume.

Ye shady groves, your verdant gloom display
To shield your poet from the burning day:
Calliope, awake the sacred lyre,
While thy fair sisters fan the pleasing fire:
The bow'rs, the gales, the variegated skies
In all their pleasures in my bosom rise.

See in the east th'illustrious king of day!
His rising radiance drives the shades away—
But Oh! I feel his fervid beams too strong,
And scarce begun, concludes th'abortive song.

To the right honorable William, *earl of* Dartmouth, *his majesty's principal secretary of state for north America*, etc.

Hail, happy day, when, smiling like the morn,
Fair *Freedom* rose *New-England* to adorn. . . .
[six lines are omitted]
Long lost to realms beneath the northern skies
She shines supreme, while hated *faction* dies:
Soon as appear'd the *Goddess* long desir'd
Sick at the view, she languish'd and expir'd:
Thus from the splendors of the morning light
The owl in sadness seeks the caves of night

No more, *America*, in mournful strain
Of wrongs, and grievance unredress'd complain,
No longer shalt thou dread the iron chain,
Which wanton *Tyranny* with lawless hand
had made and with it meant t'enslave the land.

Should you, my lord, while you persue my song,
Wonder from whence my love of *Freedom* sprung,
Whence flow the wishes for the common good,
By feeling hearts alone best understood,
I, young in life, by seeming cruel fate
Was snatch'd from *Afric's* fancy'd happy seat:
What pangs excruciating must molest,
What sorrows labor in my parents' breast?
Steel'd was that soul, and by no misery mov'd,
That from a father seiz'd his babe belov'd:

Such, such my case. And can I then but pray
Others may never feel tyrannic sway? etc. etc.

Notes

1. Omitted by Warden, Grégoire had written at this point: "J'insère ici trois de ses pièces. Le lecteur voudra bien se rappeler qu'en jugeant les productions d'une Négresse esclave, âgée de dix-neuf ans, l'indulgence est un acte de justice; d'ailleurs, la traduction n'est peut-être qu'une mauvaise copie d'un bon original" ("I insert here three of her pieces. The reader would do well to remember that, in judging the works of a nineteen-year-old slave girl, indulgence would be an act of justice. Besides, the translation is perhaps only a bad copy of a good original").

[On Jefferson on Wheatley]

Samuel Stanhope Smith*

The Poems of Phillis Whately [*sic*], a poor African slave taught to read by the indulgent piety of her master, are spoken of [by Thomas Jefferson] with infinite contempt. But I will demand of Mr. Jefferson, or any other man, who is acquainted with American planters, how many of these masters could have written poems equal to those of Phillis Whately?

["*Afric's* heir to fame"]

Joseph Brown Ladd*

. . . Here the fair volume shows the far-spread name
Of wondrous Wheatly,† [*sic*] *Afric's* heir to fame.
Well is it known what glowing genius shines
What force of numbers, in her published lines:
With magic power the grand descriptions roll
Thick in the mind, and agitate the soul.[1]

†Phillis Wheatly [*sic*], a negress, and the author of some ingenious poems, which seem to be entitled to remembrance here, although not written by a native of America. One need only peruse the following lines, extracted from her poems, to be convinced of this:

*Reprinted from Samuel S. Smith, *Essay on the Causes of Variety of Complexion and figure in the Human Species, to which are added Animadversions on Certain Remarks made in the first edition of this Essay, by Mr. Charles White, in a series of Discoveries delivered before the Literary and Philosophical Society of Manchester in England*, 2nd ed. (New Brunswick: J. Simpson, 1810), p. 269. The editions of this essay published in Philadelphia in 1787 and 1789 did not include this passage.
*Reprinted from Joseph Brown Ladd, "The Prospect of America," in *The Literary Remains of Joseph Brown Ladd, M.D.*, ed. Elizabeth Haskins (New York: H. C. Sleight, 1832), p. ixn.

"When Homer paints, lo! circumfused in air,
Celestial gods in mortal forms appear:
Swift as they move hear each recess rebound,
Earth quakes, heaven thunders, and the shores resound.
Great sire of verse, before my mortal eyes
The lightnings flash along the gloomy skies:
And as the thunder shades the heavenly plains,
A deep-felt horror creeps through all my veins."

Notes

1. Elizabeth Haskins, the editor of *The Literary Remains*, was Ladd's sister. Several of the lines here quoted differ from the version of this poem published in Wheatley's 1773 volume, suggesting that Ladd's papers included a variant manuscript of the poem. Ladd, who was born and reared in Newport, Rhode Island, the home of Wheatley's lifelong black domestic friend, Obour Tanner, may have met Wheatley to discuss their common interests.

["The most favorable evidence . . . of the capacity of the African intellect for improvement"]

Jared Sparks*

. . . In whatever order of merit they [i.e., Wheatley's poems] may be ranked, it cannot be doubted, that they exhibit the most favorable evidence on record, of the capacity of the African for intellect for improvement. The classical allusions are numerous, and imply a wide compass of reading, a correct judgment, good taste, and a tenacious memory. Her deportment is represented to have been gentle and unpretending, her temper amiable, her feelings refined, and her religious impressions strong and constant. . . .

I have not been able to find, among Washington's papers, the letter and poem addressed to him. They have doubtless been lost. From the circumstance of her invoking the muse in his praise, and from the tenor of some of her printed pieces, particularly one addressed to King George seven years before in which she compliments him on the repeal of the Stamp Act, it may be inferred, that she was a whig in politics after the American way of thinking; and it might be curious to see in what manner she would eulogize liberty and the rights of man, while herself, nominally at least, in bondage.

*Reprinted from *The Writings of George Washington*, ed. Jared Sparks, 12 vols. (Boston: Hill and Gray, 1833), IX, 297–99n. This passage is by Sparks.

["They . . . deserve a place eminently conspicuous in every private and public library"]

[William Lloyd Garrison?]*

PHILLIS WHEATLEY

Mr. George W. Light, of this city, has just published a handsome edition of the Poems of this famous African poetess, with a Memoir excellently written by one who is a collateral descendant of Mrs. Wheatley (the mistress of Phillis) and has been familiar with the name and fame of Phillis from her childhood. The Spirit of the Memoir excites our admiration, exhibiting as it does a loftiness and liberality of mind, in nowise affected by those prejudices against a colored skin which are as vulgar as they are common. We regret that the crowded state of our columns, today prevents our making an extended notice of these poems. As, however, they were all published in our third volume, and are therefore familiar to our readers, any commendatory remarks from us are unnecessary.[1] They are alike extraordinary, both as to their origin and merit; and deserve a place eminently conspicuous in every private and public library. The thanks of the friends of the colored race are due to Mr. Light, for having presented them to the public in so neat and beautiful a shape; and we cannot doubt that the edition will sell rapidly. An admirable lithographic likeness of Phillis accompanies the work.[2] The work is for sale at this office—price 50¢.

Notes

1. Founded to combat American slavery, William Lloyd Garrison's weekly, *The Liberator*, kept the name of Phillis Wheatley before its readers for years. It ran almost all of Wheatley's collected poems in its 1832 issues, February 18 through December 22; the February 18, 1832 issue also carried remarks on Wheatley from a speech by Samuel Knapp, and a brief biographical sketch by Abigail Mott; advertisements of the 1834 and 1835 reprintings of Wheatley's 1773 volume were included. Beginning on August 12, 1834, and continuing intermittently thereafter, *The Liberator* included notices of Wheatley's volume as well as Margaretta M. Odell's memoir of Phillis among its list of antislavery publications for sale.

2. This lithographic likeness was prepared from, but is not an exact copy of, the engraving found in the 1773 volume. A Mr. James Bugbee had several other copies of Wheatley struck off in 1885, and gave one to the Massachusetts Historical Society in 1886. There have been several other less faithful renderings of Wheatley which have prefaced various American reprintings of the volume. A painting said to be in London's National Portrait Gallery, and showing Brook Watson (lord mayor of London in 1796, and a friend to Phillis) handing a copy of John Milton's *Paradise Lost* to Phillis during her 1773 visit to London, does not in fact exist; Mrs. Alison Opyrchal, archival assistant at the National Gallery, reports no record of such a painting.

*Reprinted from *The Liberator*, March 22, 1834, p. 3.

[*The Liberator* on Phillis Wheatley]

William Lloyd Garrison*

#18 Phillis Wheatley, 110 p. 18mo. 37 1/2 [i.e., 37½¢]. *Memoir and Poems of Phillis Wheatley, a native African and a slave.*

The Poems were originally published in London in 1773. Many of them would do credit to a person of the highest advantages. It would do well to have them always at hand that we may have some conception of the amount of genius which slavery is murdering. The book has a beautiful lithographic likeness.

#19 *Memoir of Phillis Wheatley.* 36 pp. 18mo. 12 1/2 [i.e., 12½¢].

Besides its value, as showing what the irrepressible aspirations of a slave accomplished, it is useful, as affording encouragement to the efforts of all. It practically enforces this lesson urged by the biographer. Surely no man or woman, or child, in whatever circumstances, has occasion after this to be discouraged, in an honest exertion to add to his own usefulness, and the happiness of the world around!

[On Phillis Wheatley's Letters]

Anonymous*

Book Notice[:] *Letters of Phillis Wheatley, the Negro Slave Poet of Boston*: (Boston: Privately Printed, 1864), 8vo. pp. 19.

This pamphlet consists of seven letters from Phillis Wheatley to a young woman of her own color, Abour Tanner, of Newport, R.I., which were read by Charles Deane at a meeting of the Massachusetts Historical Society; with Mr. Deane's remarks on the occasion. Till the appearance of this brochure, we had little by which we could judge of Phillis's talent for prose composition, though her poems had been favorably known for ninety years. We agree with Mr. Deane that the letters indicate "much maturity of mind and refinement and delicacy of feeling and character."

An anonymous memoir of Phillis Wheatley was prefixed to the edition of her poems published in 1834, at Boston, by George W. Light. This memoir, Mr. Deane informs us, was written by Margaretta Matilda Odell, of Jamaica Plain.

*Reprinted from *The Liberator*, October 27, 1837, p. 4.

*Reprinted from *New England Historical and Genealogical Register for the Year 1864*, 18 (October, 1864), 394.

[". . . the merest echo of the common jingle of the day"]

James Parton*

The colored poet, Phillis Wheatley, had her admirers a hundred years ago in Boston, where her volumes can still occasionally be found. We have carefully looked over it, and cannot deny the justice of Jefferson's remarks upon it. She was a poet very much as "Blind Tom" is a musician,[1] her verses being the merest echo of the common jingle of the day. She was a poet only as Christophe[2] and Toussaint L'Ouverture[3] (those colored caricatures of Bonaparte) were generals and emperors. A fatal facility of imitation stands in the way of this interesting race, and we cannot fairly deny that facts give support to the opinion of an inherent mental inferiority. It is ninety years since Jefferson published his "Notos," and we cannot yet name one negro of pure blood who has taken the first, the second, the third, or the tenth rank in business, politics, art, literature, scholarship, science, or philosophy. To the present hour the negro has contributed nothing to the intellectual resources of man. If he turns "negro minstrel," he still imitates the white creations of that black art; and he has not composed one of the airs that have had popular success as negro melodies. . . .

Notes

1. "Blind Tom." Thomas Greene Bethune (1849–1908) was an inspired but mentally unstable black musical phenomenon, born blind in Georgia; untaught but able to play, after a single listening, pieces of music from classical masters—Beethoven, Chopin, Mendelssohn, etc., Tom was an exploited sensation managed by his former master who toured him throughout Europe, earning large sums of money from the curious—$100,000 in a single London season; prominent musical authorities and educators of Philadelphia repeatedly tested Tom and finally confessed their inability to explain his genius.

2. Christophe. Born a slave in 1767(?) on the British West Indian island of St. Christopher, Henry Christophe succeeded Jean Jacques Dessalines, who had led Haiti from 1804 (from 1805 as emperor) until he was assassinated in 1806. Declaring himself King Henry I, Christophe was eventually driven to a dramatic suicide in his Haitian palace in 1820.

3. Toussaint L'Ouverture (1743–1803). The renowned (and badly misunderstood) ex-slave was a military leader of successful Haitian slave revolts against French forces, which led to the establishment of Haiti as the first independent Negro state in the Western hemisphere. L'Ouverture was betrayed by the French, captured, and allowed to die imprisoned in the Jura mountains of France.

*Reprinted from James Parton, "Antipathy to the Negro," *North American Review*, 127 (November-December, 1878), 487–88.

["... poems ... of varying degrees of merit ..."]

Delano A. Goddard*

Phillis Wheatley, a waif brought to these shores on a slave ship from the coast of Africa, wrote youthful verses which at first attracted attention rather on account of the novelty of their origin than for any special merit of their own. Her earlier poems were first published in England, whither she had been taken in 1773 in ill health, at the age of eighteen years. These poems, gratefully inscribed to the Countess of Huntingdon, her chief friend and benefactor, and subsequently republished in this country, are of varying degrees of merit,—the best of them being simple, graceful, and not without traces of genuine poetic and religious feeling. Her memorial verses on the death of Dr. Sewall, of George Whitefield, and of Governor Hutchinson's daughter, and others, were calculated to win sympathetic interest of many persons; while her more ambitious poems, "Goliath of Gath," "Niobe Mourning for her children," and her contemplative and religious poems show great purity of sentiment and unusual gifts of poetic expression. Poverty, neglect, and a tragic death following a melancholy marriage quenched the fire just as it was beginning to light her way to hope and fame.

["... verses ... by one from whom even bad verses were too good to be expected"]

Moses Coit Tyler*

[A] prominent representative of the town of Boston in the poetry of this period is Phillis Wheatley, a gentle-natured and intelligent slave-girl, whose name still survives among us in the shape of a tradition vaguely testifying to the existence of poetic talent in this particular member of the African race. Unfortunately, a glance at what she wrote will show that there is no adequate basis for such tradition, and that the significance of her career belongs rather to the domain of anthropology or hagiology, than to that of poetry—whether American or African. Her verses, which were first published in a collected form in London in 1773, under the title of "Poem on Various Subjects, Religious and Moral," attracted for a time

*Reprinted from Delano A. Goddard, "The Pulpit, the Press, and Literature of the Revolution," in *Memorial History of Boston, Including Suffolk County, Massachusetts 1630–1880*, ed. Justin Winsor, 4 vols. (Boston: James R. Osgood, 1881), III, 147.

*Reprinted from Moses Coit Tyler, *The Literary History of the American Revolution*, 2 vols. (New York: G. P. Putnam, 1897), I, 186–87.

considerable curiosity, both in England and in America—not at all, however, because the verses were good, but because they were written by one from whom even bad verses were too good to be expected. In 1784, under her new name of Phillis Peters, she published in Boston a poem entitled "Liberty and Peace," suggested by the happy ending of the Revolutionary War. This production, however, makes no change in the evidence touching her poetic gifts.*

[". . . still a puzzle and an astonishment"]

Katherine Lee Bates*

The *Elegy in a Country Churchyard*, indeed, furnished not only verse, tone, and situation, but actual phrases to more than one formal effusion of the time. Among the poems of that phenomenal negro girl, Phillis Wheatley, a petted slave in a Boston family, is an elegy on Whitefield, two consecutive stanzas running thus:

Cou'd virtue charm the dull cold ear of Death,
Or pow'rs capacious stay the fatal blow,
Cou'd innate goodness stop the fleeting breath,
Whitefield, thou still had bless'd a world below.

Still hadst thou shone, to guide the aspiring mind,
To bid Religion's streams serenely roll,
Her ample heights or latent tracts to find,
And swell the genial currents of the soul.[1]

That a wild little black, who stood, a frail child of seven, in the Boston slave-market of 1761, clad in a rag of old carpeting, with a dim memory in her frightened heart of a far-away pagan Mother pouring out water in worship before the sun at his rising, should have been enabled, by a dozen years of Christian nurture, to produce this volume of fluent, pious, decorous verse, pranked out with all the literary elegance of the day, is still a puzzle and an astonishment. Her mind-stuff must have been at once singularly rich and singularly plastic—malleable gold of the Dark Conti-

*A little book entitled "Letters of Phillis Wheatley, the Negro-Slave Poet of Boston," and edited by Charles Deane, was privately printed in Boston in 1864,—at a time when testimony as to the intellectual capacity of the negro was much desired. But poor Phillis's efforts in prose have no more value in that direction than have her efforts in verse,—these letters being little else than pious platitudes and almost infantile platitudes expressed in extremely stilted English.

*Reprinted from Katherine Lee Bates, *American Literature* (New York: Macmillan, 1898), pp. 78–79.

nent. Her subjection to civilization is pathetic. The rare song-bird of Africa was thoroughly tamed in her Boston cage. . . . In the lines "To S.M. a Young African Painter on Seeing his works" occurs a passage of touching suggestion [lines 23–28 of that poem follow]:

But when these shades of time are chas'd away,
And darkness ends in everlasting day,
On what seraphic pinions shall we move,
And view the landscapes in the realms above?
There shall thy tongue in heav'nly murmurs flow,
And there my muse with heav'nly transport glow.

Notes

1. These two stanzas are not found in any of the three known versions of Wheatley's poem on the death of Whitefield. Bates may have confused the stanzas from one of the many other tributes to Whitefield with those from one of Wheatley's versions of her elegy.

[". . . she sings like a canary in a cage . . ."]

William J. Long*

Prominent among the minor versifiers who enjoyed a day's favor was Phillis Wheatley, the negro slave girl. In 1761 she stood, a trembling girl without name or speech, in the open slave market of Boston. Twelve years later she published, in London, a book. . . . The book created a mild sensation on both sides of the Atlantic, and no wonder! Even the inspired Psalmist once cried out, "How shall we sing the Lord's song in a strange land?" This stranger among us was violently taken from her savage mother in Africa. She remembered the horror in that mother's face as her child was snatched away. She could recall the wild, free life of the tribe,—chant of victory or wail of defeat, leaping flames, gloom of forest, cries of wild beasts, singing of birds, glory of sunrise, the stately march of the wild elephants over the silent places, Here was material such as no other singer in all the civilized world could command, and she had the instinct of a poet. We open her book eagerly, and we meet "On the death of an Infant":

Through airy roads he winged his instant flight
To purer regions of celestial light.

This is not what we expected. We skip the rest, and turn the leaves. Here is something promising, "To Imagination" [lines 13–22 follow]:

*Reprinted from William J. Long, *American Literature* (Boston: Ginn, 1913), pp. 145–46. With permission of the publishers, Ginn and Company (Xerox Corporation).

Imagination! who can sing thy source,
Or who describe the swiftness of thy course?
Soaring through air to find the bright abode,
The empyreal palace of the thundering god,
We on thy pinions can surpass the wind,
And leave the rolling universe behind.
From star to star the mental optics rove,
Measure the skies and range the realms above;
There in one view we grasp the mighty whole,
Or with new worlds amaze the unbounded soul.

It is vain to seek further, for the end is disappointment. Here is no Zulu, but drawing-room English; not the wild, barbaric strain of march and camp and singing fire that stirs a man's instincts, but pious platitudes, colorless imitations of Pope, and some murmurs of a terrible theology, harmless now as the rumbling of an extinct volcano. It is too bad. This poor child has been made over into a wax puppet; she sings like a canary in a cage, a bird that forgets its native melody and imitates only what it hears. We have called attention to her simply because she is typical of scores of minor poets of the Revolutionary period, who, with a glorious opportunity before them, neglected the poetry and heroism of daily life in order to follow a literary fashion. . . .

SELECTED REPRINTED ESSAYS

[A Review of Wheatley's *Poems on Various Subjects*]

[William J. Snelling]*

The work before us is a neat duodecimo volume, fairly printed on good paper, and ornamented with a lithographic likeness of the (we had almost said fair) authoress. It comprises upwards of a hundred pages. The Memoir prefixed is ably and feelingly written, and contains all, as we suppose, that is known of Phillis Wheatley. . . . Her mind seems to have been peculiarly susceptible of religious impressions, as indeed, we have observed most of her race are, when anyone will take the pains to teach them. At the age of sixteen she joined the Old South Church, and became an ornament to it. The little poem following may serve to exemplify the quiet piety which is characteristic of all her writings.

On Being Brought From Africa to America

'T was mercy brought me from my pagan land,
Gave [*sic,* i.e., taught] my benighted soul to understand
That there's a God,—that there's a Saviour too;
Once I redemption neither sought nor knew.
Some view our sable race with scornful-eye—
"Their color is a diabolic dye."
Remember, Christians, negroes black as Cain
May be refined, and join the angelic train.

. . . Perhaps her genius, her unquestionable virtues, the vicissitudes of her life, and her melancholy end ought to excite as much interest as the fate of Lady Jane Grey, of Mary, Queen of Scots, or any other heroine, ancient or modern; but such, I fear, will not be the case. She was a negro, and therefore entitled to no pity or regard. What matters it that a negro has talents and virtues?—what matters it that she suffers?

We turn to her poetry. It seems to us respectable, though not of a high order. Yet how many white writers of this country have enjoyed a transient reputation on much less intrinsic merit! What proportion of rhymesters, who enrich our newspapers and magazines with their effusions, can write half so well as Phillis Wheatley? She had no assistance.

*Reprinted from [William J. Snelling], "Phillis Wheatley's Poems," *Christian Examiner and General Review*, 16 (May, 1834), 169–74.

Like one of her favorite authors, "she lisped in numbers, for the numbers came." She seems to have begun to write verses as soon as she had sufficient command of the English language to express her ideas,—certainly before she could have known any thing of the rules of composition. Accordingly, we find some ill-constructed and harsh and prosaic lines, but not so many by half as in the verses of most of her contemporary American poets. That her lines are full of feeling, no one will deny who has read the extract we have already given. That she had considerable originality will be apparent from her epitaph on Dr. Sewall. [Lines 30–51 from "On the Death of the Rev. Dr. Sewell, 1769" follow.]

Lo, here, a man, redeemed by Jesus' blood
A sinner once, but now a saint with God.
Behold, ye rich, ye poor, ye fools, ye wise,
Nor let his monument your heart surprise;
'Twill tell you what this holy man has done,
Which gives him brighter lustre than the sun.
Listen, ye happy, from your seats above,
I speak sincerely, while I speak and love.
He sought the paths of piety and truth,
By these made happy from his early youth.
In blooming years that grace divine he felt,
Which rescues sinners from the chains of guilt.
Mourn him, ye indigent, whom he has fed,
And henceforth seek, like him, for living bread;
Ev'n Christ, the bread descending from above,
And ask an int'rest in his saving love.
Mourn him, ye youth, to whom he oft has told
God's gracious wonders, from the times of old.
I, too, have cause, this mighty loss to mourn,
For he, my monitor, will not return.
Oh, when shall we to his blest state arrive?
When the same graces in our bosoms thrive?

Phillis had a peculiarity of intellect which is not often met with. Her memory was very ill regulated. That it must have been uncommonly strong, in some things, is self evident, else how could she have acquired the English language in so short a time?—how could she have mastered the Latin? Yet in other matters it was very defective. It has been seen that she could remember but one solitary fact, connected with her life, previous to her seventh year. The memory of other children reaches much further back. When she composed, she could not retain her own compositions in her mind, and was obliged either to lose it or commit it instantly to paper. We offer no solution of this anomaly,—it is enough that it must have been a great disadvantage to a person of literary pursuits.

Phillis Wheatley, we think, was a precocious genius, destined very rapidly to acquire a certain degree of excellence, and there to stop for ever. As mediocrity, or even moderate merit in song, is never tolerated, we dare not hope that her works will ever be very popular or generally read; for readers never take into account the disadvantages the writer may have labored under. It is not just that they should; for otherwise the land would be flooded with bad writings, to the exclusion and discouragement of good. It is little consolation to him, who has wasted his time and money in buying and reading a wretched production, to be told that it was written by an apprentice or a woman. We do not mean by this to express any disapprobation of the publication before us, but merely to say that, singular as its merits are, they are not of the kind that will command admiration. Still the work will live,—there will always be friends enough of liberty and of the cause of negro improvement not to let it sink into oblivion, and many will desire to possess it as a curiosity. We wish the publisher success, and, if any thing we can say shall contribute to it, we shall heartily rejoice. As a friend of the Africans and of mankind at large, we are happy to record our tribute of praise in behalf of one who was an honor and ornament to her race and her kind.

Born in a land of darkness, the grasp of the spoiler first woke her from the dream of her infancy. Ruthlessly torn from home and parents, no kind arm supported her head or ministered to her wants during the horrors of the middle passage. The crack of the whip, the screams of suffocating and famishing human beings, and the clank of chains were the lullaby of her childish slumbers. Ignorant, naked, and forlorn, she stood up in a foreign land to be sold, like a beast in the market, to strangers whose pity she had not even a voice to demand. A brighter dawn flashed on her mind. Her own intelligence and energy supplied the want of instruction. In the midst of the obloquy attached to her hue, she reached an intellectual eminence known to few of the females of that day, and not common even now. The treasures of literature became hers,—the gospel shone upon her. Grateful, humble, pious, and affectionate, prosperity made no change in her heart. Flattery could not make her vain,—pleasure diminished not her gratitude,—starvation and ill usage never turned her from her duty. Her worthless husband never heard a syllable of reproach from the dying mother by the side of her dying child. She died in suffering and starvation, and is gone to take the rank which she earned, in a place where many who may despise her for a skin not colored like their own, will never come.

[". . . what African nature . . . may accomplish . . ."]

Anonymous*

This is a timely re-publication of a work, which has now become so rare, even among the bibliophiles, that it is much to be doubted whether half a dozen copies of it might be found in the country. We have ourselves met with but one, which was and is in the possession of a relative of the Mrs. Wheatley, who gave her name to the celebrated subject of the memoir prefixed to the Poems before us; and we are not sorry to perceive that, in the new edition, the interest of the whole of the old has been retained by working over the portrait of Phillis. This is said to have been, at the time it was taken, an undoubted likeness, and our friends, the Phrenologists, will certainly find in it, and in the historical accompaniment, a new paragraph for the long and learned Chapter on Heads.

. . . The style of the poems is evidently formed, in a great degree, after that of Pope, a writer now in the golden age of his fame; and, indeed, we not unfrequently meet with passages which remind us of the model so closely, that we cannot but think the original editor or printer failed to do the writer the common justice of attaching the usual marks of quotation to matter, here and there, that has very much the air of an extract. A few lines will show our meaning, and these we take from the Address to Imagination [lines 23–32]:

> Though winters frowns to Fancy's raptured eyes,
> The fields may flourish, and gay scenes arise;
> The frozen deeps may burst their iron bands,
> And bid their waters murmur o'er the sands;
> Fair Flora may resume her fragrant reign,
> And with her flowery riches deck the plain;
> Sylvanus may diffuse his honors round,
> And all the forest may with leaves be crowned;
> *Showers may descend, and dews their gems disclose,*
> *And nectar sparkle on the blooming rose.*

*Reprinted from "African Anecdotes. Memoir and Poems of Phillis Wheatley. Geo. W. Light, Boston [1834]," *Knickerbocker or New York Monthly Magazine*, 4, No. 2 (August, 1834), 85–95.

These lines, though by no means a particularly favorable specimen of the writer's ability, indicate, perhaps as sufficiently as any thing we can either cite or say, the cultivation of her literary taste and the development of her poetical genius. It must, of course, be remembered under what circumstances she commenced her career, how little encouragement she had from the example of those of her own color in those days; how incomplete at the best were the tardy sources of information and discipline which were furnished her; and especially that what she effected as a writer was the result of the whimsical leisure, after all, of a mere child—a barbarian, bought in the market—a slave! While passages of her productions, then, are characterized by the beautiful and even sublime expressions of fine thoughts, and while they are distinguished throughout by an eminent degree of that harmony for which her race are supposed to have a peculiar sensibility, it is surely little to be wondered at, if, on the whole, they should rather suggest to the philosophical mind what human, and what African nature is, and what it may accomplish under certain problematical circumstances, than furnish an intrinsic gratification to the mature taste, or a luxury to the mere lover of poetry.

The artlessness, in one sense of the word, which is for the most part a recommendation of the poems before us, is indicated also by the anecdote commented on at some length by the writer of the Memoir, that Mrs. Wheatley was in the habit of furnishing her protegé with a light, and in the cold season with a fire, in her apartment, during the night. "The light was placed upon a table at her bed-side, with writing materials, that if any thing occurred to her after she had retired, she might secure the swift-winged fancy ere it fled." . . .

However this may be, the want of retentiveness in question is not perhaps so inexplicable as our biographer seems to consider it, when he remarks that it cannot be ascribed to want of *memory*, because Phillis made rapid progress in the acquisition of language, and in other branches of knowledge. It applied only, indeed, to the combinations of her own imagination; and the simple reason must have been, chiefly, that, in the absence of every thing like intellectual discipline, or the artifice of literary conception or composition, she naturally enough merely *enjoyed*, rather than *employed*, her inventive faculties—sitting still, as it were, "lentus in umbra" [i.e., "quietly in the shadows"], and suffering the phantoms of fancy to pass over her, as Locke somewhere says, like shadows over a corn-field—in a word, not at all exercising that active, business-like attention which is equally indispensable in all departments of mental pursuit, the words themselves suggest, to *re*tention, and to recollection.

Chiefly, we say—because it is well known that, in cases of persons of apparent equal faculties in most respects, and who have availed themselves of them equally by that habitual discipline, system, and professional or practical tact which our heroine clearly lacked altogether, there is still a wide disparity, in this particular, between different individuals. The distinguished poet who has been named as the favorite of the African versifier, was probably deficient in the memory of imagination, as he resorted to the same mode of preventing the waste of his midnight fancies. Walter Scott was greatly distinguished for his retentiveness in relation to favorite subjects of contemplation, and Cuvier's memory—as his eulogist, De Candallo, says—was so remarkable in reference to *forms*, in the widest sense of the word, that the figure of an animal never left his mind, and the sight of a map or plan of a city seemed sufficient to give him an almost intuitive knowledge of the place. "Among all his talents, that memory which may be called *graphic* seemed most apparent." Phillis, whose situation, and perhaps constitution, led her to different habits of thought, cultivated a memory of *words* with diligence, and enjoyed the benefit of it in a corresponding degree. . . .

[. . . abundant proof of a degree of native genius . . ."]

Benjamin B. Thatcher*

. . . The earliest attempt in poetical composition, by Phillis, which has been preserved—though she probably made many at an earlier date—is the little poem intended to express her loyal acknowledgements to the King, (George III,) on occasion of the Repeal of the Stamp Act—an event of intense interest in all the American Colonies. It shows a degree of grammatical correctness, and a propriety of sentiment and feeling, which certainly do not disgrace the literary character of a slave at the age of fourteen years—for the piece was written in 1768. It is as follows [Thatcher has modernized spelling and punctuation]:

Your subjects hope, dread Sire, the crown
Upon your brows may flourish long,
And that your arm may in your God be strong,
Oh! may your sceptre numerous nations sway,
And all with love and readiness obey.

But how shall we the British king reward?
Rule thou in peace, our father and our Lord!
Midst the remembrance of the favors past,
The meanest peasants most admire *the last.*
May George, beloved by all the nations round,
Live with heaven's choicest, constant blessings crowned.
Great God! direct and guard him from on high,
And from his head let every evil fly;
And may each clime with equal gladness see
A monarch's smile can set his subjects free.

. . . In regard to the poetry of Phillis, it will be observed, by those who examine her works, that she has written, almost wholly, upon occasional subjects, apparently on those of mere feeling, suggested to her by the occurrence of some event in which her own sympathies were deeply interested. The subjects, accordingly, are quite as illustrative of her own heart and mind, as the style is. When this circumstance is considered, in connection with the fact that she was born, and brought up, to her eighth

*Reprinted from Benjamin B. Thatcher, *Memoir of Phillis Wheatley, A Native African and a Slave* (Boston: Geo. W. Light, 1834), passim.

year, a complete barbarian in a barbarous land; that at that period she was made a slave; that in this condition, and at the age she commenced the business of self-education; that she had to contend through life with all these circumstances, added to the prejudice commonly entertained against persons of her color, and much of the time, too, with its most trying personal sufferings—it must be admitted that her compositions furnish abundant proof of a degree of native genius which is exceedingly rare among persons of any race, class or condition. Some of them show also that she had contrived, by some means, not only to make herself familiar with the Holy Scripture, which seems to have been her favorite authority and study, but to have read and remembered not a little of ancient and modern profane history, geography, astronomy, poetry, and other matters of this kind, of which in her time it was considered no disgrace, certainly, for ladies (not to say gentlemen) of a much higher standing in society, to be much more uninformed. Few of them, we presume, would have been unwilling to acknowledge their claims to the following, had they written it—the first lines of an address to the Earl of Dartmouth, a leading English statesman, (under George III,) to whom Phillis was introduced in that country [lines 1–14 of "To the Right Honourable William, Earl of Dartmouth, His Majesty's Principal Secretary of State For North America, &" follow, q.v. above]:

. . . We will conclude our extracts from these Poems, (the whole of which have been recently republished in one small volume,) with the Lines addressed to Harvard University, at Cambridge, which, it will be seen, contain an allusion to the early history of the authoress, plainly indicative of the feeling with which she recalled so much as she knew of it:

While an intrinsic ardor prompts to write,
The Muses promise to assist my pen.
'Twas not long since, I left my native shore,
The land of errors and Egyptian gloom:
Father of mercy! 'twas thy gracious hand
Brought me in safety from those dark abodes.

Students, to you 'tis given to scan the heights
Above, to traverse the etherial space,
And mark the systems of revolving worlds.
Still more, ye sons of science, ye receive
The blissful news by messengers from heaven,
How Jesus' blood for your redemption flows.
See him, with hands outstretched upon the cross!
Immense compassion in his bosom glows;
He hears revilers, nor resents their scorn.
What matchless mercy in the son of God!
He deigned to die, that they might rise again,
And share with him, in the sublimest skies,
Life without death, and glory without end.

Improve your privileges while they stay,
Ye pupils; and each hour redeem that bears
Or good or bad report of you to heaven.
Let sin, that baneful evil to the soul,
By you be shunned; nor once remit your guard:
Suppress the deadly serpent in its egg.
Ye blooming plants of human race divine,
An Ethiop tells you, 'tis your greatest foe:
Its transient sweetness turns to endless pain,
And in immense perdition sinks the soul.

Several reflections are suggested by the facts of the preceding memoir, too obvious to be overlooked by any reader who is willing to derive benefit or pleasure from even the humblest source. One is, that genius is not limited by the Creator of man, to any color, country, or condition. The darkest skin may cover the brightest intellect, as well as the warmest heart. . . . Another is, that determination and perseverance, under favor of Providence, are sufficient to accomplish almost anything. Phillis has immortalized herself by her poems; and yet she commenced her literary career a savage and slave, ignorant of the merest rudiments of the language in which she afterwards wrote, and for some time using, in her awkward efforts to give vent to her rising conceptions, no better materials than charcoal or a piece of chalk! Surely, no man, woman, or child, in whatever circumstances, has occasion, after this, to be discouraged in an honest exertion to add to his own usefulness and the happiness of the world around.

["She expresses herself with much feeling. . . ."]

Anonymous*

. . . Her literary talents and acquirements accorded well with the intrinsic worth of her character. At the early age of fourteen, she appears first to have attempted literary composition; and between this period and the age of nineteen, the whole of her poems which were given to the world seem to have been written. Her favourite author was Pope, and her favourite work the translation of the Iliad. It is not of course surprising that her pieces should present many features of resemblance to those of her cherished author and model. She began also the study of the Latin tongue, and if we may judge from a translation of one of Ovid's tales, appears to have made no inconsiderable progress in it.

A great number of Phillis Wheatley's pieces were written to commemorate the deaths of the friends who had been kind to her. The following little piece is on the death of a young gentleman of great promise:

> Who taught thee conflict with the powers of night,
> To vanquish Satan in the fields of fight?
> Who strung thy feeble arms with might unknown?
> How great thy conquest, and how bright thy crown!
> War with each princedom, throne, and power is o'er;
> The scene is ended, to return no more.
> Oh, could my muse thy seat on high behold,
> How decked with laurel, and enriched with gold!
> Oh, could she hear what praise thy harp employs,
> How sweet thine anthems, how divine thy joys,
> What heavenly grandeur should exult her strain!
> What holy raptures in her numbers reign!
> To soothe the trouble of the mind to peace,
> To still the tumult of life's tossing seas,
> To ease the anguish of the parent's heart,
> What shall my sympathising verse impart?
> Where is the balm to heal so deep a wound?
> Where shall a sovreign remedy be found?
> Look, gracious Spirit! from thy heavenly bower,

*Reprinted from "Intelligent Negroes," pasted to inside cover of *Memoir and Poems By Phillis Wheatley* (Boston: Geo. W. Light, 1834), pp. 7–12.

And thy full joys into their bosoms pour;
The raging tempest of their griefs control,
And spread the dawn of glory through the soul,
To eye the path the saint departed trod,
And trace him to the bosom of his God.

The following passage on sleep, from a poem of some length, *On the Providence of God* [*sic*, i.e., "Thoughts on the Works of Providence" in the 1773 volume], shews a very considerable reach of thought, and no mean powers of expression:

As reason's powers by day our God disclose,
So may we trace Him in the night's repose.
Say, what is sleep? and dreams, how passing strange!
When action ceases and ideas range
Licentious and unbounded o'er the plains,
Where fancy's queen giddy triumph reigns.
Hear in soft strains the dreaming lover sigh
To a kind fair, and rave in jealousy;
On pleasure now, and now on vengeance bent,
The labouring passions struggle for a vent.
What power, O man! thy reason then restores,
So long suspended in nocturnal hours?
What secret hand returns the mental train,
And gives improved thine active powers again?
From thee, O man! what gratitude should rise!
And when from balmy sleep thou op'st thine eyes,
Let thy first thought be praises to the skies.
How merciful our God, who thus imparts
O'er flowing tides of joy to human hearts,
When wants and woes might be our righteous lot,
Our God forgetting, by our God forgot!

We have no hesitation in stating our opinion, and we believe that many will concur in it, that these lines, written by an African slave-girl at the age of fifteen or sixteen, are quite equal to a great number of the verses that appear in all the standard collections of English poetry, under the names of Halifax, Dorset, and others of "the mob of gentlemen who write with ease." Phillis Wheatley's lines are, if anything, superior in harmony, and are not inferior in depth of thought; the faults are those which characterise the models she copied from; for it must be recollected that, sixty years ago, the older authors of England were almost unknown; and till the return to nature and truth in the works of Cowper, the only popular writers were those who followed the artificial, though polished style introduced with the second Charles from the continent of Europe. This accounts fully for the elaborate versification of the negro girl's poetry; since it required minds such as those of Cowper and Wordsworth to throw off the trammels of this artificial style, and to revive the native vigor and simplicity of their country's verse.

Phillis Wheatley felt a deep interest in everything affecting the liberty of her fellow-creatures of whatever condition, race, or colour. She expresses herself with much feeling in an address to the Earl of Dartmouth, secretary of state for North America, on the occasion of some relaxation of the system of haughty severity which the home government then pursued towards the colonies, and which ultimately caused their separation and independence. [There follow lines 20–31 of the poem "To the Right Honourable William Earl of Dartmouth," q.v. above.]

A slight and curious defect of Phillis's intellectual powers might under ordinary circumstances have prevented her compositions from being ever placed on paper. This was the weakness of her memory, which, though it did not prevent her from acquiring the Latin tongue, or benefiting by her reading, yet disabled her from retaining on her mind, for any length of time, her own cogitations. Her kind mistress provided a remedy for this, by ordering a fire to be kept constantly in Phillis's room, so that she might have an opportunity of recording any thoughts that occurred to her mind, by night as well as day, without endangering her health from exposure to cold. . . . [The writer lapses back into biographical matters, and then concludes.]

Thus perished a woman who, by a fortunate accident, was rescued from the degraded condition to which those of her race who are brought to the slave-market are too often condemned, as if for the purpose of shewing to the world what care and education could effect in elevating the character of the benighted African. The example is sufficient to impress us with the conviction, that, out of the countless millions to whom no similar opportunities have ever been presented, many might be found fitted by the endowments of nature, and wanting only the blessings of education, to make them ornaments, like Phillis Wheatley, not only to their race, but to humanity.

[". . . a very respectable echo of the Papal strains"]

Evert A. Duyckinck*

The poems of Phillis Wheatley were published in London in 1773, in a thin duodecimo volume, with a copper-plate portrait, from which our engraving is taken. . . . The poems themselves show as marked indications of the feeding grounds of the readers and imitators of verse in the eighteenth century, as do those of Mistress Ann Bradstreet in the seventeenth. What in the earlier day was quaint, rude, and daring, in the latter is smooth, sounding and fluent. The formal muse of Pope, and the herd of victims whom he impaled in the *Dunciad,* had succeeded in the American colonies to the twisted efforts of *Du Bartas.* Phillis Wheatley is a very respectable echo of the Papal strains. In the first poem of the volume, addressed *To Maecenas,* she writes of Homer with an eloquence evidently derived from the glowing translation of the bright-eyed little man at Twickenham:—[lines 7–20 follow]

> While Homer paints, lo! circumfus'd in air,
> Celestial Gods in mortal form appear;
> Swift as they move hear each recess rebound,
> Heav'n quakes, earth trembles, and the shores resound.
> Great Sire of verse, before my mortal eyes,
> The lightnings blaze across the vaulted skies;
> And, as the thunder shakes the heav'nly plains,
> A deep-felt horror thrills thro' all my veins.
> When gentler strains demand thy graceful song,
> The length'ning line moves languishing along.
> When great Patroclus courts Achilles' aid,
> The grateful tribute of my tears is paid;
> Prone on the shore he feels the pangs of love,
> And stern Pelides tend'rest passions move.

One of the few allusions which we have found in the poem to her birth and condition of slavery is among these verses. She gracefully recalls the African Terence:—

*Reprinted from *The Cyclopedia of American Literature*, ed. Evert A. and George Duyckinck, 2 vols. (New York: Charles Scribners, 1856), I, 367–71.

> The happier Terence all the choir inspir'd,
> His soul replenish'd, and his bosom fir'd;
> But say, ye Muses, why this partial grace,
> To one alone of Afric's sable race;
> From age to age, transmitting thus his name
> With the first glory in the rolls of fame?

The longest piece of classicality in the volume is a paraphrase of the story of Niobe and her Children, from Ovid, in which there is one line, at least, which would do honor to any pen. Apollo is preparing the slaughter of the sons in the race-course, the moment before that arrowy devastation:—

> With clouds incompass'd glorious Phoebus stands;
> *The feather'd vengeance quiv'ring in his hands.*

This is not a translation of anything in Ovid, for that writer neglected so striking a position for his Deity. Apollo, in the Metamorphoses, goes to work at once in the most business-like manner, and covers the field with the slain in the shortest possible time. Another touch of the poetic flight of the arrow is added to the original text in the death of Sipylus:—

> Then didst thou, Sipylus, the language hear
> *Of fate portentuous whistling in the air.*

Certainly, even with the assistance of a master, it was a most generous acquisition for a female African slave to appreciate that fine classic story in this way.

The remaining poems are far from mediocrity. A large number of them belong to the class of occasional verse addressed to her friends on various family afflictions; so that she was for the time a kind of poet-laureate in the first domestic circles of Boston. Nor is the University of Cambridge, in New England, forgotten. The earnest religious feeling of the Methodists is everywhere visible. The lines, *To S. M., a Young African Painter*, on seeing his works, refer to Scipio Moorhead, a servant of the Rev. John Moorhead, of Boston, who exhibited some talent for drawing. The initials of the lady to whom the *Farewell to America* is addressed, belong to Mrs. Susanna Wright, a lady of some note for her skill in wax-work. By the favor of Mr. S. F. Haven, of Worcester, to whom we are indebted for the last two items of information, we have before us the original manuscript of two of the poems, *To the University of Cambridge*, and the lines *On the Death of the Rev. Dr. Sewall* [*sic*], written in the author's remarkably round neat hand. The earliest verses dated in the collection are those addressed *To the King's Most Excellent Majesty*, marked 1768. From this manuscript it appears that the lines on Harvard were written in 1767. . . . [The editors reprint Wheatley's letter and poem to George Washington, dated "Providence, Oct. 26, 1775, and Washington's reply of "February 2d [*sic*, i.e., 28], 1776," q.v. above.]

In Jan., 1784, the year of her death, she wrote an Elegy of fifty-two lines, *To the Memory of that Great Divine, the Reverend and Learned Dr. Samuel Cooper*, a copy of which is preserved in the Boston Atheneum. It is dedicated to the Church and Congregation assembling in Brattle street, by their Obedient Humble Servant, Phillis Peters. We have also met with the following of the same year, in the American Antiquarian Society, in four small quarto pages printed at Boston by Warden and Russell:— [The spelling and punctuation are modernized; a few words have been misprinted.]

Liberty and Peace

Lo freedom comes. Th'prescient muse foretold,
All eyes th'accomplish'd prophecy behold:
Her port describ'd, "She moves divinely fair,
Olive and laurel bind her golden hair."
She, the bright progeny of Heaven, descends,
And every grace her sovereign step attends;
For now kind Heaven, indulgent to our prayer,
In smiling peace resolves the din of war.
Fix'd in Columbia her illustrious line,
And bids in thee her future councils shine.
To every realm her portals open'd wide,
Receives from each the full commercial tide.
Each art and science now with rising charms,
Th'expanding heart with emulation warms.
E'en great Britannia sees with dread surprise,
And from the dazzling splendors turns her eyes.
Britain, whose navies swept th'Atlantic o'er,
And thunder sent to every distant shore;
E'en thou, in manners cruel as thou art,
The sword resign'd, resume the friendly part.
For Gallia's power espous'd Columbia's cause,
And new-born Rome shall give Britannia laws,
Nor unremember'd in the grateful strain,
Shall princely Louis' friendly deeds remain;
The generous prince th'impending vengeance eyes,
Sees the fierce wrong and to the rescue flies.
Perish that thirst of boundless power, that drew
On Albion's head the curse to tyrants due.
But thou appeas'd submit to Heaven's decree,
That bids this realm of freedom rival thee.
Now sheathe the sword that bade the brave atone
With guiltless blood for madness not their own.
Sent from th'enjoyment of their native shore,
Ill-fated—never to behold her more.
From every kingdom on Europa's coast
Throng'd various troops, their glory, strength, and boast.
With heart-felt pity fair Hibernia saw

Columbia menac'd by the Tyrant's law:
On hostile fields fraternal arms engage,
And mutual deaths, all dealt with mutual rage:
The muse's ear hears mother earth deplore
Her ample surface smoke with kindred gore:
The hostile field destroys the social ties,
And everlasting slumber seals their eyes.
Columbia mourns, the haughty foes deride,
Her treasures plunder'd and her towns destroy'd:
Witness how Charlestown's curling smokes arise,
In sable columns to the clouded skies.
The ample dome, high-wrought with curious toil,
In one sad hour the savage troops despoil.
Descending peace the power of war confounds;
From every tongue celestial peace resounds:
As from the east th'illustrious king of day,
With rising radiance drives the shades away,
So freedom comes array'd with charms divine,
And in her train commerce and plenty shine.
Britannia owns her independent reign,
Hibernia, Scotia and the realms of Spain;
And great Germania's ample coast admires
The generous spirit that Columbia fires.
Auspicious Heaven shall fill the fav'ring gales,
Where e'er Columbia spreads her swelling sails:
To every realm shall peace her charms display,
And heavenly freedom spreads her golden ray.

[From Wheatley's book the editors reprint "On the Death of the Rev. Mr. George Whitefield, 1770" and "A Farewell to America. *To Mrs. Susanna Wright*" [*sic*, i.e., "A Farewell to America To Mrs. S. W." in the 1773 volume]. From the original manuscript are printed "To the University of Cambridge, Wrote in 1767" and "On the Death of the Rev. Dr. Sewall, 1769," both either variants or hastily copied.]

["We prize . . . this little glimpse of your human heart . . ."]

Anonymous*

There lies before me a book of which a brief review may not at this time be inappropriate, although it cannot be classified with recent literature, and it is not now, as its title pages says it was in MDCCLXIII, "*sold by Messrs. Cox and Berry, King Street, Boston.*" Its leaves are yellow with age and its binding somewhat defaced, but its print is excellent, its leather covers strong, and it seems likely to outlive in corporeal form, if it does not also in spiritual vitality, some of its younger rivals among the "Female Poets of America." . . . It no doubt made much talk and was widely read in its day, for negro slavery, even in Boston, we cannot suppose, was prolific in such prodigies as this of a slave-girl of eighteen, only ten years from her native Africa, inditing Odes to *Maecenas* and reflections upon "*Niobe in distress for her children slain by Apollo from Ovid's Metamorphoses, Book VI, and from a View of the Painting of Mr. Richard Wilson.*" . . . Then, too, it must have created some sensation that the names of such good patriots as John Hancock and seven "ministers of the gospel" should be joined with those of the hated royal Governor Hutchinson and "notorious tories," in indorsing the Afric muse, as Phillis styles herself. Small satisfaction it must have afforded those good dames whose activity was helping to brew the Boston cup of tea poured out only a month or two after the appearance of the poems, that "Mr. Wheatley's negro-servant" had taken it upon herself to address verses to the "King's Most Excellent Majesty." The lips that were parched with long abstinence from their delectable Hysons and Souchongs, and puckered with decoctions of sage and raspberry leaves, must have found peculiarly unpronouncable the following effusion, made in gratitude for the repeal of the Stamp Act in 1768:

Your subjects hope, dread Sire,
Your crown upon your brows may flourish long,
And that your arm may in your God be strong!

* * * * * * *

*Reprinted from "A Book Notice Written for the Boston Journal," *Boston Journal,* March 9, 1875, p. 7.

May George, beloved by all the nations round,
Live with heav'n's choicest, constant blessings crown'd.
And from his head let ev'ry evil fly!
And may each clime with equal gladness see
A monarch's smile can set his subjects free.

Yet even the slave girl's obsequious muse, awed into servility to the patronage which fostered and flattered it, cannot wholly resist the infection of the atmosphere, and it strikes a note in praise of "Fair Freedom." But, lest any one should suspect it to be a taint of treason, Phillis takes care to explain (and there is a pathos in the explanation,) how it happens that she, living in a family so exemplary, could have any such Democratic notions:

Should you, my lord, while you peruse my song,
Wonder from whence my love of *freedom* sprung,
Whence flow these wishes for the common good,
By feeling hearts alone best understood.
I, young in life, by seeming cruel fate
Was snatched from Afric's fancy'd happy seat.
What pangs excrutiating must molest,
What sorrows labor in my parent's breast!
Steel'd was that soul and by no misery mov'd
That from a father seized his babe belov'd.
Such, such my case. And can I then but pray
Others may never feel tyrannic sway?

Poor Phillis Wheatley! We prize more this little glimpse of your human heart than all your platitudes on Virtue, and your affecting addresses "To a Lady on the Death of Three Relations," and your moralizings "On the Death of a Young Lady Five years of Age." We may venture also to query whether those filial tears for "the pangs excrutiating in a parent's breast" were not as acceptable to heaven as the sound orthodox doctrine of the following: ["On Being Brought from Africa to America," complete, follows; q.v. above.]

But though with the faithfulness of her race Phillis was slow in breaking the bonds of her allegiance to the patronage which had first befriended her, the instinct of freedom and the contagion of the patriotism of '75 at last triumphed. The Afric muses, full emancipation from royal bondage, was unequivically proclaimed in Feb., 1776, in lines addressed to General George Washington. These appeared in a collection of her poems published at a later date. . . .

Phillis seems to have had her own opinions about Boston society in 1773, of which she no doubt had opportunities to take observations. This is the picture she gives of it in a rebus—

A town of gayety and sport,
Where beaux and beauteous nymphs resort,
And gallantry doth reign;[1]

and in the answer to the rebus—

Boston's a town, polite and debonair,
To which the beaux and beateous repair;
Each Helen strikes the mind with sweet surprise,
While living lightning flashes from her eyes.

Harvard College also inspired Phillis's appreciative muse. Unfortunately, the page which contains the address is gone from the book, but the contents gives the title, "To the University of Cambridge in New England."

Phillis was not the sole example in Boston in 1773 of the "capacity of the negro," for she has some lines "To a Young African Painter," whom, with naivete, she addresses as "Wondrous youth," and she also intimates that he, like herself, possessed the gift of song:

Still may the painter's and the poet's fire,
To aid thy pencil and thy verse conspire.
And may the charms of each seraphic theme
Conduct thy footsteps to immortal fame!

There are some forty in number of such like poems, on various subjects—scriptural and classical—Goliath of Gath, Neptune, the Rev. Mr. Geo. Whitefield and Capt. H. D. of the 65th Regiment, Humanity and Imagination, all being alike potent over the numbers of the Afric Muse. Devoid as the book is of natural feeling and expression, it is not more so than many others of its time, when poetry was largely a synonym for pedantry. If Phillis had done no more in her ten years of life in America than merely to learn the names and the facts of history which she records, she would have accomplished more than some young ladies of her age born and bred amid all the privileges of American institutions. The facsimile of her handwriting is a model of the old school style; quite as beautiful, to my way of thinking, as the "elements" and "curves" of the modern "improved art of penmanship" of our century. . . .

Notes

1. These three lines are from "A Rebus, By. I. [J?] B." (James Bowdoin?); the next four lines are from "An Answer to the Rebus, By the Author of These Poems" (i.e., by Phillis Wheatley).

Phillis Wheatley, the Negro Poetess

John R. Slattery*

"One swallow never makes a summer," was the remark of a Southern gentleman, made to the writer after reading the sketch of Benjamin Banneker, the negro astronomer, which appeared in the Catholic World for December, 1883. In this sketch of Phillis Wheatley appears a second *swallow*. Neither do two swallows make a summer. But more are at hand. And as a multitude of those little birds betoken the near approach of that season in which Nature is most lavish of her gifts, so let us hope that a brighter day, indicative of a fairer show for the colored race, is about to dawn, when their capabilities and abilities will be acknowledged—let us not say as human, but far more generally. . . .

Phillis' first attempt at poetry was probably made in a spirit of gratitude at securing through her forced exile the knowledge, imperfect as it was, of God and the Saviour whom he sent. The poem, written when she was about fifteen, thus runs:

On Being Brought from Africa to America

'Twas mercy brought me from my pagan land,
Taught my benighted soul to understand
That there's a God, that there's a Saviour too;
Once I redemption neither sought nor knew.
Some view our race with scornful eye:
"Their color is a diabolic dye."
Remember, Christians, negroes, black as Cain
May be refined and join th'angelic train.

. . . Her knowledge of the classics was seen in some of her poems—for instance, the first in her published poems, and addressed to Maecenas, evidently imitating Horace in this respect. From it are the following lines [lines 21–40 of "To Maecenas" follow]:

Great Maro's strain in heavenly numbers flows,
The Nine inspire, and all the bosom glows.
Oh! could I rival thine and Virgil's page,

*Reprinted from John R. Slattery, "Phillis Wheatley, the Negro Poetess," *Catholic World: A Monthly Magazine of General Literature and Science*, 39 (July, 1884), 484–94.

Or claim the Muses with the Mantuan sage,
Soon the same beauties should my mind adorn,
And the same ardors in my soul should burn;
Then should my song in bolder notes arise,
And all my numbers pleasingly surprise.
But here I sit and mourn a grov'ling mind
That fain would mount and ride upon the wind.

Not you, my friend, these plaintive strains become—
Not you, whose bosom is the Muse's home;
When they from towering Helicon retire
They fan in you the bright, immortal fire.
But I, less happy, cannot raise the song;
The falt-ring music dies upon my tongue.

The happier Terence all the choir inspired,
His soul replenished, and his bosom fired.
But say, ye Muses, why this partial grace
To one alone of Afric's sable race?

At the name of *Terence* Phillis has this foot-note: "He was an African by birth." Proud[,] the poor girl was to claim as her countryman the immortal comedian of imperial Rome. "Terentio non similem dices quempiam." ["You might say there is no one like Terrence."] For Terence, "genere Afer, civis Carthaginiensis" ["African born, citizen of Carthagenia"], was one of the captive slaves of Scipio Africanus, though afterwards his boon companion.

. . . The following stanzas, taken from a poem entitled, "On Virtue," give evidence of an aspiration which many think above her despised race, too grovelling, as they fancy, for anything higher than the brute [lines 1–10 of the poem follow]:

O thou, bright jewel! in my aim I strive
To comprehend thee. Thine own words declare,
Wisdom is higher than a fool can reach.
I cease to wonder, and no more attempt
Thine heart t'explore, or fathom thy profound.
But, O my soul! sink not into despair:
Virtue is near thee, and with gentle hand
Would now embrace thee, hovers o'er thine head.
Pain would the heav'n-born soul with her converse;
Then seek, then court her for her promised bliss.

Phillis naturally was of a religious turn of mind; in fact, all her poems breathe a spirit of piety, and we must deeply regret that the church, the mother and mistress of all that is noble and lofty, was a stranger to her. . . . The following lines from her poem, "On the Death of the Rev. Dr. Sewall [*sic*], 1769," will give some notion of the piety of

Phillis, who was then in her sixteenth year [lines 30–51 of the poem follow, q.v. above]:

. . . In 1773, shortly after her arrival [in London], Phillis, urged on by her many admirers, published her poems. This is the only complete edition of her writings, a few of them having previously appeared in Boston in pamphlets. This edition is a small volume of one hundred and twenty-four pages containing thirty-seven poems, together with a rhyming charade by some person, answered in rhyme by our poetess.

. . . In the course of this sketch are given enough extracts to enable the reader to form a fair estimate of the girl's powers. Two further selections are here added. The first is from a poem addressed to a lady on the death of three relations [lines 1–8 follow]:

> We trace the pow'r of death from tomb to tomb,
> And his are all the ages yet to come.
> 'Tis his to call the planets from on high,
> To blacken Phoebus, and desolate the sky;
> His, too, when all in his dark realms are hurled,
> From its firm base to shake the solid world;
> His fatal sceptre rules the spacious whole,
> And trembling nature rocks from pole to pole.

A friend, no mean votary of the Muses himself, especially in lyrics and sonnets, to whom were sent Phillis' poems, thus writes: "It seems to me that 'Hymn to the Evening' is one of the best things in the book. She is less artificial here than elsewhere. Towards the end of this poem she reminds me somewhat of Newman." ["An Hymn to the Evening," complete, follows, q.v. above.]

. . . The reader will be astonished, no doubt, that a slave-girl should write so many poems from the fifteenth to the twentieth year of her age—a time of life when most girls are given to all giddiness. The lofty sentiments of her mind are still more wonderful when Phillis' race is remembered. The wandering child of the worst-treated among men, she seems in some measure to have tasted of those lights which the God of nature bestows, thus realizing, though never so faintly, the prophecy, "Before him the Ethiopians shall bow down." There was a like astonishment in London in her own days. It was mooted about that no slave-girl could do what Phillis did. It was simply impossible. So strong were the suspicions afloat that the publisher felt constrained to get a solemn declaration in defence of the girl's claims to be the author. We give it here entire with the signatures, among which are some names familiar in American history. . . . [The attestation follows; also reprinted are excerpts from Jared Sparks's comments on the manuscripts of Wheatley's poem and covering letter to George Washington, dated "Providence, Oct. 26, 1775"; Washington's letter of February 10, 1776, to Joseph Reed concerning Wheatley's letter; and Washington's letter of February 28, 1776, to "Miss Phillis," for all of which, see above.]

[. . . she made her mark, and her place . . . is secure"]

Benjamin Brawley*

. . . At the time when she was most talked about, Phillis Wheatley was regarded as a prodigy, appearing as she did at a time when the achievement of the Negro in literature and art was still neglible. Her vogue, however, was more than temporary, and the 1793, 1802, and 1816 editions of her poems found ready sale. In the early years of the last century her verses were frequently to be found in school readers. From the first, however, there were those who discounted her poetry. Thomas Jefferson, for instance, said that it was beneath the dignity of criticism. If after 1816 interest in her work declined, it was greatly revived at the time of the anti-slavery agitation, when anything indicating unusual capacity on the part of the Negro was received with eagerness. When Margaretta Matilda Odell of Jamaica Plain, a descendant of the Wheatley family, republished the poems with a memoir in 1834, there was such a demand for the book that two more editions were called for within the next three years. For a variety of reasons, especially an increasing race-consciousness on the part of the Negro, interest in her work has greatly increased within the last decade, and as copies of early editions had within recent years become so rare as to be practically inaccessible, the reprint in 1909 of the volume of 1773 by the A.M.E. Book concern in Philadelphia was especially welcome.

Only two poems written by Phillis Wheatley after her marriage are in existence. These are "Liberty and Peace," and "An Elegy Sacred to the Memory of Dr. Samuel Cooper." Both were published in 1784. . . . The little octavo volume of 124 pages contains 39 poems. One of these, however, must be excluded from the enumeration, as it is simply "A Rebus by I. B.," which serves as the occasion of Phillis Wheatley's poem, the answer to it. Fourteen of the poems are elegiac, and at least six others are occasional. Two are paraphrases from the Bible. We are thus left with sixteen poems to represent the best that Phillis Wheatley had produced by the time she was twenty years old. One of the longest of these is "Niobe in Distress for Her Children Slain by Apollo, from Ovid's Metamorphoses, Book VI, and from a View of the Painting of Mr. Richard Wilson." The

*Reprinted from Benjamin Brawley, *The Negro in Literature and Art in the United States* (New York: Duffield, 1913), pp. 10–32.

poem contains two interesting examples of personification (neither of which seems to be drawn from Ovid), "fate portentous whistling in the air," and "the feather'd vengeance quiv'ring in his hands," though the point might easily be made that these are little more than a part of the pseudo-classic tradition. The poem, "To S. M., a Young African Painter, on seeing his Works," was addressed to Scipio Moorhead, a young man who exhibited some talent for drawing and who was a servant of the Rev. John Moorhead of Boston. From the poem we should infer that one of his subjects was the story of Damon and Pythias. Of prime importance are the two or three poems of autobiographical interest. . . . In the lines addressed to William, Earl of Dartmouth, the young woman spoke again from personal experience. Important also in this connection is the poem "On Virtue," with its plea:

> Attend me, Virtue, thro' my youthful years!
> O leave me not to the false joys of time!
> But guide my steps to endless life and bliss.

One would suppose that Phillis Wheatley would make of "An Hymn to Humanity" a fairly strong piece of work. It is typical of the restraint under which she labored that this is one of the most conventional things in the volume. All critics agree, however, that the strongest lines in the book are those entitled "On Imagination." This effort is more sustained than the others, and it is the leading poem that Edmund Clarence Stedman chose to represent Phillis Wheatley in his "Library of American Literature." The following lines are representative of its quality [lines 13–22 follow, q.v. above]. . . . Hardly beyond this is "Liberty and Peace," the best example of the later verse. The poem is too long for inclusion here, but may be found in Duyckinck's "Cyclopedia of American Literature," and Heartman and Schomburg's collected edition of the Poems and Letters.

It is unfortunate that, imitating Pope, Phillis Wheatley more than once fell into his pitfalls. Her diction—"fleecy care," "vital breath," "feather'd race"—is distinctly pseudo-classic. The construction is not always clear; for instance, in the poem, "To Maecenas," there are three distinct references to Virgil, when grammatically the poetess seems to be speaking of three different men. Then, of course, any young writer working under the influence of Pope and his school would feel a sense of repression. If Phillis Wheatley had come on the scene forty years later, when the romantic writers had given a new tone to English poetry, she would undoubtedly have been much greater. Even as it was, however, she made her mark, and her place in the history of American literature, though not a large one, is secure.

Hers was a great soul. Her ambition knew no bounds, her thirst for knowledge was insatiable, and she triumphed over the most adverse circumstances. A child of the wilderness and a slave, by her grace and culture she satisfied the conventionalities of Boston and of England. Her brilliant conversation was equaled only by her modest demeanor. Everything about her was refined. More and more as one studies her life he becomes aware of her sterling Christian character. In a dark day she caught a glimpse of the eternal light, and it was meet that the first Negro woman in American literature should be one of unerring piety and the highest of literary ideals.

["... one of the most interesting curiosities"]

Vernon Loggins*

... The main body of Phillis Wheatley's verse belongs to that class of poetry which we call occasional. Eighteen out of her forty-six poems which are known to have come down to us are elegies. It has been said that she wrote them as consolatory poems at the request of friends. Five are on ministers, two on the wives of a lieutenant-governor and a celebrated physician, and the rest on unknown persons, including a number of children who died in infancy. The material is in each instance conventional, true to the traditions of the elegy in an elegy-making age, especially in Boston, where the writing of poems of condolence and epitaphs had been in great vogue since the days of Anne Bradstreet and Urian Oakes. The treatment is in accord with neoclassical standards. Whatever feeling there is, is impersonal and artificial; the method for achieving effect is mainly that of hyperbole; the ornamentation is elaborate and sumptious [*sic*], with frequent invocations of the Muses, allusions to pagan gods and Biblical heroes, overuse of personification, and pompousness of diction. "To the Rev. Mr. Pitkin on the Death of His Lady," which suggests the general mood of the elegies, opens in this strain—

> Where Contemplation finds her sacred Spring;
> Where heav'nly Music makes the Centre ring;
> Where Virtue reigns unsullied, and divine,
> Where Wisdom thron'd, and all the Graces shine;
> There sits thy Spouse, amid the glitt'ring Throng;
> There central Beauty feasts the ravish'd Tongue;
> With recent Powers, with recent Glories crown'd,
> The choirs angelic shout her welcome round.

Six of the poems were inspired by public events of importance, such as the repeal of the Stamp Act, the appointment of Washington as commander-in-chief of the Revolutionary forces, the betrayal of General Lee into the hands of the British, and the return of peace after the close of the Revolution; and a number of minor happenings, such as the voyage of a friend to

*Reprinted from Vernon Loggins, *The Negro Author: His Development in America to 1900* (New York: Columbia Univ. Press, 1931), pp. 22–29.

England, and the providential escape of an acquaintance from a hurricane at sea. These, like the elegies, are affected, written with an exaggerated dignity, with a straining attempt to force high eloquence.

But not all of Phillis Wheatley's poems are occasional. Following the New England custom of versifying selections from the Bible, begun back in the early days when The *Bay Psalm Book* was compiled, she worked out paraphrases of eight verses from the fifty-third chapter of Isaiah, and of the passage in the first book of Samuel which describes David's fight with Goliath. It is unnecessary to say that her neoclassical couplets deaden entirely the fire of Isaiah's rhapsody; she was so far away from the true Biblical ardor that she opened the paraphrase by invoking the "heav'nly muse." Her "Goliath of Gath" is more successful. In hearing the following lines one might feel that he is listening to the steady music of the opening lines of Pope's version of the *Iliad:*

> Ye martial pow'rs, and all ye tuneful nine,
> Inspire my song, and aid my high design.
> The dreadful scenes and toils of war I write,
> The ardent warriors, and the fields of fight:
> You best remember, and you best can sing
> The acts of heroes to the vocal string:
> Resume the lays with which your sacred lyre,
> Did then the poet and the sage inspire.

Also among her better achievements is the adaptation of that portion of the sixth book of Ovid's *Metamorphoses* which tells of Niobe's distress for her children. This classical paraphrase belongs to the small group of poems for which Phillis Wheatley did not look to her New England predecessors for models. Her pieces on abstractions, including "Imagination," "Recollection," and "Virtue," probably owe their subject matter to English rather than to American influences. And her companion hymns, "Morning" and "Evening," place her among those eighteenth century poets, numerous in England, who felt so greatly the splendors of Milton's "L'Allegro" and "Il Pensoroso" that they attempted imitations.

What one most wishes Phillis Wheatley had done, she left undone: she wrote too rarely about herself. Her intimate personal interests were ignored. She composed verses on the deaths of those who meant little to her, but, so far as we know, she remained silent after the deaths of Mrs. Wheatley and Mrs. Lathrop [i.e., Mary Wheatley, who married the Reverend John Lathrop in 1771] and her own children. She dwelt at length on the common notions of her day regarding liberty, but she neglected almost entirely her own state of slavery and the miserable oppression of thousands of her race. In all of her writings she only once referred in strong terms to the wrongs of the Negro in America. The reference is in the poem addressed to the Earl of Dartmouth upon his appointment as George III's secretary for North America [lines 20–21 from this poem follow, q.v. above]. . . . But with all of her outward neglect of self, Phillis Wheatley was too honest to veil her true personality in what she wrote. The sincerity of childhood and the delicacy of young womanhood, uniform in both the black race and the white, are constantly reflected, even when she is most artificial. Her gentle character, so often commented upon, lies revealed in every poem and letter.

But the dominant trait in her personality, which her writings reveal, is a capacity for intense religious faith. Without that faith she probably would never have written a line. She was not devout with the primitive adoration of a Jupiter Hammon, but with a belief balanced and controlled by Puritan training, such a belief as that of any other member of the Old South Church who might have seen worth in the emotionalism of George Whitefield. Every poem which was born in her mind, even the adaptation from Ovid, came forth filled with religious feeling. Her letters to Obour Tanner are to a great extent dissertations on the mercies and goodness of God. The only wholly subjective poem which came from her pen, "On Being Brought from Africa" proves what religion was in her life. [This poem, complete, follows, q.v. above.]

It is interesting to speculate what her thinking might have been if it had not been nurtured by the Puritanism of eighteenth century Boston and by the simple doctrines of the Countess of Huntingdon's circle. But speculate as we will, we cannot conceive of a philosophical system, whether based on the assumption that the savage is noble and superior or on any other assumption, which might have replaced her deep trust in the God of the Puritans.

That which is most important in a consideration of her work is her talent—a talent all the more difficult to explain because it is contradictory, in one respect spontaneous and intuitive, and in another respect rational and exceedingly self conscious. Her success in absorbing the music of Alexander Pope, master of England's neoclassical verse-makers, gives her poems their highest claim to distinction; and it seems that she was not aware of what she was doing when she achieved that success. We are told that there were three books in the Wheatley library for which she had a particularly srong affection—the Bible, a collection of tales from classical mythology, and Pope's Homer. Her first publication, the elegy on Whitefield, shows that she was familiar with Gray. We know that after her visit to England she possessed a Milton, and that after 1774 she owned a collection of Shenstone's poems. There is reason to believe that she read every poem which she could find, whether in book, magazine, newspaper, or broadsheet. But it was Pope's translation of Homer which taught her most. We have already noticed, in the quotation from "Goliath of Gath," how near she could come to her great master's idiom whenever her subject matter gave her the opportunity. In writing the following lines from "Thoughts on His Excellency Major General Lee," she was probably thinking of the first book of Paradise Lost, but it is Pope's music which she reproduced [lines 39–44 follow]:

> While thus he spake, the hero of renown
> Survey'd the boaster with a gloomy frown,
> And stern reply'd: "O arrogance of tongue!
> And wild ambition, ever prone to wrong!
> Believ'st thou chief, that armies such as thine
> Can stretch in dust that heaven-defended line?"

Even in her one poem in blank verse, "To the University of Cambridge, in New-England,"[1] . . . the line, with its strong rise, marked caesura, and hastened fall, is that of Pope. Indeed, reproduction of Pope's versification characterizes all of her poems with the exception of the few which she wrote in lyrical measures. She lived during the age when the poetical fashion in America was to imitate Pope; and while John Trumbull, Timothy Dwight, Joel Barlow, the Philip Freneau of the political satires, and numerous others among her contemporaries caught more of his general spirit, she perhaps excelled them all in reproducing his rhythms. Her power to attain this place of eminence must be pronounced as due to her instinct for hearing the music of words, an instinct which was possibly racial. As in Jupiter Hammon and many other Negro poets, in her the strange sense for imitating sound exercised itself of its own will. She never mentioned Pope, and only rarely touched upon themes such as he treated; but before she began writing, she had read his Homer with her deep-searching ear open for impressions which were to endure. Another Negro poet, Alberry A. Whitman, was a century later than Phillis Wheatley to come perhaps as near reproducing the sonorousness of Byron's *Childe Harold* as any one else has ever come. But a more exact parallel to her genius for imitating sound is to be found in the extraordinary musicianship of Thomas Green Bethune, the Negro pianist, commonly known as "Blind Tom." For a period of over forty years, down to the time of his death in 1908, his unique concerts were exploited on vaudeville and music-hall stages both in Europe and in America. Although blind and mentally unbalanced, he possessed the power of imitating the playing of the most skilled pianists. All that he needed in order to interpret a movement from a Beethoven sonata was to hear it played. While the nuances which make the virtuosos escaped him, his reproduction of rhythm, tempo, melody, and harmony was exact.

But Phillis Wheatley was reproducing the more subtle sounds of words, and those words were carrying ideas. She possessed not only a musical precocity comparable to Bethune's but a clear, logical mentality that created images which in most instances are true and precise. In her ability to write with all the practical common-sense control demanded by the neoclassicists is exhibited a still greater psychological puzzle than in her talent for music. Like all neoclassical poets she borrowed images freely. One finds in her poems the favorite eighteenth century *clichés*, such as *vaulted skies, roving fancy, crystal shower, feathered warbler, smiling fields, graceful tresses,* and *pensive bosoms.* One also finds an imagination imitating with a remarkable accuracy. The images indicated by italics in the following lines are the invention of a mind working with precision and with a clear recognition of the nice artistic adjustment:

> All-conquering Death! by thy resistless pow'r
> *Hope's tow'ring plumage falls to rise no more!*
>
> *We trace the pow'r of Death from tomb to tomb*
> And his are the ages yet to come.
>
> *The frozen deeps may break their iron bands,*
> *And bid their waters murmur o'er the sands.*
>
> Aeolus in his rapid chariot drive
> *In gloomy grandeur* from the vault above:
> Furious he comes. His winged sons obey
> Their frantic sire, *and madden all the sea.*
>
> He drops the bridle on his courser's mane,
> *Before his eyes in shadows swims the plain.*
>
> *Swift thro' his throat the feather'd mischief flies,*
> Bereft of sense, he drops his head, and dies.

Images of like character abound in Phillis Wheatley's poems. They are not direct copies, and they cannot be created by a mind that is not master of itself. They prove as well as the smooth music in Phillis Wheatley's verse her genius at imitation. And it is not too much to presume that if she had been taught by a Wordsworth, who would have convinced her of the value of turning to her sincere religious self for her subjects and of using an idiom drawn out of her own personality, her work would stand on its own merit rather than on the fact that she, a Negro and a slave, produced it. If she had not fallen under the sway of the New England elegists and of Pope and his school, she might today be considered one of the ornaments in American literature as well as one of the most interesting curiosities.

Notes

1. "On Virtue," in the 1773 volume, is also in blank verse.

The Personal Elements in the Poetry of Phillis Wheatley

Arthur P. Davis*

The most frequently stated criticism of Phillis Wheatley is that she was too highly objective in her writing, that adhering too closely to the tenets of her neo-classic training and background, she failed to tell us enough about herself, her personal feelings and thoughts. This view has been expressed in varying forms by practically all of the scholars who have written concerning the fascinating little eighteenth century poetess.

Among the modern critics, James Weldon Johnson was perhaps the first to complain about this shortcoming. Writing in 1922, he comments not only on Phillis Wheatley's lack of race-consciousness but also on what he feels is a certain smugness in her attitude:

> But one looks in vain for some outburst or even complaint against the bondage of her people, for some agonizing cry about her native land. In two poems she refers definitely to Africa as her home, but in each instance there seems to be under the sentiment of the lines a feeling of almost smug contentment at her own escape therefrom.[1]

In 1925 Vernon Loggins published his excellent study, *The Negro Author*, giving in it the most thorough and scholarly treatment of Wheatley's poems that we have. Although highly flattering in his praise of the Negro poetess, Loggins too regrets that she was reticent about herself:

> What one most wishes Phillis Wheatley had done, she left undone; she wrote too rarely about herself. Her intimate personal interests were ignored. She composed verses on the deaths of those who meant little to her, but, so far as we know, she remained silent after the deaths of Mrs. Wheatley and Mrs. Lathrop and her own children. She dwelt at length on the common notions of her day regarding liberty, but she neglected almost entirely her own state of slavery and the miserable oppression of thousands of her race.[2]

Echoing closely the sentiment of Loggins, Benjamin Brawley in 1935 wrote the following comment: "What one misses in the poems of Phillis

*Reprinted from *Phylon: The Atlanta University Review of Race and Culture*, 12, No. 2 (2nd Quarter, 1953), 191–98. With permission of *Phylon*.

Wheatley is the personal note. Like others who were of the school of Pope, she was objective in her point of view, . . ."[3]

In 1941 the editors of *The Negro Caravan* (and I am one of them) joined in the chorus of regret concerning Miss Wheatley's failure to unbosom herself, particularly on the matter of slavery:

> In only one poem, that addressed to the Earl of Dartmouth . . . does she express any resentment, and then fairly detached, against slavery. This was of course in line with her neoclassic models. Just as Phillis Wheatley shared their preference for the elegant and ornate, so she shared their dislike for self-revelation. Phillis Wheatley seemed to shrink from this even more shyly, however, than even Pope her master, and certainly more than such American contemporaries as Freneau and John Trumbull.[4]

And in 1945, Richard Wright, commenting on the modern Negro's estrangement from his cultural and intellectual background because of prejudice, praises in contrast the "complete identification" of Phillis Wheatley with her age and community. After quoting Miss Wheatley's well-known verses "On Imagination," Wright makes the following statement: "Whatever its qualities as poetry, the above poem records the feelings of a Negro reacting not as a Negro, but as a human being."[5]

It is hardly necessary to summarize what the above critics have said. They all state or imply that Phillis Wheatley because of her identification with the literary viewpoint of her age simply did not write enough about slavery or herself. For four of these critics, she was disappointingly objective; for the fifth she was refreshingly and fortunately "detached," and as a consequence, she was free to write "not as a Negro, but as a human being."

What these critics have said is largely true, and yet the implications of their statements give a picture which is essentially false. After reading the above comments (and they are typical), we get the idea that Phillis Wheatley was a pathetic little Negro girl who had so completely identified herself with her eighteenth century Boston background that all she could write was coldly correct neo-classical verse on dead ministers and even deader abstractions. As a matter of fact she is not as devoid of racial and personal feeling as such statements tend to make us think; and it will be the purpose of this paper to show, through a re-examination of her poetry, that Phillis Wheatley does speak of her own problems more often than is commonly recognized.

The first thing that impresses the close reader of Miss Wheatley's verse is that in spite of the generally held contrary opinion she is definitely race conscious. Although she never belabors the issue, she keeps reminding the reader that she is not just a poet, but an "Afric" poet. Phillis Wheatley seems to realize full well the propaganda value of her race and condition, and she uses both to advantage. For example, in the poem "To the University of Cambridge, in New England" she admonishes the students to avoid sin, but she underscores this advice with the line: "An Ethiop tells you, 'tis your greatest foe." The admonition to shun sin certainly does not need the peculiar or special backing of an Ethiop to make it effective, but Phillis Wheatley has in mind the obvious contrast between her own disadvantage as a slave just recently brought from a pagan land and the silver-spoon opportunities of these Harvard young men. This sort of contrast is implied in much of her poetry. Using her race and her lowly position as a frame of reference, she points up the message currently given. We find the same approach in a poem addressed "To His Honor the Lieutenant Governor on the Death of His Lady." After describing the beauties of the late wife's heavenly existence, she says abruptly to the husband:

> Nor canst thou, Oliver, assent refuse
> To heav'nly tidings from the *Afric Muse*.

This racial underscoring also occurs in other ways. In the opening lines of "On Recollection" we find the racial tag:

> Mneme, begin. Inspire, ye sacred Nine,
> Your *ven'trous Afric*, in her great design.

There is no obvious reason for designating her race in an objective and abstract poem of this sort, but consciously or unconsciously Phillis Wheatley realizes the advantage of the race label and inserts it. She does the same thing in "A Hymn to Humanity" (to be considered below in another respect) when she asks the question: "Can *Afric's Muse* forgetful prove?" Her race awareness appears in yet another way in "To Maecenas" (also to be considered below). In this piece she mentions three great poets—Homer, Virgil, and Terence. The last-named is included for one reason only, he is an *Afric* genius; and as such she is proud of him, so proud in fact that she brackets him with two men who are not only infinitely superior to him in excellence but who write in a totally different field.

Far from being shy about her race and native land, Phillis Wheatley is sometimes capable of special pleading on that score. This is apparent in the following lines from "On the Death of the Reverend Mr. George Whitefield":

> Take him [Christ], ye wretched, for your only good,
> Take him, ye starving sinners, for your food;
> Ye thirsty, come to this life-giving stream;
> Ye preachers, take him, for your joyful theme;
> Take him, my dear Americans, he said,
> Be your complaints on his kind bosom laid:
> *Take him, ye Africans, he longs for you;*
> *Impartial Saviour* is his title due;

Washed in the fountain of redeeming blood,
You shall be sons, and kings, and priests to God.[6]

Phillis Wheatley gives one or two lines to each of the other groups listed here but four to "ye Africans." Unlike the men of this world Christ is "impartial" (she uses the word here and elsewhere in a strictly racial sense); he "longs" to help Africans because of their unhappy condition and will make them "sons, and kings, and priests to God." All through this passage there runs the obvious theme of escape through leveling which was Christianity's primary appeal to the slave. Phillis had experienced in her own life the power of Christianity to open doors before closed to her. Though still a slave she was a Christian "sister" even to her owners and a "saint" in the Boston of her day. It was the only way for Africans to enter into the "kingdom" both here and hereafter. Realizing this fully, she underscores the appeal.

Let us examine now the two best known racial passages in the Wheatley poems. The first of these is "On Being Brought from Africa to America," the only poem in which she is totally subjective:

'Twas mercy brought me from my *pagan land*,
Taught my benighted soul to understand
That there's a God—that there's a Saviour too;
Once I redemption neither sought nor knew.
Some view our sable race with scornful eye,
'Their color is a diabolic dye.'
Remember, Christians, Negroes black as Cain
May be *refined*, amd join th'*angelic train*.

"Refined" seems to be the key word here. It is one that she likes, and she uses it in emphatic positions in at least four other poems.[7] As an African and a slave, Phillis Wheatley had felt the "scornful eye" all too often, but she knows that refinement furnished at least partial escape from that evil. And by refinement she had in mind not only Christian salvation but intellectual and cultural improvement as well. Her whole life was a serious and determined effort to acquire this sort of transforming refinement; and in the last two lines above—the lines with the imperative "remember"—she seems to be serving personal notice to the effect that she had achieved some measure of success on that score. There is a certain positiveness and assurance in these verses which impresses.

The second of these better known racial passages is that found in the verses "To the Right Honorable William, Earl of Dartmouth." It is Phillis Wheatley's strongest and most forthright utterance on slavery:

Should you, my lord, while you peruse my song,
Wonder from whence *my love of Freedom sprung*,
Whence flow these wishes for the common good,
By *feeling* hearts alone best understood,
I, young in life, by *seeming cruel fate*

Was snatched from *Afric's fancied happy seat;*
What pangs excruciating must molest,
What sorrows labor in my parent's breast!. . .
Such, such my case. And can I then but pray
Others may never feel *tyrannic sway*?

The above lines speak for themselves on the subject of freedom, but they take on added strength and significance when compared with the objective passages on the same theme in "Liberty and Peace" and "His Excellency General Washington." In the latter poems (q.v.) Freedom is a typical neo-classic abstraction; but the personal reference in this poem makes it as strong a protest against slavery as a slave could utter and expect to have his work published in a slave-holding community. Several critics, among them James Weldon Johnson, have been irritated by the so-called smugness expressed in the phrases "seeming cruel fate" and "Afric's fancied happy seat." Phillis Wheatley also takes the same attitude towards her homeland in the verses "To the University of Cambridge, in New-England," in which she refers to Africa as a "dark abode" and a "land of errors and Egyptian gloom." But to accuse her of smugness in this respect is to overlook the most important subjective element in these phrases. Phillis Wheatley is speaking here not as a native of Africa but as a Christian, and to the Christian Phillis, Africa or Asia or any other land which did not know and accept Christ could never be a truly "happy seat." In short she writes upon two levels. As a little African girl it was cruel to be snatched from her parents, but to find Christ as a result of this misfortune was more than ample compensation for this "seeming cruel fate." We must always bear in mind that Phillis Wheatley was deeply religious, and that her religion was inextricably tied up with practical everyday considerations such as acceptance in the best circles of her time. This talented little girl made the most of her Christianity, tying it in neatly with the added appeal that her racial and pagan background gave to it. This is not to say that she was opportunist or hypocritical. She was simply human and highly intelligent.

Another important subjective element in Phillis Wheatley's work is her concern with excellence as a poet. It is only fair to state here that many of the phrases she uses to characterize herself are the conventional ones typical of neo-classic writing; but there are others which seem to have unusual pertinence. For one thing, she is keenly aware of her own handicaps in the matter of education and status, referring to herself as a "groveling mind,"[8] "a languid muse in low degree,"[9] and "the last and meanest of the rhyming train."[10] One notes that each of these phrases has a menial connotation. In spite of her position, however, she is convinced that "an intrinsic [natural] ardor"[11] prompts her to write; she wishes to cultivate virtue to learn "a better strain, a nobler lay";[12] and time and time again she calls on the

Celestial Muse, my arduous flight sustain
And *raise* my mind to a seraphic strain![13]

As stated above, phrases and passages of this sort may be conventional utterance, but in certain lines of the poem "To Maecenas" Phillis Wheatley seems to be voicing real disappointment at poetic failure:

Oh! could I rival thine and Virgil's page,
Or claim the Muses with the Mantuan sage;. . .
Then should my song in bolder notes arise,
And all my numbers pleasingly surprise:
But here I sit and mourn a grov'ling mind,
That fain would mount and ride upon the wind.

Not you, my friend, these *plaintive strains* become;
Not you, whose bosom is the Muses' home. . . .
But I, less happy, cannot raise the song;
The faltering music dies upon my tongue.

The *happier Terence* all the choir inspired,
His soul *replenished*, and his bosom fired;
But say, ye Muses, *why this partial grace*
To one alone of Afric's sable race; . . .

Even after we discount the exaggeration and disparagement typical of such poems, we find that Phillis is saying in no uncertain words that she cannot expect to equal Terence as a poet because his position was "happier" than hers. Terence, who was also an African, had once been a slave but had gained his freedom presumably because of his excellence as a poet. At this time Phillis was still in bondage and as a result of her unhappy position and "grov'ling mind" the "faltering music" dies upon her tongue. One notes also that the poetess seems just a little piqued that the "partial" muses had allowed only one poet of "Afric's sable race" to achieve world fame. In short this whole Terence passage is highly personal because of its racial and status comparisons.

Phillis Wheatley, however, always had one consolation, one unfailing support—her religion. Even though she could not equal her countryman Terence in this world, there was always that second chance in the world-to-come. In the verses "To S. M., A Young African Painter, on Seeing His Works," she seems as confident of this second chance as Browning:

But when these shades of time are chased away,
And darkness ends in everlasting day,
On what seraphic pinions shall we move,
And view the landscape in the realms above!
There shall thy tongue in heav'nly murmurs flow,
And there my muse with heav'nly transport glow; . . .

And finally let us examine those few poems of Phillis Wheatley which touch on personal relationships. Our limited knowledge of the poet's life is a serious handicap in considering these pieces, but the verses say enough to show at least certain basic traits in the young lady. Strangely enough, of the three poems to be considered, the one, "A Farewell to America," addressed to Mrs. Susannah Wheatley, the poet's mistress, seems the most stilted. Phillis was being sent to England for her health. The following lines are the only poetic reference to her mistress that we have:

> Susannah mourns, nor can I bear
>   To see the crystal shower,
> Or mark the tender falling tear
>   At sad departure's hour.
>
> Not unregarding can I see
>   Her soul with grief opprest;
> But let no sighs, no groans for me,
>   Steal from her pensive breast.

There is much more feeling in the "Hymn to Humanity," addressed to one S. P. G., Esq.:

> For when thy *pitying eye* did see
> The languid *muse in low degree;*
>   Then, *then at thy desire,*
> Descended the *celestial Nine;*
> *O'er me methought they deigned to shine,*
>   And deigned to string my lyre.
>
> Can *Afric's muse* forgetful prove?
> *Or can such friendship fail to move*
>   *A tender human heart?*

We do not know who S. P. G. is, but it is obvious that he encouraged or helped Phillis in the writing of poetry. He is evidently an eminent person, and she is grateful that his "pitying eye" sought her out. There is a certain warmth in the last three lines entirely lacking in the lines to Mrs. Wheatley.

In the verses "On the Death of the Reverend Dr. Sewall" we find the strongest personal utterance in any of her poems:

> "Sewall is dead." Swift-pinioned Fame thus cried.
> "Is Sewall dead?" my trembling tongue replied . . .
> How oft for us the holy prophet prayed!
> How oft to us the Word of Life conveyed!
> *By duty urged my mournful verse to close,*
> I for his tomb this epitaph compose. . . .
> Listen, ye happy, from your seats above;

> *I speak sincerely, while I speak and love . . .*
> *I, too, have cause this mighty loss to mourn*
> For he, *my monitor*, will not return.

It would be good to know just how Dr. Sewall helped Phillis, just how he urged her "mournful verse to close" [end?]. Did he advise her to stop writing funeral elegies? We of course do not know, but we need no biographical help to get the full import of the last three lines above. In them the young poetess has dropped the objective tone habitually used in these elegies and speaks in the first person, straight from the heart.

One gets the impression from these personal utterances that Phillis Wheatley was not so much the victim of her neo-classic training as of a congenital reserve. She seems to keep a perpetual guard on her emotions, holding them under rigid control. And when, as happens on occasion, she inadvertently lowers the guard in a brief personal passage, she seems immediately to regret it and then to run for shelter on the safe ground of religious generality. For example, after the strong lines quoted above expressing gratitude to S. P. G., Phillis, as though ashamed of such warmth, concludes the stanza with the following cliché:

> Immortal Friendship laurel-crowned
> The smiling Graces all surround,
>   With ev'ry heav'nly Art.

With these verses she has destroyed completely the intimate mood created in the first half of the stanza, changing the friendship of a "tender human heart" into an immortal and "laurel-crowned" abstraction with little or no real meaning. Afraid that she has been too "human," she hastily seeks sanctuary in her customary religious platitude. It is this kind of guarded and grudging subjectivity which characterizes all of the personal passages in the poems of Phillis Wheatley.

In summary then, after a close reading of her poetry, one finds that Phillis Wheatley has written a few passages expressing stronger-than-customary personal feeling; that she does tell us some things concerning her ambitions and desires as a poet; and that above all else, she is definitely race conscious in her writings. These findings do not invalidate the opinions expressed by the critics quoted above, but they do tend to soften and tone down the charge of stern and unyielding objectivity which for too long has dominated all criticism of Phillis Wheatley.

Notes

1. James Weldon Johnson, *The Book of American Poetry* (New York, 1922), p. xxvii.
2. Vernon Loggins, *The Negro Author* (New York, 1925), p. 24.
3. Benjamin Brawley, *Early Negro American Writers* (Chapel Hill, 1935), p. 34.
4. Sterling Brown, Arthur P. Davis and Ulysses Lee, *The Negro Caravan* (New York, 1941), pp. 233–234.

5. St. Clair Drake and Horace R. Cayton, *Black Metropolis* (New York, 1945), p. xxxiii. The Introduction to this work was written by Richard Wright.

6. The italics in this and other quotations in this article are mine. I have used them to call attention to pertinent words, phrases, and passages.

7. See the following poems: "To a Lady on Her Husband's Death," "Hymn to the Morning," "Hymn to the Evening," and "To the Reverend Thomas Amory."

8. "To Maecenas."

9. "A Hymn to Humanity."

10. "Niobe in Distress . . ."

11. "To the University of Cambridge . . ."

12. "On Virtue."

13. "Thoughts on the Works of Providence."

Matilda's "On Reading the Poems of Phillis Wheatley, the African Poetess"

Eugene L. Huddleston*

If Matilda's poetry accurately reflects his experiences, he was a New Yorker, a Revolutionary, a Western traveler, a patrician, and a sentimentalist—at least on topics like friendship, death, home, and religion.[1] His twenty-odd poems published in the *New York Magazine* from 1795 to 1797 display no particular literary merits, but because of their topicality they do help elucidate the cultural and intellectual history of the period. "On Reading the Poems of Phillis Wheatley . . ." in particular attracts attention because its subject is the young slave whose *Poems* (1773) went through five editions before 1800 and who was courteously received by General Washington at his headquarters in Cambridge and visited by Benjamin Franklin during her stay in London.[2] Of special interest are its application of the Great Chain of Being to the question of racial equality and its appearance in a relatively long-lived journal of the Federalist era whose readers represented an informed if somewhat conservative level of opinion.[3] If these readers valued perspicuity—that most vaunted stylistic accomplishment of the Augustans—then they must have passed over Matilda's offering, for it is frustratingly obscure.[4] Penetrating this obscurity requires examining the poem formally and ideologically and then comparing it with other productions of the author in the *New York Magazine*—a procedure that may elucidate the thinking of a man who, although anonymous, likely represented a prevalent mode of political and social awareness in the Federalist era.

"On Reading the Poems of Phillis Wheatly, the African Poetess."

His servile lot the beast of burden bears.
Unstung by memory, and unvext with cares.
With glad release returning evening smiles,
And food and slumber closes all his toils.
  If Afric's sable sons be doom'd to know
Nought but long bondage and successive woe,
Why did just Heav'n their sun-born souls refine

*Reprinted from *Early American Literature*, 5, No. 3 (Winter 1970–1971), 57–67. With permission of *Early American Literature*, and the author.

With passions, virtues, as our own, divine?
What tho' the sanguine flushes that adorn
Our limbs with tinges like the roseate morn,
Ah, partial Nature! on the race be lost,
Yet leave them peace and freedom still to boast:
For, as a just gradation still we find,
Up from the grov'ling to the enlighten'd mind,
And all the graces of the human form
Allied, in system, to the meanest worm;
The unfavor'd race in shade are meant to be
The link between the brutal world and we.
In flowers we see that beauteous order rise
From earth to purest substance of the skies,
Rough and unformed in its first degree,
More polish'd verdure in the next we see,
The third claims perfect beauty to its share,
And breathes its fragrant soul in kindred air.
Free and impartial still, the gifts of Heaven
In just degrees to all mankind are given:
This boasts of mental, that corporeal grace,
Or the vain merits of a beauteous face:
And these no grace, no scientific art,
But all the nobler virtues of the heart.
As our's their souls with great ambition glow,
Or melt in softer sympathy of woe.
Long did the hapless race in bondage groan,
In grief unheeded, and in worth unknown.
And long in vain their weeping genius bore
The sighs of sorrow to the eternal shore.
Oft when the Lover in some fav'rite grove,
Told the soft raptures of successful love,
Rude ruffian force the guiltless youth would tear
From all that love and nature render'd dear,
To unrelenting Rigour's cruel sway,
To drudge his fond unhappy soul away.
'Tis done! at length the long-withheld decree
Goes forth, that Afric shall be blest and free;
A PHILLIS rises, and the world no more
Denies the sacred right to mental pow'r,
While, Heav'n-inspired, she proves *her Country's* claim
To Freedom, and *her own* to deathless Fame.

New-York. MATILDA

In form, Matilda's encomium for the poetess whose name had become synonymous with Negro equality adheres closely to the same neo-classic conventions that Phillis herself was so widely admired for having mastered. It is not surprising that Matilda approved of her poetry, for whether Matilda's talent was wholly "natural" like Phillis' or, as what was more likely, was sharpened by a formal study of rhetoric and belles lettres, they both undoubtedly came under similar stylistic influences. The attempt to satisfy a uniform and proven standard of excellence common to men of taste everywhere guided both Matilda and Phillis in their stylistic and prosodic endeavors.[5] Both accepted the superiority of the heroic couplet;[6] both used periphrasis, personification, apostrophe, inversion, and elevated diction to embellish and aggrandize their expression;[7] and evidently both intended metaphors to supply vivid analogical images to the imagination rather than to objectify complex modes of the poet's own thought and feeling—a case in point being Matilda's two image clusters, one involving a "beast of burden" and the other a "Lover" being abducted, presumably by slave traders.[8]

The title reveals Matilda's work as one of the most common types of eighteenth-century poetry, yet as an occasional poem it hardly touches upon the event of reading Phillis' poems and concentrates instead on rationalizing the intellectual standing of her race. On the surface Matilda is doing what so many other writers did with the "sable Muse" after her discovery—citing her to illustrate the mental equality of Negroes with white Europeans.[9] The closer one examines the poem, however, the more he discovers ambiguities that complicate this apparently benevolent intention. Attempting to follow the poet's reasoning on the mental status of Blacks leads to a necessary entanglement with the central concept—and central ambiguity—of the poem: the Great Chain of Being, that grand scheme of universal order and harmony so admirably suited to the intellectual temper of the eighteenth century.[10]

Americans of the early national period became acquainted with the idea mainly through Pope's *Essay on Man*, and in its unrivaled couplets expounding the principles of continuity, plenitude, and gradation they found justification of man's dual nature and for the world's seeming chaos—"A mighty maze! but not without a plan," as Pope so hopefully put it.[11] Because man's middle estate in the order of creation from God to animalcule is the main concept of the Chain metaphor, it was inviting to apply the principle of hierarchy to the problem of racial differences. Winthrop Jordan has well summarized the thinking of those "natural philosophers" of the eighteenth century who were tempted to find gradations not only between man and animal but also within the genus *Homo:* "Clearly mankind was formed not in one image but in many. Clearly men were not equal in energy, talent, manner, and elegance of form. If all other created beings were ranked upon a grand scale, why not Man? Could it be that the Creator had graded mankind from its noblest specimens to its most brutal savages?"[12] It could be, indeed, as demonstrated by the considerable polemics generated by the question in the latter part of the eighteenth century.[13] By the time Matilda's poem was published in 1797, most of intellectual America knew that both apologists for slavery and naturalists obsessed by a rage for order were using gradation as expounded in the Great Chain of Being to justify the low estate of Negroes.

Matilda's poem is clear enough in this respect: because of their color Negroes "are meant to be / The link between the brutal world and we"—the "we" presumably being the exalted white readers of the poem. Here there is no mistake about the poet's meaning, for blackness—or "shade" as Matilda euphemistically puts it—provided the strongest of all physiognomic evidence that Negroes belonged at the bottom of the human scale and white Europeans at the top.[14] The chief difficulty is determining what the author thinks about qualities of Blacks other than color.

Nature, so the poet argues, has not impartially distributed to each race desired human qualities, for even though Blacks share with Whites souls refined by identical "passions" and "virtues," they were created deficient in color and hence accorded an inferior status in life. Pursued in detail, the reasoning in the first three verse paragraphs goes something like this: The "beast of burden" endures its "servile lot" because it does not know any better. If the Negro, like the beast, must endure "long bondage," why then did Nature endow Blacks with "passions, virtues, as our own, divine?" Further, why did Nature (or "Heav'n") deprive the "race" of the sanguine flushes that adorn / Our limbs with tinges like the roseate morn" and yet endow them (in their native land) with "peace and freedom"? If one accepts the tenets of the Great Chain of Being, he must accept as fact that black is a mark of inferiority:

> For, as a just gradation still we find,
> Up from the grov'ling to the enlighten'd mind,
> And all the graces of the human form
> Allied, in system, to the meanest worm;
> The unfavor'd race in shade are meant to be
> The link between the brutal world and we. (ll. 13–18)

Flowers provide for the poet apt illustration from nature of the hierarchical ranking arising from differences in degrees of beauty.

Lack of clear transition to the next verse paragraph intensifies the already difficult task of discovering with certainty the direction of the poet's thinking. Evidently he wants to establish that qualities other than physiognomy can assign humans their ranks in the Chain of Being. If Matilda's thought is fuzzy here, perhaps it is a result of the problem that proponents of the Chain faced in deciding whether gradation was to be applied to groups or individuals and in finding a single criterion for ranking.[15] Common belief held that men, individually and collectively, are unequal not only in appearance but also in mental capacities, or "faculties," such as memory, reason, imagination, and the moral sense.[16] By assuming varying capacities among men, the poet keeps himself from having to admit the complete inferiority of Negroes that his statement making them the link between men and beasts would seem to imply.

Although he does not introduce specific faculties into the poem, he does suggest that an unequal distribution of mental attributes among "mankind" makes impossible a single criterion of rank in the Chain of Being. Some divisions of mankind—he does not specify whether groups or individuals—have "grace" of body or of mind, and others have beauty alone. Blacks (presumably the referent of "these" in line twenty-nine), even though lacking in "grace" and "scientific art," nevertheless possess "nobler virtues of the heart," a term synonymous with the "passions" and "virtues" mentioned in line eight as being shared with Whites. Here, by introducing the heart-head dichotomy, the poet implies equality for the Negro on the basis of his "sensibility"—that is, his sensitivity to moral and aesthetic beauty.

The next verse paragraph illustrates specifically the inherent capacity of Negroes for deep feeling and their genius for its expression, even though repressed by long "bondage." Depicted as within a "fav'rite grove" reciting verse (one assumes), the Lover resembles the happy shepherd from a classical pastoral. The locus of this pastoral landscape is unclear: if Africa why is he already in bondage (line 33) and if America why is he rapturous? In either case, the joyous recitation of this "guiltless youth" will remain forever unknown, for amid his performance he is taken forcibly from his pleasures to a life of "unrelenting" hard labor.

In the conclusion, which finally introduces Phillis, the poet cleverly produces a "long-withheld decree" of undetermined origin that bids her rise and end the artistic oppression of her race illustrated by the silenced "Lover" of the preceding paragraph. Her appearance furthermore provides a way out of the dilemma raised by the poet regarding the apparent inferior status of Negroes resulting from color; for, "Heav'n-inspired," she has demonstrated to the world "the sacred right to mental pow'r" of her race, while at the same time assuring her own fame and serving the cause of her country.

The foregoing reading of Matilda's poem has tried to impose a plan where one is seldom apparent, for a lack of coherent transitions, in addition to inconsistencies and ambiguities, complicates precise determination of meaning. One discovers unclear transitions not only between paragraphs but also from couplet to couplet, where it is not always certain whether the poet is repeating an idea, developing it dialectically, or illustrating it. The author's confused syntax, evidently impelled by the demands of meter and rhyme, results in ambiguities such as the failure to specify to whom "the world no more / Denies the sacred right to mental pow'r"—her race? Phillis? "Afric?"—and whether this "right" is the same as that of Whites. A major inconsistency is in the recurrence of "mental." Is the term limited to intellect or does it include the total faculties of consciousness?[17] In the conclusion it seems to mean intellect, yet in the fourth verse paragraph the poet had specifically ruled out the "mental," or intellectual, equality of the race and had assigned it "virtues of the heart" among attributes of the mind allotted in varying degrees to men. If the poet intends "mental" to refer to mental faculties, then admitting equality on such broad grounds is admitting very little.

Reading the poems of Phillis Wheatley has taught Matilda very little—only to be equivocal. While denying her race fundamental equality, based on low status in the Chain of Being, he grants it mental power—whatever the term includes—based on Phillis' genius. If all of Matilda's efforts in the *New York Magazine* were equally obscure, one might assume that the Wheatley poem merely illustrates idiosyncratic thought processes. That he could attack other subjects with less obfuscation, however, suggests that his ambiguous stand on racial equality, not to mention his failure to deal with the issue of slavery, results from a divided sensibility—a conflict in the author's consciousness between the values of his intellectual milieu and the values derived from his adjustment to new conditions in a new land. The Republic of Letters, to which his publications attest his aspiration to belong, enforced its preoccupation with status by demanding, in Pope's words, that "ancient rules" be esteemed, for "to copy nature is to copy them." His experiences as an American, this "new man" of Crèvecoeur's, challenged him to reject authority and to accept freedom for the individual as a natural right.

In the purely literary realm there is no contest when the two sets of values conflict. Matilda never learned, for instance, that a pastoral elegy is not a suitable vehicle for the theme of Indian warfare. "Elegy, Supposed to be Written on the Banks of Detroit River" was composed in response to a poetical invitation from his friend Lt. Col. dePeyster, British commander of Fort Detroit from 1779 to 1784, to eulogize with his "matchless pen" the Englishmen who lost their lives. "Like heroes, e'en the French agree," in Pontiac's Rebellion of 1763.[18] Imposed on Matilda's decasyllabic quatrains are all the usual trappings of graveyard gloom; but instead of a rural churchyard the setting is the American wilderness, specifically "the uncultur'd shore" of the Detroit River, "where mighty lakes through narrow limits flow" and instead of an "unletter'd swain" two British officers—Dalyell and Campbell, one of whom was executed by the Indians and the other killed in ambush outside the fort—are the recipients of moralistic encomiums.

The conflict between authority and experience manifested in the contradictions between form and content in Matilda's frontier poetry is but one illustration of his divided sensibility. He also exhibits a conflict between what George Santayana was later to describe in his analysis of the Genteel Tradition as a female intellect *vs.* a male will.[19] Several of his poems suggest a gentleman of taste nourishing his sensitivity to beauty, both moral and aesthetic, in a manner approved by contemporary philosophers of the "moral sense" school. As a man of feeling, he cultivated the delicate susceptibilities of his heart through effusions like "Sonnet to Resignation" and "Ode to Melancholy," the topographical imagery of the latter poem lending some interest to the otherwise commonplace mortuary landscape through which personified Melancholy conducts the poet: "Lead me from all the busy throng," he pleads, "to *Abraham's* fatal plains" or "to some more contiguous grave" on the Hudson or "to *Flatbush'* dreary plains, / Where universal horror reigns / O'er each unnoted tomb."[20]

Matilda's deliberate cultivation of Sensibility and Benevolence prompts occasional emotional excesses anticipating Byronism. Even though *Childe Harold's Pilgrimage* was still more than a decade in the future, one hears definite echoes of it in the *Weltschmerz* of "Elegy Addressed to the River St. Lawrence," in which the poet, forced to wander far from home by "the stern decree of adverse Fate," seeks in "the war of elements" waged "on Ocean's barren shore" an elemental force to match "the gloomy temper" of his soul.[21] Lord Byron often turned in his distress to his half-sister; Matilda, alone on the "raging" St. Lawrence, finds comfort in thoughts of his father, whom he calls "partner of my heart" and who, in addition to "benevolence and justice," is blessed "with every firm and milder virtue." Matilda's loyalty is unflagging:

> How oft a pensive wanderer, distant far,
> In foreign lands reluctant doom'd to roam:
> Again, I said, a father's tender care
> Shall cheer my soul and give the sweets of home.

In addition to such sentimentalism, induced by a thought-feeling dichotomy, Matilda's political views—at least those expressed poetically—attest to a divided consciousness. His love of liberty—a theme running through several of his poems—vies for ascendancy with a need for security derived from a rigid moral code and the authority of established institutions. His evaluation of Pontiac as a Noble Savage in his Detroit River elegy is based on Pontiac's "patriot zeal" in uniting "scatter'd tribes" in order to "repel invasion, and retrieve the land." But in the same poem the rebel Logan's barbarity, a foil to Pontiac's nobility, derives from the Mingo chief's reputedly debased "moral sense":

> Not *Logan's* fame e'er the verse inspire:
> *Logan*, undaunted in the martial strife:
> But, more ferocious than the tyger-sire,
> From his own infant crush'd the guiltless life.

In his poems of the frontier Matilda projects the image of a gentleman for whom established modes of Eastern refinement hold much stronger attraction than the crudities and disorder associated with empire building. "The Traveller Returned" and "Elegy Addressed to the River St. Lawrence" both celebrate the poet's homecoming to New York after apparently fruitless wanderings "on distant wild and cheerless shores. / Where thund'ring Niagara roars." In the one, he complains of the "Ignorance" and "cheerless Superstition" that hold sway on "rude St. Lawrence's dreary coast," and in the other, bidding the "unfriendly shores" of the St. Lawrence a "last farewell," he maintains that the "sublime" scenery of the area is no compensation for the mental poverty of its "tenants . . . / Lock'd in the gloom of intellectual night." Here, unlike home, are no "books or friends" to "afford resource."[22]

Warring with Matilda's desire for refinement and order was his love of liberty, manifested in his poetical support of the Revolution. In verses dated 1780, he chastised a young man for leaving America at the beginning of the War:

> No longer be deceiv'd, mistaken youth,
> Nor trust the voice of interest for truth;
> The servile sons of men, in silent pain,
> Too long have yielded to the regal chain.[23]

Notwithstanding his support of rebellion, he clearly believed that too much liberty would unleash anarchic forces. His poetical loyalty to George Washington, "in whom all public, private virtues blend," as late as 1797 is evidence that his political sympathies were Federalist.[24] Certainly the dual attitude implicit in verses addressed to Thomas Paine as author of *The Age of Reason* demonstrates that conservative religious principles circumscribed Matilda's love of liberty.[25] Because the "distinguished fame" of the "great reformer" was already assured by his promotion of human rights, he could have retired from public life, like General Gates, with glories intact. But men are imperfect; how else account for his "nefarious" determination to undermine religion, "the source of virtue, and the spring of joy"? Setting himself up as the sole arbiter of reason, Paine failed to recognize its limitations:

> The use of reason, rightly understood,
> Is but to soften ill and heighten good:
> But oft, as diverse passions, interests blend,
> The means are inefficient to the end:
> What state was e'er thro' Time's long circuit known,
> To rise from error by her aid alone?

When put to the test, Religion supplies the "arms" needed to meet life's crises, "while weaker Reason from the conflict flies."

In the face of the divided mentality that the poem on Paine so well sets off, one can more easily understand the ambivalent attitudes toward race in Matilda's poem on Phillis Wheatley. He accepted the Chain of Being, and the Negro's place in it, because it provided a system of order and stability in harmony with the author's genteel political and intellectual proclivities. On the other hand, as with most informed Americans after the Revolution, equality for Matilda was more than a slogan; it was the basis for a new form of government. In Winthrop Jordan's words, it had been "naturalized, legalized, politicized, and nationalized."[26] And a man who consciously cultivated Benevolence and Sensibility as a means of moral self-improvement (as he and most of his contemporaries had learned to do) could hardly overlook the boost to the ideal of equality given by Miss Wheatley's performance as a Black Augustan poet.

If Matilda's literary tradition had provided him with a stereotype for humanizing Negroes, he would have seized it; instead, the only precedent for treating Blacks was to wax indignant over the immorality of slavery and the inhumanity of slaveholders. It was proving easy enough to place the American Indian into polarized stereotypes of Noble and Ignoble Savage sanctioned by the current vogue for primitivism both in England and America. And students of the problem generally agreed that if Indians could only adopt the white man's values and mode of life, they could be accepted as social equals.[27] But Negroes, because of their unfortunate color and physiognomy, presented a problem that neither primitivists nor reformers could handle. No one attempted to idealize Black culture or make it picturesque, nor did reformers interested in abolishing slavery seek to assimilate Negroes into American society. Matilda easily enough made Pontiac a Noble Savage, and undoubtedly he was tempted to sentimentalize Phillis along the same lines. But having no guides to follow, he was in effect forced to keep her out of the poem.

In offering Phillis the praise that seemed due her in the equalitarian spirit of the times, Matilda was willing to grant that she demonstrated that Negroes possessed "mental pow'r"—whatever he meant by that term—but he stubbornly clung to the idea that black in the scale of nature was a deficiency and was sufficient reason for the low estate of the race in the Great Chain of Being. He and those of his contemporaries who had been through the Revolution and who subscribed to its ideology—of "government founded on a moral theory, . . . on the indefeasible hereditary Rights of Man," in Paine's words—discovered that "though they could not easily defend the Negro's color . . . they could—and had to—defend his character.[28] "On Reading the Poems of Phillis Wheatley, the African Poetess" forcefully attests to the significance of color in racial prejudice, for try as he might, Matilda could not accept as an equal the most widely acclaimed Black artist of her day.

Notes

1. Assumptions about Matilda's life were gleaned from the following poems, all in the *New York Magazine*: "The Traveller Returned," 6 (1795), 375–76; "Lines Addressed to a Young Gentleman who Left America at the Commencement of the late Revolution. Written nearly at that Time," 6 (1795), 502–03; "Elegy Addressed to the River St. Lawrence," 6 (1795), 445; "To Lieutenant-Colonel D[ePeyste]r, on Reading his Song on the Charms of the Riviere Rouge . . . ," II [n.s.] (1797), 269. The poet's insistence on the power of sympathy is particularly demonstrated in "Ode to Melancholy," II [n.s.] (1797), 215–16; "To an Absent Friend," I [n.s.] (1796), 272; "Epistle to the Author of the Age of Reason," II [n.s.] (1797),

495–97. Matilda's identity can only be conjectured. Likely he was on the staff of Major Ephraim Douglass, whom Col. dePeyster cordially received as representative of the new government, July 1783, at Detroit. See Silas Farmer, *History of Detroit and Michigan* (Detroit, 1889), I, 263.

2. Matilda's poem, appearing fourteen years after Phillis' death, was published in the *New York Magazine* (as were all of his cited hereafter), I [n.s.] (1796), 549–50. For Phillis' reception by Washington and Franklin, see *The Poems of Phillis Wheatley*, ed. Julian D. Mason (Chapel Hill, 1966), p. 88, and *The Writings of Banjamin Franklin*, ed. Albert H. Smyth (London, 1907), VI, 96.

3. Among the notables who initially subscribed to the magazine were President Washington, Vice-President Adams, Governor Clinton, DeWitt Clinton, Matthew Carey, Evert Duyckinck (senior), William Dunlap (also an anonymous contributor), John Fenno, Baron Steuben, Philip Schuyler, Tammany Society, and Calliopean Society.

4. Lord Kames in *Elements of Criticism* (Edinburgh, 1762, II, 256) stated that "communication of thought being the principal end of language, it is a rule that perspicuity ought not to be sacrificed to any other beauty [of language] whatever."

5. Kames in *Elements of Criticism* (III, 365), affirmed that in both morals and the fine arts a "common standard" determines excellence.

6. Wheatley's use of the couplet is more adept than Matilda's; in the former's "Liberty and Peace," for example, only one pair of rhymes—"prayer" and "war"—seems violently yoked, whereas Matilda's poem has at least six awkward pairings. As forced as many of them seem (*e.g.* "more" and "pow'r"), Kathryn DeBoer's "The Rhymes of Philip Freneau: A Reflection of Eighteenth Century American Pronunciation" (*Speech Monographs*, 33, March, 1966, 50–56) suggests that Matilda's choices largely reflected cultivated usage; *e.g.* (p. 56), ". . . the frequent rhyming of words like *join* and *fine* indicates that the vowels of the two words were considerably closer together than . . . in present speech." Certainly Matilda's rhyming "grove" with "love" (ll. 37–8 was not exceptional; in William Livingston's popular "Philosophic Solitude" (1747) the pairing appears three times (lines 11–12; 55–56; 452–453).

7. Periphrasis, which Lord Kames (III, 136–44) believed "hath a happy effect in preventing the familiarity of proper names," occurs in "Afric's sable sons," "unfavor'd race," and "hapless race"; personification in "Rigour's cruel sway," and "just Heav'n"; apostrophe in "Ah! partial Nature"; inversion in the opening line; and elevated diction in epithets like "sanguine flushes" and "roseate morn."

8. Ernest Lee Tuveson analyzes Kames on the effects of images on the imagination in *The Imagination As a Means of Grace* (Berkeley, 1960), pp. 153–56.

9. Winthrop D. Jordan explains this use of Wheatley in *White over Black: American Attitudes toward the Negro*,1550–1812 (Chapel Hill, 1968), pp. 283–84.

10. In purpose the poem is persuasive. Gordon E. Bigelow in *Rhetoric and American Poetry of the Early National Period* (Gainesville, 1960), has explained that persuasive poetry often derived its form from rules of classical oratory because in this era there was "no sharp distinction between rhetorical and poetical modes of discourse." However, other than the facts that the poem offers praise and is composed of a series of enthymemes, it does not exhibit enough characteristics (*e.g.*, formalistic divisions and highly ornamented style) of epideictic verse—the declamatory mode that Matilda's poem most resembles—to make formal rhetorical analysis worthwhile.

11. The American popularity of the *Essay on Man* is discussed in Agnes M. Sibley, *Alexander Pope's Prestige in America, 1725-1835* (New York, 1949), pp. 22–56.

12. Jordan, p. 223.

13. See Jordan (Chap. 13) for arguments on the "rightful place" of Negroes "in a natural order which derived from divine decree."

14. In the eighteenth century, "no matter how one wished to describe the majority of

men (tawny, copper, yellow, olive, brown), Negroes were black and Europeans, happily, were white. Black remained the opposite of white. Newton's *Opticks* had shown black for what it was—a deprivation." So reasoned Europeans in general, according to Jordan, p. 253.

15. Jordan, p. 224.

16. Jefferson, for instance, wrote in *Notes on . . . Virginia* (ed. William Peden, Chapel Hill, 1955, p. 139): "Comparing them [Negroes] by their faculties of memory, reason, and imagination, it appears to me, that in memory they are equal to the whites; in reason much inferior . . . ; and that in imagination they are dull, tasteless, and anomalous."

17. Both meanings were current in the eighteenth century. See *OED*, definitions nos. 17 and 18 under "mind."

18. "On reading the foregoing Ode to Melancholy [by Matilda]. By Lieutenant-Colonel D*******R, commanding Detroit" [dated "Detroit, 1782"]. This poem immediately preceded Matilda's "Elegy . . . Written on the Banks of Detroit River," II [n.s.] (1797), 216–18.

19. For this and similar metaphors used by Santayana see Douglas L. Wilson (ed.), *The Genteel Tradition: Nine Essays by George Santayana* (Cambridge, 1967), pp. 9, 40, 82.

20. "Ode to Melancholy," II [n.s.] (1797), 215–16.

21. VI (1795), 445.

22. Both titles cited in footnote 1.

23. "Lines Addressed to a Young Gentleman who Left America at the Commencement of the late Revolution. Written nearly at that Time," 6 (1795), 502–03.

24. Matilda praises Washington in several poems. See "The Progress of Liberty: Inscribed to the late Commander in Chief of the American Armies," II [n.s.] (1797), 327–30; "On Hearing the Brave Unfortunate Paschal Paoli had Engaged in the Russian Service. Written in 1779," I [n.s.] (1796), 496; "Inscription for the Pedestal of a Bust of Washington" [dated "May 1797"], II [n.s.] (1797), 608.

25. "Epistle to the Author of the Age of Reason. Occasioned by Reading the first Part of that Performance," II [n.s.] (1797), 495–97.

26. Jordan, p. 270.

27. See Bernard W. Sheehan, "Paradise and the Noble Savage in Jeffersonian Thought," *William and Mary Quarterly*, 26 (July 1969), 327–59.

28. Jordan, p. 281.

Phillis Wheatley—Soul Sister?

R. Lynn Matson*

Feelin' tomorrow like I feel today,
Feelin' tomorrow like I feel today,
I'll pack my grief and make my getaway.
Bessie Smith, "St. Louis Blues."

Phillis Wheatley has been condemned for more than a century by whites and blacks alike for failing to espouse in any way the plight of her race. No one denies that she was a genius; no one denies her the right to be called a poet; no one denies that she was an extremely clever imitator; but almost all deny that Phillis Wheatley was race conscious, or what could be called by any stretch of the imagination a protester of slavery. The common view, in effect, is that she was the white man's ideal of a good "nigger"—so good, in fact, that she was almost white.

Vernon Loggins, who has written the most extensive criticism on her poems, says, "She dwelt at length on the common notions of her day regarding liberty, but she neglected almost entirely her own state of slavery and the miserable oppression of thousands of her race."[1] Loggins goes on to say, "Like the rest of neoclassical sentimental verse, her poems offer slight interest to the modern reader."[2] He sums her up as a clever imitator, nothing more.[3]

James Weldon Johnson was also disappointed with Miss Wheatley:

> . . . But one looks in vain for some outburst or even complaint against the bondage of her people, for some agonizing cry about her native land. In two poems she refers definitely to Africa as her home, but in each instance there seems to be under the sentiment of the lines a feeling of almost smug contentment at her own escape therefrom.[4]

The modern anthologizers of black verse seem to follow the same worn path of opinion concerning Phillis Wheatley:

> . . . If this ex-slave had dared to put into her poetry more than just that of Miss Wheatley, if she had had the strength to give all that was really hers,

*Reprinted from *Phylon: The Atlanta University Review of Race and Culture*, 33, No. 3 (Fall, 1972), 222–30. With permission of *Phylon*.

> and not that which others had given her, she might have become a really important figure and not, as she is now, a literary curio.[5]

> . . . Phillis Wheatley . . . the first poet of African descent to win some measure of recognition, had almost nothing to say about the plight of her people. And if she resented her own ambiguous position in society, she did not express her resentment.[6]

Even Julian Mason, Jr., who is to be thanked for recently bringing out a new authoritative edition of Phillis Wheatley's poems and letters, says of her:

> . . . The neoclassical influence also may have been responsible for the fact that there is little about Phillis herself in her poems. She certainly leaves the reader of her poems only slightly aware of her being a Negro and a slave.[7]

One of the most recent, and perhaps most devastating, condemnations of Phillis Wheatley is shown by her exclusion from the popular anthology of writings by Negroes *Dark Symphony* (MacMillan, 1968). Phillis has often been the recipient of backhanded compliments, such as the following by Arthur Schomburg (one time secretary of the Negro Society for Historical Research), "There was no great American poetry in the eighteenth century, and Phillis Wheatley's poetry was as good as the best American poetry of her age."[8] But seldom has she been ignored wherever black writing was discussed. This leads one to surmise that Phillis Wheatley is hardly appreciated among the black intelligentsia in this age of extreme race consciousness—a miscarriage of justice, because Phillis Wheatley has much to offer black (and white) readers of today. Not only is she America's first accomplished black poet (a fact that by itself should insure her a safe place in our literary history), but her poetry is a record of a Negro's survival in our white culture. Though Phillis Wheatley may not have been a black nationalist (and of course such a stand would have been impossible considering the time and her position), nonetheless she was very race conscious, very aware of her position as a slave, and not at all "smug" in this position (as comparatively desirable as it may have been) in the Wheatley household. In fact, it can be shown that she protested slavery, after her fashion, often implicitly through the use of various escape themes in her poetry.

Before dismissing the critics, however, it must be stated that there was at least one early Wheatley admirer who saw that Phillis was not color blind. He is Arthur Schomburg, quoted above:

> . . . Phillis Wheatley is a jewel—priceless to the literature of the Negro in America. Her name stands as a beacon light to illuminate the path of the young, who will surely pass every year. Let us with diligence weave to her memory as affectionate and loving a feeling for her sacrifice, *in keeping*

> *with the manifested race pride shown in her poems,* that they may stimulate us to nobler deeds and loftier purposes in life.[9]

For a man who has brought out such a careful edition of Phillis Wheatley's work, Mason's comment above—that "there is little about Phillis herself in her poems"—is truly surprising. More than ten years before Mason's edition of Phillis Wheatley's poems, an article appeared in *Phylon* by Arthur Davis entitled "Personal Elements in the Poetry of Phillis Wheatley."[10] Davis does an excellent job of fulfilling the objectives of his title, and there is no need here to rehash his findings. One of his themes, however, may be expanded—the idea of Phillis Wheatley's race consciousness. He mentions the several (and obvious) instances in which Phillis refers to herself as *Afric* or *Ethiop*. She does this in part no doubt to capitalize on her reputation as the famous black poetess of Boston, but it also suggests that she is proud of her blackness.

It is not true that Phillis Wheatley was "smug" and unconcerned about her black brothers and sisters. A look at her letters makes this clear. In a letter dated May 19, 1772, to Obour (or Arbour) Tanner, also a slave girl, we can see Phillis expressing a sort of black unity. (And in the letters to this girl one can imagine that Phillis was most at ease and frank, although she could not let her guard down completely since the letters were usually delivered by white acquaintances.) Phillis is speaking of their fortunate deliverance to a Christian country. She is obviously responding to some news about blacks when she says, "It gives me very great pleasure to hear of so many of *my nation* seeking with eagerness the way of true felicity."[11] "My nation" is Africa. In another more guarded letter to Obour Tanner (October 30, 1773) she writes:

> . . . What you observe of Esau is true of all mankind, who, (left to themselves) would sell their heavenly birth rights for a few moments of sensual pleasure . . . *Dear Obour, let us not sell our birthright for a thousand worlds,* which indeed would be as dust upon the balance.[12]

Ostensibly she is talking about religious matters, but would it be going too far to expect that a person of Phillis Wheatley's intelligence could write intentionally ambiguous passages, and that "birthright" might be a racial allusion? The possibility becomes even more probable when one considers her position—a slave who enjoys all the benefits of a kind and enlightened family, a position to be guarded, and yet an enslaved muse, infinitely more intelligent than many of her white "betters." We must keep this in mind when looking later at what are possible double meanings in her poems. First, however, it is necessary to look at one more letter of Phillis's that shows her special concern for her black race. Having heard of "two Negro men" who were desirous of returning to Africa to preach the gospel, she tells the Reverend Samuel Hopkins:

> . . . My heart expands with sympathetic joy to see a distant time the thick cloud of ignorance dispersing from the face of *my benighted country*. Europe and America have long been fed with the heavenly provision, and I fear they loath it, while Africa is perishing with a spiritual Famine. *O that they could partake of the crumbs, the precious crumbs, which fall from the table of these distinguished children of the kingdom.*
> . . . Ethiopia shall soon stretch forth her hands unto God.[13]

Phillis Wheatley considered herself extremely fortunate in being brought to America, not because she was well-treated here, not because she was at least physically comfortable in slavery, but because America was where she discovered Jesus Christ. From evidence such as this passionate letter it would seem that she was not smug or self-satisfied but instead deeply concerned for the spiritual welfare of her people.

The overpowering concerns of Phillis Wheatley's life were God and salvation. In understanding her feelings about being black and a slave, it is crucial to examine her view of life in relation to God and salvation. It is important to keep in mind that she was once a pagan. This, in addition to her being a Negro, gives her a decidedly different (non-white) slant on religion.

Concerning Negroes and Christianity, LeRoi Jones has said:

> . . . One of the reasons Christianity proved so popular was that it was the religion, according to older Biblical tradition, of an oppressed people. . . . In the early days of slavery, Christianity's sole purpose was to propose a metaphysical resolution for the slave's natural yearnings for freedom, and as such it literally made life easier for him.[14]

Judging from her poems and what little we know about her life, it appears that Phillis Wheatley's most emotional religious experience came from the preaching of the Reverend George Whitefield. Whitefield was a Boston evangelist, known for his spirited sermons and his concern for orphans and other unfortunates. Although he defended slavery on biblical grounds, he was quite sympathetic to the plight of Negroes.[15] Other than the elegy on Whitefield's death, we have no record of Phillis's writing about him. However, it is probable that her attraction to his type of preaching arises out of a racial predilection for religious emotionalism.

We are fortunate to have an eyewitness account of one of Whitefield's performances from another slave poet, Gustavus Vassa:

> . . . When I got into the church I saw this pious man exhorting the people with the greatest fervor and earnestness, and sweating as much as I ever did while in slavery on Montserrat beach. . . . I was very much struck and impressed with this; I thought it strange that I had never seen devines exert themselves in this manner before, and was no longer at a loss to account for the thin congregations they preached to.[16]

About Whitefield's preaching and Negroes, Loggins says:

> . . . The Christianity which Whitefield and his emotional predecessors preached in America brought to the Negro a religion which he could understand, and which could stir him to self-expression. He responded to it with enthusiasm, allowed his imagination to run riot with it, loved it with passion. *It afforded him a mental escape from this wretchedness of his social position. . . .*[17]

This emotional, participatory reaction to religious preaching was the same kind of reaction found later at camp meetings, out of which in turn came the Negro spiritual and a whole progression of black music from Blues to Soul.

The question now facing us is did Phillis Wheatley have what could be called an escapist view of death and Christianity? Arthur Davis points to the following passage in the poem "On the Death of the Rev. Mr. George Whitefield," saying "All through this passage there runs the obvious theme of escape through leveling which was Christianity's primary appeal to the slave."[18]

> Take him [Christ], ye wretched, for your only good,
> Take him, ye starving sinners, for your food;
> Ye thirsty, come to this life-giving stream;
> Ye preachers, take him, for your joyful theme,
> Take him, my dear Americans, he said,
> Be your complaints on his kind bosom laid;
> Take him, ye Africans, he longs for you;
> Impartial savior is his title due;
> Washed in the fountain of redeeming blood,
> You shall be sons, and kings, and priests to God.[19]

The theme of escape expressed in these last four lines becomes even more apparent in another version of the same poem (probably published in England). Here these lines read:

> Take him, ye Africans he longs for you,
> Impartial savior is his title due.
> *If you will walk in Grace's heavenly Road,*
> *He'll make you free, and Kings, and priests to God.*[20]

We can only guess at why the poet changed "He'll make you free" to "You shall be sons" in the Boston version of the poem. Did she feel that she was being too obvious, and, in order to protect herself, felt the need to delete a personal reference and insert an abstraction?

Another of Phillis Wheatley's great concerns was death (18 of her 46 poems are elegies). Her elegies are usually dismissed as the mere sentimental effusions of a young black girl. They certainly are sentimental, even bathetic in some cases, but what is overlooked is this same theme of escape, in this case, escape (freedom) through death. In "On the Death of a Young Lady of Five Years of Age" Phillis writes:

From dark abodes to fair ethereal light
The' enraptured innocent has wing'd her flight;
On the kind bosom of eternal love
She finds unknown beatitude above.
This know, ye parents, nor her loss deplore,
She feels the iron hand of pain no more:

. . . . . .

Let then no tears for her henceforward flow,
No more distress in our dark vale below,

. . . . . .

Freed from a world of sin, and snares, and pains,
Why would you wish your daughter back again?[21]

The poet goes on to tell the parents to endure until "Yourselves, safe are landed on the blissful shore."[22] One must also notice in these poems the metaphors of death as a flight or a voyage over water which later became so popular in Negro spirituals. In "To a Lady on the Death of Three Relations" Phillis Wheatley describes the dead as,

From bondage freed, the exulting spirit flies . . .

. . . . . .

Weep not for them, who with thine happy mind
To rise with them, and leave the world behind.[23]

While in another elegy, the dead

Invite you there to share immortal bliss
Unknown, untasted in a state like this.
With tow'ring hopes, and growing grace arise,
And seek beatitude beyond the skies.[24]

Heaven is a place "Where grief subsides, Where changes are no more, / And life's tumultuous billows cease to roar."[25] On the death of the Reverend Dr. Sewell (1769) Phillis writes:

See Sewell number'd with the happy dead.
Hail, holy man, arriv'd th' immortal shore,

. . . . . .

Thrice happy saint! to find thy heav'n at last
What compensation for the evils past.[26]

Some would say that these lines could be dismissed as mere clichés and poetic conventions of the day. Indeed they could if they came from the pen of a white poet, but since they come from the soft-spoken Negro slave of John Wheatley, and a slave who was probably a genius, perhaps the lines take on an added significance. Perhaps Phillis Wheatley was much more shrewd than she is given credit for.

Even Phillis Wheatley's severest critics admit that there are two or three poems in which she does seem to make some reference to her own position. One of these much-quoted poems is "To the Right Honorable

William, Earl of Dartmouth . . ." The Earl of Dartmouth had just been appointed Secretary of State for the Colonies, and Phillis is addressing him, ostensibly on the subject of America's liberty:

> No more America in mournful strain
> Of wrongs, and grievance unredress'd complain,
> No longer shalt thou dread the iron chain,
> Which wanton tyranny with lawless hand
> Had made, and with it meant t' enslave the land.
>   Should you, my Lord, while you peruse my song,
> Wonder from whence my love of Freedom sprung,
> Whence flow these wishes for the common good,
> By feeling hearts alone best understood,
> I, young in life, by seeming cruel fate
> Was snatch'd from Afric's fancy'd happy seat:
> What pangs excruciating must molest,
> What sorrows labour in my parents breast?
> Steel'd was that soul and by no misery mov'd
> That from a father seiz'd his babe belov'd
> Such, such my case. And can I then but pray
> Others may never feel tyrannic sway?[27]

The last stanza is usually cited as an example of Phillis speaking out (not too harshly) on slavery, which indeed she is. But what is overlooked, by critics who cite only this stanza, is its relation to the rest of the poem. Why does she suddenly insert some very personal references to herself right in the middle of a poem about American freedom? The last stanza above makes a very curious juxtaposition with the first stanza. This juxtaposition gives the poem a whole new slant. It suddenly becomes more forceful, even angry. "Wanton tyranny" with its "lawless hand" in juxtaposition with Phillis's biographical details makes strong language indeed. But yet, she always keeps her guard up, never leaving herself unprotected.

This use of possible double meaning and ambiguity becomes more and more clear to the close reader of Phillis Wheatley's poems. One tip-off to this deliberate use of ambiguity is in the nature of some of her revisions. A prime example is in "To the University of Cambridge, in New England (1767)." This is one of her few peevish poems. Here she is admonishing the gallant young Harvard men to avoid sin and sloth and to make the most of their fortunate positions. The last stanza of the published 1773 version of the poem reads:

> Improve your privileges while they stay,
> Ye pupils, and each hour redeem, that bears
> Or good or bad report of you to heav'n.
> Let sin, that baneful evil to the soul,
> By you be shunned, nor once remit your guard;
> Suppress the deadly serpent in its egg.
> Ye blooming plants of human race devine,

An Ethiop tells you 'tis your greatest foe;
Its transient sweetness turns to endless pain,
And in immense perdition sinks the soul.[28]

This is hardly a strong admonition. But after all, how presumptuous could a little slave girl be in addressing the young white aristocracy? However, the manuscript version of this stanza is more illuminating:

Improve your privileges while they stay:
Caress, redeem each moment, which with haste
Bears on its rapid wing Eternal bliss.
Let hateful vice so baneful to the soul,
Be still avoided with becoming care;
Suppress the sable monster in its growth,
Ye blooming plants of human race, divine,
An Ethiop tells you tis your greatest foe;
Its transient sweetness turns to endless pain,
And brings eternal ruin on the soul.[29]

The published version has obviously been toned down, made milder. But why did she delete completely the line "Suppress the sable monster in its growth" in favor of "deadly serpent?" Could she have been afraid that "sable monster" might have been interpreted as the enslaved black race?[30] Keep in mind that Phillis at this time would have been approximately the same age as these young dandies, and had an insatiable thirst for knowledge. It does not seem unreasonable that she might have felt strong resentment over this privileged class not taking their opportunities seriously enough, while her own educational and social opportunities were definitely limited. She had much cause to be bitter, yet more cause to hide it.

In his article, Arthur Davis points to Phillis's constant striving for poetic excellence (and lamenting her lack of it) as an example of a personal element in her poetry. We may go a step further and say that this is a continuation of the escapist or flight theme examined earlier. Like Baudelaire's albatross, beautiful and free in flight, but ugly and awkward out of the air, Phillis Wheatley longed to soar to poetic heights. She could be free metaphorically, at least. In "To Maecenas" she envies Virgil, and especially Terence (an African).

But here I sit and mourn a grov'ling mind,
That fain would mount and ride upon the wind. . .

. . . . . .

But I, less happy, cannot raise the song;
The faltering music dies upon my tongue.[31]

And finally let us look at "To S.M., a young African Painter, on Seeing His Works," a poem in which she swells with pride over this black artist's accomplishments. She is telling him her hope that they can be better artists in the freedom of the next world:

But when these shades of time are chas'd away,
And darkness ends in everlasting days,
On what seraphic pinions shall we move,
And view the landscapes in the realms above?[32]

But sadly, she is brought back to her present state, and ends her poem with "Cease, gentle muse! the solemn gloom of night/Now seals the fair creation from my sight."[33] It is obvious that she is talking about poetic inspiration. What is not so obvious, and we should allow Phillis Wheatley this possibility, is that her writing on the figurative level corresponds exactly with her real position in life. It is entirely probable that the slave whom she is addressing in the poem would interpret such phrases as "shades of time" and when "darkness ends" much differently than a white man of the day would.

Phillis Wheatley was not a great poet; but then neither was the American poetry of the eighteenth century a remarkable literature. She can be dismissed as just another mediocre versifier without doing her a great injustice (although some of her poems have real merit, comparatively). But she cannot be dismissed, as she has been, on the grounds that she abandoned her race and completely assimilated into the slave society. If she is not exactly a soul sister, she is certainly a distant relative.

Notes

1. Vernon Loggins, *The Negro Author* (Port Washington, Kennikat Press, 1964), p. 24.
2. Loggins, p. 16.
3. Concerning her imitating Pope, he says; "Her power to attain this place of eminence must be pronounced as due to her instinct for hearing the music of words, an instinct which was possibly racial." Loggins, p. 27.
4. James Weldon Johnson, *The Book of American Negro Poetry* (New York, Harcourt, Brace Co., 1922), p. xxvii.
5. Rosey E. Poole, *Beyond The Blues* (Lympne Hythe Kent, Hand and Flower Press, 1962), p. 14.
6. Robert Hayden, ed., *Kaleidoscope, Poems by American Negro Poets* (New York, Harcourt, Brace, 1967), p. xx.
7. Phillis Wheatley, *The Poems of Phillis Wheatley, ed. by Julian Mason, Jr.* (Chapel Hill, University of North Carolina Press, 1966), p. xxv.
8. *Phillis Wheatley, Poems and Letters*, ed. by Charles F. Heartman (New York, Privately Printed, 1915), p. 19.
9. Heartman, p. 19. (Italics here and elsewhere are mine.)
10. *Phylon*, XIV (June, 1953), 191–198.
11. Phillis Wheatley, in Mason, *op. cit.*, pp. 103–104.
12. Mason, p. 106.
13. Mason, p. 110.
14. Leroi Jones, *Blues People* (New York, Wm. Morrow, 1963), p. 39.
15. Phillis Wheatley, in Mason, *op. cit.*, p. 67.
16. Loggins, *op. cit.*, p. 4.

17. *Ibid.*

18. In *Phylon, op. cit.*, 194.

19. *Ibid.*, 193.

20. Phillis Wheatley, in Mason, *op. cit.*, p. 70.

21. Phillis Wheatley, in Heartman, *op. cit.*, pp. 88–89.

22. *Ibid.*

23. *Ibid.*, p. 86.

24. *Ibid.*, pp. 68–69.

25. *Ibid.*, p. 61.

26. *Ibid.*, pp. 34–35.

27. *Ibid.*, pp. 73–74.

28. *Ibid.*, p. 33.

29. Phillis Wheatley, in Mason, *op. cit.*, pp. 63–64.

30. In the poem "To Maecenas" Phillis refers to Negroes as "Africa's sable race." Heartman, *op. cit.*, p. 90.

31. *Ibid.*, pp. 89–90.

32. *Ibid.*, pp. 58–59.

33. *Ibid.*

[On "The barter of her soul"]

Merle A. Richmond*

. . . The poetic world of Phillis Wheatley was circumscribed by rigid boundaries; by the decasyllabic line in the heroic couplet, by the ornate diction of neoclassicism and the ritualistic obeisances it prescribed. Within these boundaries of meter and language other narrowing constrictions defined the thoughts and emotions that inhibited her poetic world.

Conforming to neoclassical ritual, she constantly addressed the Muses, singly or collectively, in such terms as these: Celestial Muse, heavenly Muse, Muse divine, sacred Nine, indulgent Muse, gentle Muse, tuneful Nine, tuneful goddess, sacred choir, blooming graces. . . .

In the effulgent imagery of neoclassicism the sky became ethereal space, ethereal train, starry train, heavenly plains, Phoebe's realms, orient realms, azure plain, empyereal skies. The earth appeared as this vast machine, rolling globe, dusty plain, dark, terrestrial ball.

The verse is peopled with figures from the Greek and Roman classics, literary and mythological; Homer and Virgil and Terence are here, as are gods and goddesses in profusion, and such place names as Helicon, Olympus, and Parnassus. . . .

In some critical analysis, the decasyllabic couplet, which attained its apogee with Pope, is perceived as an appropriate reflection of a harmonious confluence between science and religion in the early eighteenth century. . . . Wheatley's vision of the universe was etched most explicitly in "Thoughts on the Works of Providence":

> ARISE, my soul; on wings enraptured, rise,
> To praise the Monarch of the earth and skies,
> Whose goodness and beneficience appear
> As round its centre moves the rolling year. . .
> Adored forever be the God unseen,
> Which round the sun revolves, this vast machine. . .

In Wheatley's verse there is, indeed, a harmony between the symmetrical pattern and the apprehension of a well-ordered universe. There

*Reprinted from *Bid The Vassal Soar: Interpretive Essays on the Life and Poetry of Phillis Wheatley and George Moses Horton* (Washington, D.C.: Howard University Press, 1974), pp. 54–66. With permission of Howard University Press.

is a third part of this harmony: the human condition. In her view, . . . there is no serious discord between man and the divinely enacted laws of nature. Nor is there much concern with the contradictions in man . . . With her benign disposition . . . her emphasis is on human redemption, not on wickedness and folly. . . .

So her poetry does not rise to the greatness that truly expresses the spirit of an age, but such poetry is rare, and there was none of it in Colonial times. . . . But she was a *black* poet, and it is not enough to say that the quality of her verse was as good as that of her best white contemporaries. She also has to be assessed in terms of her own identity.

Not until recently has black scholarship attempted to assess her in explicitly black terms. The more traditional view among black scholars was presented by James Weldon Johnson, who wrote:

> Phillis Wheatley has never been given her rightful place in American literature. By some sort of conspiracy she is kept out of most of the books, especially the textbooks on literature used in schools. Of course, she is not a *great* American poet—and in her day there were no great American poets—but she is an important poet. Her importance, if for no other reason, rests on the fact that, save one, she is the first in order of time of all the women poets of America. And she is among the first of all American poets to issue a volume. . . .[1]

It is not a matter of making allowances for her antecedents (that is, for her blackness and her slavery), but of taking them properly into account. This is attempted explicitly by the black critic J. Saunders Redding and in a curiously inverse way by the black novelist Richard Wright.

In his lecture on "the Literature of the Negro in the United States," Wright read passages from the works of Alexander Pushkin and Alexander Dumas and made the obvious point that nothing in those passages suggested they were written by Negroes. "The writings I've just read to you," he went on, "were the work of men who were emotionally integrated with their country's culture; no matter what the color of their skins, they were not really Negroes. One was a Russian, the other a Frenchman." Then he posed the question: has any American Negro ever written like the Russian poet and the French novelist? And he replied that one, only one, had done so—Phillis Wheatley . . .

Wright sketched an idyllic picture of her condition—she "was accepted into the Wheatley home as one of the family, enjoying all the rights of the other Wheatley children . . . she got the kind of education that the white girl of her time received." As a consequence of her integration, he argued, she was able to articulate a "universal note" that was in total harmony with the Colonial culture. Only later on, he said, did a distinct "Negro literature" take form as a reservoir of bitterness and despair and rebellion. . . . She "was at one with her colonial New England culture,"[2] just as Pushkin and Dumas were with theirs.

But was she? Is the comparison with Pushkin and Dumas valid? She was born an African; the two men were born Russian and French. She entered her incarnation as Phillis Wheatley, a naked child, a slave, forcibly abducted and cruelly transported. They were born into social status and moderate means. Pushkin, the son of landed gentry and a reluctant attendant at the czar's court, was three generations removed from the black slave who was his maternal grandfather. Dumas, the son of a French general, traced his lineage to a black grandmother and a wealthy French colonist in Haiti. Such genealogical traces of blackness in the Russian and Frenchman had no real bearing on their lives or social status. . . . For Wheatley blackness was an ever-present reality that made its heavy imprint on her life.

Wright could say about Pushkin that "he went to the schools of his choice; he served in an army that was not Jim Crow, he worked where he wanted to; he lived where he wanted to. . . ." Wheatley did not serve in any army, but she did serve a church where she was consigned to a "Nigger Pew" or "Nigger Heaven." She did not live or work where she wanted to, not even when she was free. . . . Wright's sketch of Wheatley's condition is much too idyllic. . . . To be sure she was favored by kind and considerate masters, but the question still remains whether benign slavery, with its subtle discriminations, is the same as the freedom that Dumas and Pushkin enjoyed. It isn't, and the distinction makes dubious the identity that Wright discerned. It may be said that in Pushkin and Dumas, the oneness with the respective national culture was a natural extension of their social being. . . . With Wheatley, there is a nagging sense of the contradiction between her cultural assimilation and her social situation. . . .

It is to this contradiction that critic Redding addresses himself, arriving at a judgment that is the opposite of Wright's. What Wright hails as Wheatley's triumph, Redding deplores as her failure. "There is no question but that Miss Wheatley considered herself a Negro poet: the question is to what degree she felt the full significance of such a designation," Redding wrote. ". . . Not once . . . did she express in either word or action a thought on the enslavement of her race; not once did she utter a straightforward word for the freedom of the Negro."

Redding quotes the lines from the poem to the Earl of Dartmouth:

> I, young in life, by seeming cruel fate
> Was snatched from Afric's fancied happy seat.

and comments:

> "Seeming cruel" and "fancied happy" give her away as not believing either in the cruelty of the fate that had dragged thousands of her race into bondage in America nor in the happiness of their former freedom in Africa. How different the spirit of her work, and how unracial (not to say

> unnatural) are the stimuli that release her wan creative energies. . . . It is this negative, bloodless, unracial quality in Phillis Wheatley that makes her seem superficial, especially to members of her own race. . . . First and last, she was the fragile product of three related forces—the age, the Wheatley household, and New England America. Her work lacks spontaneity because of the first, enthusiasm because of the second, and because of the third it lacks an unselfish purpose that drives to some ultimate goal of expression.[3]

. . . It is easy enough to characterize the quality of personality mirrored in the poetry—negative, bloodless, unracial, chilly. The difficult question is what made her so. . . .

For this we must revert to the frail, near-naked native of seven displayed for sale on a Boston dock. At that age the native African culture and values are not firmly imbedded, certainly not with the depth and strength needed to withstand the powerful and assimilative impact of the new culture into which she was thrust. She has no defenses against Puritan certitude and self-righteousness, no resources for *critical* assimilation. To begin with she does not have a chance, and then two specific factors reinforce the process which is better described as inundation than assimilation.

One is her precocity, and the Wheatley's appreciation and cultivation of it. She is encouraged with patronizing kindness. Privileges and material rewards are compensation for piety and for poetry that respects the prevailing conventions in theme and style. . . . These are formative years, and the subsequent years are so disordered and, as it turns out, so brief that they do not modify the initial mold.

The first factor is complemented by the second, her isolation from the society of slaves and its subculture. . . . Further, as the first significant black writer in North America she faced a problem that her successors were to face. She wrote for a white audience. . . .

Perhaps the first significance of Phillis Wheatley is as a laboratory, test-tube exemplar of what was done to black identity, to black pride and self-awareness, by the institution of slavery with all its accessories of custom, culture, and ideological rationales. . . . What emerges most starkly from her poetry and her private correspondence is the near surgical, lobotomy-like excision of a human personality with warmth and blood and the self-assertiveness that is grounded in an awareness of one's self and relationship of this self to contemporary society. The religious moralisms that lard her letters to Obour Tanner are a poor form of sublimation, a substitute for the expression of emotional response to personal experience. The poems are vicarious in theme and imitative in style. In the circumstances it hardly could have been different. She was permitted to cultivate her intelligence, to develop her feeling for language and her facility in its use, but one thing was she not permitted to develop: the sense of her own identity as a black poet. And without this there could be no personal distinction in style or the choice of themes that make for greater poetry. The barter of her soul, as it were, was no conscious contract. Enclosed by a cloying embrace of slavery at a tender age, alternatives did not at first intrude, and later, when she might have chosen one, she was drained of the will and perception to do so. . . .

It may be idle to speculate about her true potential, but surely, given the evidence of her intelligence and talent, it is a permissible assumption that it was far greater than the one realized with the oppressive restrictions imposed upon the flowering of her own personality as a black poet. . . .

Phillis Wheatley is not a great figure in American literary history, but she is a tragic one. It is the tragedy rather than the poetry of Phillis Wheatley that has the more enduring relevance for American life. Elements of the tragedy have far more contemporary urgency than is evoked by the echoes of her poetry. To those in the present black generations, who are involved in the assertion and definition of black identity, in the rekindling of black pride, she can represent, with rare purity, the initial deprivation of that which they seek to regain.

To the contemporary black militant, the poetry will indeed seem "superficial" and "chilly," assuming he reads it at all, and there is little reason to believe he will. The tragedy should be more germane. If this is so, then it is conceivable that in striking some militant blow for freedom, in a spirit of retribution and poetic justice, he might say, "This one is for you, baby."

Notes

1. James Weldon Johnson, *The Book of American Negro Poetry*, p. xxiii.
2. Richard Wright, *White Man, Listen!* (New York, Doubleday, 1964), pp. 74–79.
3. J. Saunders Redding, *To Make A Poet Black* (Chapel Hill, University of North Carolina Press, 1939), pp. 8–11.

Analysis of Selected Poetry of Phillis Wheatley

Angelene Jamison*

During the last twelve or fifteen years, as we have witnessed a progressive interest in the history and culture of Black Americans. This interest includes, particularly, Black Americans who are considered pioneers in demonstrating the talents and gifts of the Afro-Americans. One of these pioneers is Phillis Wheatley and an example of this growing interest in her literary contributions was expressed in the November, 1973, Poetry Festival in her honor at Jackson State College in Mississippi.

Although records show that Lucy Terry had written a poem as early as 1746, Briton Hammon had written a short slave pamphlet by 1760 and Jupiter Hammon had written some poetry by 1761, Phillis Wheatley was the first Black American to succeed in getting a book of poems published. Her book, *Poems on Various Subjects, Religious and Moral,* was published in England in 1773. An examination of early Black American literature shows that Phillis Wheatley is often the first Black poet included in the anthologies and the only one mentioned for the Revolutionary Period. Moreover, in any discussion of early Black American poetry, the name of Phillis Wheatley is almost always among the first, if not *the* first one to be mentioned.

Phillis Wheatley was a poet of the latter half of the eighteenth century who happened to be Black. Despite her position as a slave and despite the growing interest in the slave issue in Bostonian circles, of which she was a marginal part, she did not address herself in any significant degree to the plight of her people. She wrote to Whites, for Whites and generally in the Euro-American tradition at that time. That is, Phillis Wheatley was influenced by neo-classicism. And much of her poetry reflects various stylistic characteristics of Alexander Pope and his followers. "On Being Brought from Africa to America," "Hymn to Evening," and many of her other poems reflect her ability to use effectively Pope's heroic couplet. Also, as Julian D. Mason, Jr. points out in his introduction to the *Poems of Phillis Wheatley*, the "mixing of Christian and classical in the many invocations in her poem . . ." reminds one of Milton.[1]

*Reprinted from *Journal of Negro Education*, 43, No. 3 (Summer, 1974), 408–16. With permission of *Journal of Negro Education* and the author.

Among the themes which permeate the poetry of Phillis Wheatley are Christian piety, morality, virtue, death, praises of classical heroes, and a celebration of abstractions such as the poems "On Recollection" and "Imagination." There are very few poems in which Phillis Wheatley points to her experiences as a Black and a slave. Her poetry embraces White attitudes and values, and it characterizes Phillis as a typical Euro-American poetess. She was detached from her people and her poetry could never be used as an expression of black thought.

How then does the teacher of Black literature deal with Phillis Wheatley from a Black perspective? It is obvious that she should not be excluded from any study of Black American poets or Black literature, especially since she is representative of Black contributions of the Revolutionary Period. On the other hand, it will be highly impossible to make her Black, and it will be unnecessary to glorify her as a model for young Black poets. What we must do then is to bring a new interpretation to her poetry, one that contributes to the intellectual and spiritual growth of those we are teaching.

Since Phillis Wheatley wrote primarily for the Whites and since we are concerned with re-examining her life and works in terms of their significance to us, it is important to analyze the image that those for whom she wrote had of her. Many were astonished at the poetry of Phillis Wheatley and showered her with praises because they had not expected such capabilities from an African. This kind of response was typical of those Whites who were willing to recognize the talents of Blacks. To them, Blacks who made contributions were always the exception and never the general rule regardless of the circumstances under which Blacks made their contribution.

Julian D. Mason, Jr. cites the example of William Joseph Snelling, a White Boston writer who spoke favorably of Phillis Wheatley, his comments appearing in the May, 1834 edition of *The Christian Examiner*. Snelling marveled at the level of intelligence reached by Phillis, but he felt that her poetry would receive lasting admiration from only those who were sympathetic towards Blacks.[2] Even though he made some positive comments about Phillis Wheatley, Snelling was operating under the assumption that Blacks were inferior and incapable of intellectual pursuits. He did not see her poetry as highly exceptional when compared to eighteenth century standards, but he was awed by the fact that here was a Black who could at least make attempts at expressing herself in poetry. And since Phillis's poetry was white-oriented, Snelling seemed to have been convinced that she had intellectual potential.

Although Phillis Wheatley generally received some favorable comments from Whites during her lifetime and afterwards, there were also those Whites who harshly criticized her poetry purely on a racial basis. People like Thomas Jefferson were blinded by her color and their prejudices against Blacks. In his "Notes on Virginia," Thomas Jefferson said:

> Misery is often the parent of the most affecting touches in poetry. Among the Blacks is misery enough, God knows, but no poetry. . . . Religion, indeed, has produced a Phillis Wheatley; but it could not produce a poet. The compositions published under her name are below the dignity of criticism.[3]

Many of the other so-called critics who ridiculed the works of Phillis Wheatley fall into the category of White racists who refused to recognize any merits in the contributions of Blacks.

More important to us than the attitudes of Whites toward Phillis Wheatley are those of Blacks, and here the attitudes are just as diverse as those of Whites. Perhaps the first Black to pay tribute to Phillis Wheatley was Jupiter Hammon who wrote a poem to her in 1778 entitled "An Address to Miss Phillis Wheatly [*sic*], Ethiopian Poetess, in Boston who came from Africa at eight years of age, and soon became acquainted with the gospel of Jesus Christ." By referring to her in his title as an "Ethiopian Poetess," Hammon acknowledged her ancestry and her creative abilities. However, the main thrust of the poem to Phillis Wheatley is that she should be thankful to God for "bringing thee from the distant shore, / To learn his holy word."[4] It is implicit in the poem that Jupiter Hammon was much more concerned with Phillis's salvation than he was with her poetry, and he wanted Phillis to give all praises to God for any gifts she might have had.

More recent black critics of Phillis Wheatley have been more concerned with examining her image as a Black rather than saving her soul. Several critics have pointed to her ability to write poetry, but they have critically questioned her race consciousness. J. Saunders Redding, in his book, *To Make A Poet Black*, says, ". . . the extent to which she was attached spiritually and emotionally to the slave is even slighter" than the extent she felt herself a Negro poet.[5] He goes on to say that "she is chilly," and he holds Pope's neo-classicism responsible.[6] Benjamin Brawley also points to Phillis Wheatley's lack of reference to race, but he seems to feel that she had no alternative but to model herself after writers with whom she was familiar.[7]

Statements like those of J. Saunders Redding and Benjamin Brawley have been compounded by more militant critics and readers of Phillis Wheatley. After reading various poems of Phillis Wheatley, the first comment of most students is that she was not Black enough and of course they are correct. But we must move beyond that kind of statement into reexamining the poetry in light of the implications of her lack of race consciousness to the development of black thought.

Phillis Wheatley was a woman of African descent. However, when examining certain poems where she makes direct and indirect references to herself as an African, it is obvious that she lacked pride in her heritage. Her reference to herself as an Ethiopian gives no evidence that she had embraced the culture from which she was taken; rather it was a means of humbling herself. In her poem, "To The University of Cambridge in New England," she requested that the students take advantage of all the opportunities presented to them and guard themselves against sin. In the concluding lines of the poem she pleaded:

> Ye blooming plants of human race divine
> An Ethiop tells you 'tis your greatest foe;
> Its transient sweetness turns to endless pain
> And in immense perdition sinks the soul.[8]

Here she refers to the students, who were obviously White, as practically God-like, and she warns them against the pitfalls of evil. Her statement that "an Ethiop tells you . . ." reflects a lack of self-worth particularly within the context of the poem. If an Ethiop is aware of the danger of sin, then certainly these "blooming plants of human race divine," those who belong to the best race, should also be aware. It would seem that Phillis, one who thought it necessary to warn these White students of the deadly potential of sin, would have included in her poem the greatest sin of slavery which had been committed upon her.

Her concept of herself as a poet was no better than her concept of herself as a Black. When writing poems to those for whom she had an extreme admiration, she felt it necessary to apologize for even attempting to address these Whites in poetic form. As a matter of fact, Phillis once implied in a response to the answer to a poem she had written to a gentleman in the Navy, that her poetry could never equal the poem she had received from him. In the same poem, after having placed herself in an inferior position, she states: "Then fix the humble Afric muse's seat / At British Homer's and Sir Isaac's feet."[9] At this point, she is just humble and submissive enough to believe that the African muse belonged at the foot of the European.

Phillis Wheatley's self-image as it is reflected in her poetry is strongly related to her religious attitudes. The poem, "On Being Brought from Africa to America," shows her gratitude for having been taken from what she perceived as a pagan land, brought to America and taught Christianity. Her lines, "Some view our sable race with scornful eye, / Their colour is a diabolic die,"[10] are indicative of some awareness of the existing attitude of Whites toward Blacks. And in the last two lines of the poem, "Remember, *Christians, Negroes,* black as *Cain,* / May be refined and join th'Angelic train,"[11] she articulates that Blacks too have the opportunity to be saved. However, "Remember, *Christians, Negroes,* black as *Cain*" does not clarify whether she perceives Christians and/or Blacks can be black as Cain. The ambiguity indicates that possibly before Blacks can be equal to Christians, if ever, they must be refined. The lines also indicate Phillis Wheatley's acceptance of the curse of Cain and its racist implication.

To Phillis, God was an impartial and merciful Savior whose works deserved all praises from mankind. In the final lines of "Thoughts on the Works of Providence," she muses, "To him, whose works array'd with mercy shine, / What songs should rise; how constant, how divine!"[12] This God had been taught to Phillis Wheatley by Whites and her feelings towards Him enhanced her humbleness and submissiveness. Much of her poetry reflects the qualities she perceived as necessary in order to meet God's approval and, consequently, be received in Heaven. Graciously and without question, Phillis Wheatley accepted the religion of the oppressor who had enslaved her. She never looked at her position as a slave as a contradiction to the goodness and graciousness of God.

Just as Phillis did not see a contradiction in the White man's concept of religion, neither did she see the contradiction in his concept of freedom. In no area does Phillis Wheatley's White orientation present itself more than in her poems dealing with freedom. In "To His Excellency General Washington," after humbling herself and apologizing for what she perceived as possible inaccuracies in an introductory letter, Phillis Wheatley moves on to express her patriotism and her undying faith in the "honorable" General Washington. She praises his gallantry and sees him as "first in peace and honors," and "fam'd for thy valour, for thy virtues more."

Not only does she exalt Washington, but his armies and their art of war as well. She is inspired by their great quest for freedom from Great Britain and she makes it clear to Washington that she supports him.

> Proceed, great chief, with virtue on thy side,
> Thy ev'ry action let the goddess guide.
> A crown, a mansion, and a throne that shine,
> With gold unfading, Washington! be thine.[13]

This clearly shows how supportive Phillis Wheatley was of the events, ideologies and even the hypocrisies of the White world. Washington and other American Revolutionists felt the strain of their bondage and yet they thought nothing of holding Blacks in bondage. Phillis Wheatley, who spoke of Washington's honor and courage in fighting for the freedom of the colonies, made no mention in her poem of those enslaved by the so-called "honorable" Washington and other Whites.

In another poem, "On Liberty and Peace," Phillis Wheatley sees Columbia as being firmly protected by Heaven in the quest for freedom and peace. She sees Britain, in its efforts to maintain control over the colonies as a cruel and vicious menace, and she strongly supports other countries which come to the aid of the colonies in their fight for freedom. The blood that was shed in the war, the lives that were lost on both sides, the land that was destroyed were all necessary to Phillis because she felt heaven had ordained that Columbia be free, and as she points out "Freedom comes array'd with charms divine, / And in her Train Commerce and Plenty Shine."[14] Throughout the poem, "Liberty and Peace," she makes reference to the fact that some divine aid will always guide the path of Columbia, and that Columbia will be a model for peace.

Where e'er Columbia spreads her swelling sails:
To every Realm shall peace her charms display,
And heavenly Freedom spread her golden ray.[15]

Phillis saw the very country which enslaved her and other Blacks as one deserving some heavenly protection. How could she be so removed from the plight of her people and the attitude towards her people as to glorify those who were responsible for that wretched condition of slavery? Did she feel that bringing peace to the colonies would bring peace and freedom to Blacks? It is clearly substantiated that she was brainwashed to the point of expressing totally the sentiments of Whites without giving any consideration to the fact that the white "heroes" of the American Revolution were concerned only about themselves. Blacks, to most of them, were a means of supplying labor and the questions of the freedom of Blacks had nothing to do with the freedom of Whites from the mother country.

Some readers of Phillis Wheatley might argue that her poem, "To the Right Honourable William, Earl of Dartmouth, His Majesty's Principal Secretary of State of North America, & & &" is a strong indication of her awareness of the position of Blacks in this country and her own plight particularly. From that poem, most refer to the following lines:

Should you, my lord, while you peruse my song,
Wonder from whence my love of freedom sprung,
Whence flow these wishes for the common good,
By feeling hearts alone best understood,
I young in life, by seeming cruel fate
Was snatch'd from Afric's fancy'd happy seat.
What pangs excrutiating must molest,
What sorrows labour in my parents' breast?
Steel'd was that soul and by no misery mov'd
That from a father seiz'd his babe belov'd:
Such, such my case. And can I then but pray
Others may never feel tyrannic sway?[16]

In this stanza Phillis Wheatley seems to be trying to explain why she has concerned herself in her poetry with the freedom of the American colonies. Her reason which is weakly supported is that she was taken from her homeland, which she describes as "Afric's fancy'd seat." The implication here is that Africa may not have been as happy as imagined. Moreover, she talks about the pain and suffering endured by her parents but she never makes reference to having suffered herself. Slavery is not mentioned nor is it clearly implied. Also, as J. Saunders Redding points out "seeming cruel" and "fancy'd happy" give her away as not believing even in the cruelty of the fate that had dragged thousands of her race into bondage in America nor in the happiness of their former freedom in Africa.[17]

In the last two lines of this stanza she is obviously talking about Whites when she says, ". . . and can I then but pray / Others may never feel tyrannic sway." because Blacks already felt this tyranny.

Thus, Phillis Wheatley's poem to the Earl of Dartmouth provides no evidence of her Blackness nor does it show that her orientation was anything other than white. She was a poet who happened to be Black and it is a mistake to refer to her as a Black poet. However, it is much to the credit of Black people that a slave girl was able to get a book of poems published at such an early age and during the seventeen hundreds. But in any literary analysis of the poetry of Phillis Wheatley from a Black perspective, we must accept the fact that her poetry is a product of a White mind, a mind that had been so engulfed in the education, religion, values, and the freedom of Whites that she expressed no strong sentiments for those who had been cast into the wretchedness of slavery by those she so often praised with her pen. Any student who is exposed to Phillis Wheatley must be able to recognize that her poetry expressed the sentiments of eighteenth century Whites because her mind was controlled by them, her actions were controlled by them, and consequently her pen.

CONCLUSION

My aim in presenting a literary analysis of Phillis Wheatley from a Black perspective has not been to deny her ability as a poet of the eighteenth century. Instead, I have presented a way of examining her that, I feel, gets at the truth of her life and works. I have also presented a way of teaching Phillis Wheatley that clearly defines to the students (1) who she was; (2) what influenced her, and (3) the results of this influence.

By critically looking at the works of Phillis Wheatley, I have discussed a method by which she can be taught, one which promotes the development and awareness of Black students. Of course, Phillis Wheatley can be taught as a poet of the eighteenth century tradition, if the teacher is concerned with teaching poetry only for poetry's sake. But, if a teacher is committed to the growth of strong Black minds, he must not ignore Phillis Wheatley's white orientation simply because she was Black and achieved recognition for her poetry. Teaching Phillis Wheatley from a Black perspective shows that she was simply an eighteenth century poet who supported, praised and imitated those who enslaved her and her people.

Notes

1. Julian D. Mason, Jr., editor, *The Poems of Phillis Wheatley* (Chapel Hill, University of North Carolina Press, 1966), p. xxii.

2. Mason, pp. xxxviii–xl.

3. Thomas Jefferson, "Notes on Virginia," *The Writings of Thomas Jefferson,*

1781–1784, ed. Paul Lecester Ford (New York, G.P. Putnam's & Sons, 1894), 111, 246.

4. Jupiter Hammon, "An Address to Miss Phillis Wheatly [*sic*], Ethiopian Poetess, in Boston who came from Africa. . . ," *Early Black American Poets*, ed. William H. Robinson (Dubuque, Wm. C. Brown Publishing, 1971), p. 9.

5. J. Saunders Redding, *To Make A Poet Black* (Chapel Hill, University of North Carolina Press, 1939), p. 9.

6. Redding, p. 11.

7. Benjamin Brawley, *Early Negro American Writers* (Chapel Hill, University of North Carolina Press, 1953), p. 34.

8. Phillis Wheatley, "To the University of Cambridge in New England," *The Poems of Phillis Wheatley*, ed. Julian D. Mason, Jr. (Chapel Hill, University of North Carolina Press, 1966), p. 5. (All further citations from the poems of Phillis Wheatley will be taken from this edition and publication.)

9. Phillis Wheatley, "Phillis' Reply to the answer in Our Last by the Gentleman of the Navy," p. 86.

10. Phillis Wheatley, "On Being Brought from Africa to America," p. 7.

11. Wheatley, p. 7.

12. Phillis Wheatley, "Thoughts on the Works of Providence," p. 23.

13. Phillis Wheatley, "To His Excellency General Washington," p. 90.

14. Wheatley, p. 94.

15. Wheatley, p. 95.

16. Wheatley, "To the Right Honourable William, Earl of Dartmouth, His Majesty's Principal Secretary of State for North America, &c," p. 34.

17. Redding, *op. cit.*, pp. 10–11.

Do Birds of a Feather Flock Together?

Margaret G. Burroughs*

Phillis Wheatley appears to many or most persons familiar with her, as a black poet who did little for the liberation of the African-American people, in her poetry, or in other forms of social action. But it must be remembered that little is known of her life, apart from her writing.

There is one fact that can be documented which suggests that there was more to her social concern than meets the eye. The circle in which she moved in England consisted of an organized group of social radicals who were engaged at the time of her visit in encouraging slave insurrections in America, and immediately after her visit, in helping those insurrections with massive assistance. This group, religious in form, though deeply involved in politics, was called the Evangelical Movement.

Her two chief hosts and sponsors in England, around whom contacts centered, were the closely associated Countess of Huntingdon and Earl of Dartmouth.[1] Lady Huntingdon was the foremost financial angel, and Lord Dartmouth was her second-in-command foremost British statesman, in the leadership of the Evangelical Movement. The Evangelicals were religious reformers who expressed emotion in worship, contrary to current standards, were active in controversial social reforms, and received most of their support in England from the working people and other poor, and in the Western Hemisphere from the black people, the Native Americans, the poorer frontiersmen, and other elements of the poor or unaffluent. For these reasons the English establishment, church, state, trade and landed interests, condemned the Evangelicals, though titled, wealthy or politically powerful members such as Huntingdon and Dartmouth escaped some of the prosecution. The three clergymen who founded and led the Evangelical Movement were John Wesley, whose followers later established the Methodist Church, his brother Charles Wesley, who wrote the Evangelical or Methodist hymns, and George Whitefield, who conducted the first great mass revivals in America in the 1740's, protracted camp meetings known as The Great Awakening.

What has not been previously put together in the contract of African-

*Reprinted from *Jackson State Review*, 6, No. 1 (Summer, 1974), 61–73. With permission of the author.

American history is that Evangelicals were also engaged in the furthering of slave insurrections.

Phillis Wheatley's first poem was written "On the Death of George Whitefield." To Lady Huntingdon she dedicated her book of poems, and it was the circle around the Countess and Lord Dartmouth who saw to it that the book was published. To Lord Dartmouth Miss Wheatley dedicated her most interesting poem in terms of Black liberation, and with him she corresponded from America. She considered them her friends, and their attitudes a new experience for her. To an African-American friend she wrote:

> The friends I found there among the nobility and genteel, their benevolent conduct towards me, the unexpected and unmerited civility and complaisance with which I was treated by all, fills me with astonishment.[2]

This decent behavior was undoubtedly related to the social ethics held by the Evangelicals.

Charities for various causes were always the most usual form of Evangelical social concern, and practically the only one which remained after what had been a radical movement settled down into piety and denominationalism in the middle and late 19th Century.[3] But as a dynamic movement from the middle of the 18th to the early 19th Century, the Evangelicals successfully led in causes deemed dangerously and damnably radical by the establishment. William Wilberforce was one of the leading Evangelicals, and apart from the Quakers, received much of the early support for the British Abolitionist Movement from Evangelicals. The First Factory Act (1833), regulating working conditions, was led to success in Parliament by the Evangelicals' representative, Lord Shaftesbury.

The British Abolitionist Movement was not organized until 1787, three years after Phillis Wheatley's death. But there had been antislavery activity in the generation before, some of it extremely militant, and the Evangelicals were deeply involved.

Miss Wheatley's associate, the Countess Huntingdon, like other Evangelicals of that time, did not hesitate to disobey the law or the established order for her principles. Her special role as financer of the Evangelical Movement was to establish bases for general Evangelical activity, rather than direct action against slavery. She usurped the powers of the Bishop of the Church of England, founding Church of England chapels of Evangelical persuasion without authorization, staffed by Evangelical ministers. Every peer was entitled to a private chapel, but the Countess multiplied chapels into a virtual denomination. When the Anglican Church recovered from its confusion and disorganization in the face of her bluff, and outlawed the Countess of Huntingdon's chapels, the rest of the establishment joined the ecclesiastical in branding her a criminal as well as a heretic. And her chapels continued as independent churches.

In the meantime in the same militant spirit, Phillis Wheatley's other chief associate in England, the Earl of Dartmouth, was about his special witness: direct action in the struggle for freedom of the colored peoples. He organized and chaired a fund-raising committee for Moor's Indian School in Connecticut, an academy offering free education to Native Americans. The school was soon named Dartmouth, and moved to New Hampshire where it could be closer to the western Native American Nations and the militant remnants of destroyed east-coast Nations who had taken refuge in what is now Vermont. The representative of Moor's school or Dartmouth College with which the Earl worked was the Reverend Samson Occum, a Native American.[4] It should be noted that most New England Native American communities today are African-American in membership, and that the ancestral as well as social relationships of African-Americans and Native Americans was already well under way in the late 18th Century: Crispus Attucks of Boston, with his Native American last name, and Jean-Baptiste Du Sable of Chicago, with his Native American wife and associates, were not isolated phenomena. It would be surprising if Dartmouth College, so long as its endowment was used for its stated purpose, did not include persons of African ancestry in its student body. As for Samson Occum himself, it is apparent from his given name that his parents believed that strong persons should tear down edifices of oppression. The origin of his last name is moot, whether from a Native American word, such as the place name Accomac, or from an African word, such as the common Akan name Accompong. The connection between the Reverend Mr. Occum and Phillis Wheatley was not only through Lord Dartmouth. They also corresponded directly.[5]

In other contexts the Evangelicals' furthering of a Native American school might not seem very militant action. But in the politics of the 1760's it was explosive. Britain had taken over the formerly French fur trade, and American colonists, seeking more Native American land and the further 'removal' of Native Americans, feared that Britain might act as the protector of the Native American Nations. The Nations, too, were well aware of the political situation, and therefore became Britain's staunch allies during the American Revolution. In this context the Evangelicals' religious zeal and conscience for the Native Americans was also radical political action, for the Empire against the colonists, and for the Native American against those who sought to complete his genocide.

The other special concern of the Earl of Dartmouth was the support of slave insurrections. It was carried out through his office as a cabinet member. In 1765 he had joined the British Cabinet as President of the Board of Trade and Plantations, the body in charge of affairs relating to the American Colonies. He was again in the Cabinet between 1772 and 1775, as Secretary of State for the Colonies, a new office which included the Presidency of the Board of Trade and Plantations. After 1775, to the end of the American Revolution, he remained in the Cabinet as Lord Privy Seal (a more general office), but for several years continued to receive voluminous reports from the Colonies, and to be one of the Government's specialists on American affairs.

Dartmouth therefore was the cabinet member responsible for the preparation for, and opening moves of, the War of the American Revolution. The Prime Minister, in seeking his acceptance of the office, told him: "You know the nature of the American Department much better than I do." Not only had Dartmouth been involved with the Native American school in the North, but also the Evangelicals had been much concerned with social service work in Georgia. The Evangelical movement in the Colonies, "The Great Awakening," had been at least as great as the movement in Britain. Throughout the Colonies there were American and British Evangelicals at work, regularly reporting to or visiting Dartmouth and the other Evangelical leaders in Britain.

As Secretary of State for the Colonies at the time of their revolt, these were Dartmouth's tasks: defense of religious toleration for Catholics in French Quebec, a British policy which infuriated the Protestant leaders of the American Revolution; control of Westward migration, which again enraged adherents of the American Revolution who sought swift possession of Native American lands; organization of a new British Crown Colony of Vandalia in the West, inhabited by 'outcasts' of the east-coast colonies, as an ally for the British cause against the rebels; the establishment of a full-scale military alliance between Britain and the Native Americans against their common enemy. One of the general duties of the office was the receiving of intelligence, much of it secret, and surely Dartmouth's most delicate task was that of co-ordinating and aiding massive slave revolts against the slave-holders who supported the American Revolution.

Prior to the American Revolution his agents in America instructed confidential army officers and civil servants in the strategy of a British-Black alliance against the rebellious colonists.[6] Besides distributing information on the secret contingency strategy among those who would carry it out, the American agents of the Evangelical Secretary of State for America also contacted slave insurrectionary leadership, and joint plans were made.

Between 1767 and 1769, the Royal Governor of South Carolina remained neutral between planter militia and escaped slave guerrilla troops during a two-year war, and at the end mediated the conflict! In return the black guerrillas referred to themselves as "The Friends of the Government," meaning the British government, against the rebellious colonists.[7] In Boston in 1768 an army officer was accused by the local authorities of encouraging slave insurrection to drive the "Liberty boys to death"; that is, the party of rebellious colonists.[8] There were rumors to the same effect in Connecticut.[9] In Boston again, six years later, Dartmouth in office again, the Royal Governor and a high-ranking army officer were engaged in further strategic discussions with the enslaved black community.[10] The next year, 1775, black persons in bondage in North Carolina were engaged in a plan to join other Loyalists on the frontier, where British arms would be supplied, and they would be free to organize their own military and civil government."[11] The Royal Governor of North Carolina was privy to such plans.[12] And in that same year Lord Dunmore, Royal Governor of Virginia, was working out detailed plans for the coordination of slave insurrections with the operations of Native American allies and such British regulars as would be available in the Virginia sector.[13]

When war broke out, the plan was translated into action, still under the coordination of Dartmouth.[14] Virginia's Governor Dunmore issued a military emancipation proclamation: freedom for all slaves of rebels who joined the British cause. Many responded. Next the same proclamation was issued for all the colonies by the British High Command. Hundreds of thousands of the enslaved escaped from the plantations and Southern agriculture ground to a long halt, worsening the American Continental Army's shortness of provisions. Tens of thousands of self-liberated Blacks joined the British. Black redcoats went into battle with white sashes across their breasts emblazoned in black letters with the words "Liberty to Slaves." Richmond, the capital of Virginia, fell for a time to British regular and Black troops, the rebel Governor Jefferson fleeing ignominiously. Georgia (including what is now Alabama), South Carolina and North Carolina were retaken from the rebels by the combined British and Black forces. Until Cornwallis trapped himself on the Yorktown peninsula and the French fleet cut him off, the American Continental Congress was considering a negotiated peace, with the deep South remaining British West Indian colonies. At the War's end the British High Command refused to yield to General Washington's demand for the return of Britain's freedmen allies, and some ten thousand sailed away with the British Navy. Some became the nucleus of Nova Scotia's Black community. Some pioneered in the establishment of Sierra Leone. Others settled in the West Indies. Records have not been found, or studied, to determine the fate of these. Black students and scholars, including Dr. Benjamin Quarles, the specialist on this topic, expect to find that promises were betrayed, in this case, that the Black veterans were re-enslaved upon landing in the West Indies. Of course American Revolutionary spokesmen would claim as much. But Dr. Quarles' source for this fear is simply another pessimist, without hard data.[15] Two pieces of evidence suggest that the Black Loyalists may not have been betrayed in the West Indies. Population statistics in a recent history of the Bahamas show that the rate of increase at this time of the "free" Black population was much greater than that of the enslaved.[16] And the West India Regiment, founded in 1795, today the Armed Forces of Jamaica, was called down to the 20th Century by the alternate name "The First South Carolina Regiment."[17] It is difficult to believe that the proud Black soldiers of this unit would have used this name if many Black Loyalist veterans had been re-enslaved.

The British-Black alliance and military emancipation policy were prior to the official founding of the British Abolitionist Movement, but this came just four years after the end of the American Revolution. The first success of the new organization, enabling it to become a mass movement, was the passage of legislation granting land to the freedmen veterans, a project initiated by the leader of the Nova Scotia freedmen.

The planning and launching of the sweeping southwide slave insurrection was a form of witness exercised by the Evangelical peer, Lord Dartmouth, already an enemy of slavery. It may be argued that he was acting as a cabinet minister, a realistic political leader of Britain, that the Black alliance and military emancipation were military strategies. And of course this is true. But it was surely not coincidence that the minister of the government chosen to coordinate this political warfare was the Evangelical representative, whose religion's social radicalism already included the anti-slavery witness. In Dartmouth radical social ethics and the needs of government were united. If plans leaked, or actions were condemend in parliament, the radicalism could be blamed on the Evangelical Movement rather than on the government. More important, Dartmouth's concern, knowledge, contacts and experience as an Evangelical radical qualified him for this delicate work of secret service subversion.

It is interesting that it was to Dartmouth that Phillis Wheatley wrote these lines:

> Should you, my lord, while you peruse my song
> Wonder from whence my love of Freedom sprung. . .
> I, young in life, by seeming cruel fate
> Was snatched'd from Afric's fancy'd seat. . .
> Such, such my case. And can I then but pray
> Others may never feel tyrannic sway?

It is one of the several references to Black liberation in her poetry, and the strongest. It is plausible that she selected this message for this man because she knew, and approved, the radicalism of his anti-slavery commitment.

Dartmouth was by no means the only Evangelical leader to engage in such militant expression of anti-slavery sentiment. At the very beginning of the Evangelical Movement, in the 1740's, George Whitefield's representative for South Carolina, a Carolinian, Hugh Bryant, preached at camp meetings that the Coming of the Lord would be accompanied by universal slave insurrection, and prophesied that the seas would open as of old and that the Black people would march, dryshod, home to Guinea.[18] Superstitious perhaps, if taken literally, but it was surely an expression, in the most militant context, of Pan-African consciousness.

Before and during the American Revolution, the Evangelical ministers sent out from England to America by John Wesley preached emancipation, forbade church membership to slaveholders, and won a disproportionate number of Black converts. During the Revolution, as the Blacks arose throughout the South, these ministers continued their work, often suffering jail or mob violence in the cause of God, King and Emancipation. After the War, America saw to it that all these Evangelical ministers were deported, and organized a new Methodist Church on the totally American basis of welcome to slaveholders and segregated pews.[19] It was against these changes that Richard Allen protested, and with his fellows of the older Evangelical form of Methodism organized the historic African Methodist Episcopal Church.

The roots of this ongoing connection between the Evangelicals and radical anti-slavery activism can be traced back to the founding of the Evangelical Movement. The three clergymen founders of the Evangelicals, Whitefield and the Wesleys, had studied at a school maintained by the leading theologian of an older religious movement, the Nonjuror Church of the early 18th Century, William Law, who had also influenced the family of the Countess of Huntingdon. They were profoundly influenced by his teachings, that conversion must be a deeply felt experience expressed in an ethically high and dedicated way of life.[20]

The Nonjuror Church through its most distinguished thinker, William Law, the forerunner of the Evangelicals, was the semi-underground religious arm of the entirely underground, illegal Jacobite Party of Britain. The Jacobites were those who sought, often by revolution, to overturn the ruling monarchs of Britain and to restore the exiled House of Stuart to the throne. The House of Stuart is usually associated with absolute monarchy, against the rule of parliament and the royal houses that submitted to Parliament. But this reactionary character of the Jacobite Party, if it was reactionary,[21] did not apply to its relation to the poor. Over many decades of unsuccessful conspiracy and abortive revolts, the number of aristocrats supporting the House of Stuart diminished, while the proportion of the desperate classes of society grew.[22] In 1741 Governor Oglethorpe of South Carolina warned other colonial governments that Nonjuror clergymen in disguise were working throughout the colonies with slaves and indentured servants towards slave insurrection. One such, a Nonjuror minister acting for the Jacobite Party, after activities in Black settlements around Philadelphia, especially near the border of the slavery colony of Delaware, went to New York City, where he became liaison between the enslaved and other poor of that city, and the exiled House of Stuart with its allies, France and Spain. Plans were established for seizure of the city, aid from a French or Spanish fleet, and establishment of New York as a Stuart domain, under an Irish Governor for the indentured servants and a Black King (in the local sense of the term) for the African-American people. Religious encouragement was provided jointly by the

Nonjuror Church and the West African religious organization of the Holy Spirit Shango. The public buildings of the city were successfully burned down, but no fleet arrived, and the revolt was suppressed with much bloodshed. The Nonjuror minister was hanged along with the Black and indentured servant leaders.[23]

Four years later, in 1745, the Stuart "Pretender" to the British throne, Charles Stuart, "Bonny Prince Charlie," landed in Scotland, rallied the Highland clans for a march on London, and issued a military emancipation proclamation: all persons bound in servitude to enemies of the House of Stuart who would rally to his cause were declared free.[24] In substance it was identical to the proclamation issued thirty years later by Virginia's Governor Dunmore and the British High Command in America.

It is clear that the Nonjuror Church, and its political sponsor the Jacobite party, followed a strategy of alliance with the enslaved and military emancipation in the 1740's practically identical to the policies held by the Evangelicals in the 1770's. This is not likely to be unrelated to the three clergymen organizers of the Evangelical Movement's receiving their education in unorthodoxy from the greatest theologian of the Nonjuror Church, William Law.

What was Phillis Wheatley's political relationship to the Evangelicals, her hosts and sponsors in London, and her continuing correspondents? Her biographer thinks her politics to have been those of the American Revolution, judging from her poetry favoring the American cause and her letter to George III, congratulating him on his repeal of the Stamp Act, which had been so hated by the American colonists.[25] Neither writing is decisive. She was a chattel slave owned by American Revolutionists during the War, and could not have refused assignments without grave danger of reprisal. As for the repeal of the Stamp Act, Loyalists joined Rebels in relief at the end of that crisis. If it is true that she was an advocate of the American Revolution, she was an unusual one, in that she had many good friends among the most militant, subtle and ruthless of Loyalists in England. Perhaps like Prince Hall, who had worked with British Masons until the British Army left America, or Richard Allen, who had loved the Loyalist Methodists but, when they disappeared, joined the American Methodists as long as he could stomach them, Phillis Wheatley was caught in situations of relative powerlessness and necessary accommodation, a not uncommon part of the Black experience.

We must assume that she recognized the radicalism of her English friends; nothing indicates that Phillis Wheatley was stupid. Was their relation to her one of patronization only, or charity in the narrow sense? It is possible. But the Evangelicals of this time leave an impression of a more visceral form of Christian duty than the piety of a century later. In one respect at least their relation to her was more than narrow charity: the publication of her book of poems in that year 1773, in its dramatic demonstration of African humanity and intelligence, was inevitably helpful to the Earl of Dartmouth and other Evangelicals in the political tasks of securing more personal commitment to the new strategies from military and civil aides, and the support of British public opinion for the military emancipation policy.

Was Miss Wheatley one of the Evangelicals, in their radicalism? (More properly, was she at one with the Black insurgents, to whose militancy the Evangelical conscience and the needs of the Empire were responding?) Her poetry's lack of radical commitment to Black freedom is no proof that she was not. Until recently Black poets, like other poets, by no means always expressed in their art the same concerns expressed in more directly political aspects of living.

As research now stands, it is just as likely as not that she was one of them, when and where she could be. Research in the Dartmouth papers and other related sources in Britain are more likely to reveal the answer than further research in America, where the victory of the American Revolution obscured many truths, by the later reluctance to preserve the record, or to recall it in written memoirs.

It may be relevant to the issue of Miss Wheatley's personal convictions that the American and British versions differed for her first published poem (1770) on the death of George Whitefield. The version circulated in Boston has the great Evangelical leader say, regarding the Black people's acceptance of Jesus and the results for the Black people:

> "Take him, ye *Africans,* he longs for you,
> "*Impartial Saviour* is his title due:
> "Wash'd in the fountain of redeeming blood,
> "You shall be sons, and kings, and priests to God."[26]

The poem states that the true Jesus is no racist, and that in the Kingdom of God, Black people shall be among the rulers, civil and ecclesiastical. The London version repeats these statements, but adds another:

> "Take him, ye *Africans,* he longs for you,
> "*Impartial Saviour* is his title due:
> "If you will walk in Grace's heavenly Road,
> "He'll make you free, and Kings and Priests to God."[27]

The poem demands the abolition of slavery publicly, at this early date of 1770. Either the author, or her agent in Britain, reworded it so. For sure, this wording would not have been popular in the Colonies, except among the enslaved.

Perhaps Phillis Wheatley's principles should be evaluated, not by the reactions of today's readers, but by those of her contemporary audience, her Black audience. At her death, an anonymous poet of Boston, as part of her obituary, states that the Black community already poetically inclined, loved her poetry and her.

> So Phillis tun'd her sweet mellifluous lyre;
> (Harmonious numbers bid the soul aspire)
> While AFRIC'S untaught race with transport heard,
> They lov'd the poet, and the muse rever'd.[28]

In the meantime, ignorant of so much about her except her *published* poems, we can say this much with certainty: Miss Wheatley's associates in England, those who published her book, those to whom she dedicated her poems and with whom she corresponded, the Evangelicals, were radical supporters of slave insurrections in America, the combined result of ethics and politics, a distinct tradition of at least thirty years past and of more than thirty years to come. If the Continental Congress had possessed an intelligent counter-intelligence service, Phillis Wheatley might have been interned for the duration as a security risk, on the principle of guilt by association.

Notes

1. Phillis Wheatley, *The Life and Works of Phillis Wheatley*, edited by G. Herbert Renfro, Washington, D.C., 1916. The author of the present article wishes to thank Hugo P. Leaming, of the history faculty of the University of Illinois at Chicago Circle, for his help in gathering historical studies of 18th Century British political movements.

2. Phillis Wheatley to Obour Tanner, Oct. 30, 1773, in Phillis Wheatley, *The Poems of Phillis Wheatley*, edited by Julian D. Mason, Jr., Chapel Hill, 1966, p. 106.

3. Some British labor historians have seen Methodism as a force which turned working people away from labor organization and politics. Yet there is also a strong tradition among some Methodists that in the beginning their movement was radical, in a number of ways. The solution proposed here is chronological: a watershed in the early 19th Century between the old (radical) and new (charitable) Evangelical movement.

4. Articles on Lady Huntingdon and Lord Dartmouth in the *Dictionary of National Biography*, Oxford, 1917–. Article on Dartmouth College in the *Encyclopedia Britannica*.

5. Phillis Wheatley, *Life and Works*, edited by G. Herbert Renfro.

6. For Dartmouth as a cabinet member, see B. D. Bargar, *Lord Dartmouth And The American Revolution*, University of South Carolina, 1965, pp. 27, 35, 68 ff., 125 ff., 170 f., 186 ff. This work goes little into Dartmouth's Evangelical leadership, and not at all into the British military emancipation policy. For evidence of British preparation for aid to slave insurrections and Dartmouth's leadership see letters of General Gage to Governor Dunmore, Governor Joshiah [*sic*] Martin to Lord Dartmouth, Dartmouth to Dunmore, Gage to Guy Carleton, and Gage to Dartmouth, all 1775, quoted or cited in Benjamin Quarles, *The Negro in the American Revolution*, Chapel Hill, 1961, p. 21 f., notes 5, 6, 8, 9, 10.

7. South Carolina, Royal Council, *Proceedings*, Oct. 5, 1767. South Carolina, Commons House of Assembly and Royal Council, Joint Session, *Preceedings*, Nov. 5, 1767. Commons House of Assembly, *Journal*, Jan. 8–Aug. 9, 1765. Richard T. Hooker, ed., *The Carolina Backcountry on the Eve of the Revolution*, Chapel Hill, 1953, pp. 171 f., 175. 183, 207 n., 242 n., 279 n.

8. Herbert Aptheker, *American Negro Slave Revolts,* New York, International Publishers, 1943, p. 199, n. 104.

9. *Ibid.*, p. 88, n. 25.

10. *Ibid.*, p. 87.

11. *Ibid.*, p. 88.

12. Letter, Joshiah Martin to Dartmouth, in work cited in footnote 6.

13. Dunmore correspondence cited in footnote 6.

14. Sources cited in second part of footnote 6.

15. The story of the Black Loyalists is told in Benjamin Quarles, *The Negro in the American Revolution,* cited above.

16. Michael Craton, *A Histor'i of the Bahamas,* London, Collins, 1963.

17. Sir Harry Johnston, *The Negro in the New World,* London, 1910.

18. M. Eugene Sirmans, *Colonial South Carolina,* Chapel Hill, 1966, p. 231.

19. Daniel De Vinne, *The Methodist Episcopal Church and Slavery, A Historical Survey,* New York, 1857. This work presents the old *vs.* the new Evangelical movement thesis, with statistics and other details. Even then the Church's knowledge of its own history had become blurred.

20. Article on William Law, *Dictionary of National Biography.*

21. Parliament in the 18th Century was under the control of the Whig party of the great landlords. The issue between Jacobites (or Tories) and Whigs was between absolute monarchy and virtually absolute aristocracy. See Herbert Butterfield, *George III And The Historians,* London, Collins, 1957. George III was raised in a circle much influenced by the Jacobites, and as King was close to the Evangelicals in his religion. (B. D. Bargar, the work cited, p. 11.) Early in his career Dartmouth had been kept from close contact with the King because his Evangelicalism was too similar to the King's faith, and might bear too much influence. Later the King felt a special affection for Dartmouth and his religion. (*Ibid.*, and Article on Dartmouth in the *Dictionary of National Biography.)*

22. Sir Charles Alexander Petrie, *The Jacobite Movement,* London, 1948, Volumes 1 and 2.

23. Daniel Horsmanden, *The New York Conspiracy,* New York, 1810, reprint by Beacon Press, Boston, 1971.

24. Petrie, the work cited, Volume II.

25. Phillis Wheatley, *Life and Works,* edited by G. Herbert Renfro.

26. Phillis Wheatley, *The Poems of Phillis Wheatley,* edited by Julian D. Mason, Jr., p. 10.

27. *Ibid.*, p. 33 f.

28. *Ibid.*, p. xvii. ("Eulogy on The Death of a Late Celebrated Poetess," by Horatio, in *Boston Magazine,* December, 1784.)

Phillis Wheatley: The Dark Side of the Poetry

Terrence Collins*

In a recent article in *Phylon*,[1] R. Lynn Matson credibly argues that the poems of Phillis Wheatley exhibit the beginning of a poetry of protest, albeit surreptitiously. Though he rightly dismisses much Wheatley criticism as overlooking essential elements discoverable in the poems and letters (more readily available now with Julian D. Mason's fine edition of the poems and letters),[2] on the whole one senses throughout Matson's presentation an element of wishful thinking that finds in Wheatley a racial and political precocity difficult to reconcile with the facts of her slave life and with the evidence of the poems and letters themselves. In interpreting the thrust of Phillis Wheatley's consciousness of race as disguised resentment of the institution of slavery, he has addressed only one aspect of a highly ambivalent attitude. A more educative purpose to which a reexamination of Wheatley's life and work might be put is to see in the poems a gauge of the depths to which what has come to be called the slave mentality—or self-hate by blacks based on introjection of the dominant culture's estimate of their worth—penetrated and to some extent, we are told, still penetrates the collective mind of Black America.[3]

Since her enslavement was hardly typical of even the mildest versions of New England slavery, a short biographical sketch, implied in many of Matson's comments, seems essential for inquiry into the racial attitudes of Wheatley as they emerge in the poems and as they relate to her estimate of her own worth as a black person.[4]

Phillis Wheatley was owned by the Boston tailor John Wheatley. Mr. Wheatley gave the following sketch of her origins in a letter of introduction to the 1773 edition of her poems:

> Phillis was brought from Africa to America, in the year 1761, between seven and eight years of age. Without any assistance from school education and by only what she was taught in the family, she, in sixteen months time from her arrival attained the English language, to which she was an utter stranger before, to such a degree, as to read any, the most difficult part of the sacred writings, to the great astonishment of all who heard her.

*Reprinted from *Phylon: The Atlanta University Review of Race and Culture*, 36, No. 1 (March, 1975), 78–88. With permission of *Phylon*.

> As to her writing, her own curiosity led her to it; and this she learned in so short a time, that in the year 1765, she wrote a letter to the Rev. Mr. Occum, the Indian minister, while in England.[5]

The tone of this letter as well as the indication that she was admitted to the inner circle of family education and religion suggest that hers was not a life typical of American slavery.

Such indeed was the case. When the Wheatley family obtained her, she was sickly and weak, fitted only for housework, and soon became the personal attendant for Mrs. Wheatley and a companion for a daughter, Mary Wheatley. In this capacity she was exempted from the usual lot of slaves and was encouraged toward refinement and cultivation. Margaretta Matilda Odell, an abolitionist biographer, relates the following:

> A daughter of the family, not long after the child's first introduction to the family, undertook to learn her to read and write; and while she astonished her instructress by her rapid progress, she won the good will of her kind mistress by her amiable disposition and the propriety of her behavior. She was not devoted to menial occupations, as was first intended; nor was she allowed to associate with other domestics of the family, who were of her own color and condition, but was kept constantly about the person of her mistress.[6]

Odell further indicates that Wheatley was nurtured on "the best English writers" with Mary, and that she was "encouraged to converse freely with the wise and learned" of Boston's polite circles. She further notes that Phillis, unlike slaves prior to that time, was received as a member of Boston's Old South Church congregation with the Wheatley family. Significantly, all of these tokens of special favor were shown to the slave Phillis prior to the added notoriety afforded her by the publication of her poems in the 1773 volume.

During 1773, Phillis was sent to England in the company of Nathaniel Wheatley, a son in the family, in order that she might recover her health—a further indication that her position as a slave was indeed out of the ordinary. While in England she was befriended by Selina Hastings, the Countess of Huntingdon, who introduced her to London polite society and who eventually arranged for the publication of her poems. The extent to which she was encouraged to mix freely in these aristocratic circles is indicated by the gifts she received (the Lord Mayor of London presented her with a folio copy of *Paradise Lost*, for instance) and by her being favored with an audience with George III, which was prevented only by her premature return to America at the news of Mrs. Wheatley's impending death.

Thus Phillis Wheatley's life during the years in which all but a few of her extant poems were written was both comfortable and cultivated. From 1774 until her death, however, her fortune changed for the worse. Still popular enough to be noticed by George Washington in 1776 as the result of a flattering poem in his honor, little is known of her after her manumission and marriage in 1778, except that her husband was an unsuccessful dabbler who brought Phillis to poverty and to a premature death, nearly unnoticed, in a cheap boarding house in 1784.

The few details of Wheatley's life which are available to us suggest that she was in no ordinary sense of the word a slave, nor was she in any way subject to the more tangible hardships characteristic of even New England slavery during the years in which she wrote the poems of the 1773 collection. In fact, if the account of Odell (a relative of the Wheatley's) is accurate, Phillis was entirely cut off from the slaves around her (her correspondence with Arbour Tanner being the one noticeable exception). On the other hand, she was not in any real way a part of the dominant culture: although she mixed with white society, it was always as an exception, as a guest, as a showpiece novelty. As a result, one must guess that she lived in a neutral zone, neither black nor white—and her poems stand as a record of this ambivalence, as an indication that the slave mentality went deeper than the surface of her life.

Not surprisingly, then, Wheatley stands at the head of a long line of black American artists who, more or less unwittingly, give expression in their work to hatred of or at least an ambivalence toward their blackness. J. Saunders Redding generalizes about the literature of black Americans and calls it a "literature of necessity," a literature "motivated by the very practical desire to adjust to the American environment."[7] The literature that springs from the unique motivation is likewise unique. In Redding's analysis, it is marked by a "cultural dualism":

> Of course writing by Negroes is different. The difference stems from the fact of their distinctive group experience in America. The cultural dualism of the American Negro is very real, and nearly all the Negro writers of more than local reputation have expressed it in one form or another. . . .[8]

Redding's assertion that there exists in the work of black authors a strain of racial alienation finds eloquent affirmation in James Baldwin's "Autobiographical Notes." Generalizing from his own experience, Baldwin says of the dilemma faced by the black artist in America:

> The most crucial time in my development came when I was forced to recognize that I was a kind of bastard of the West; when I followed the line of my development I did not find myself in Europe but in Africa. And this meant that in some subtle way, in some really profound way, I brought to Shakespeare, Bach, Rembrandt, to the stones of Paris, a special attitude. Those were not really my creations, they did not contain my history, I might search in them in vain for any reflection of myself. . . . At the time I saw that *I* had no other heritage which I could possibly hope to use. . . . I would have to appropriate those white centuries, I would have to make them mine—I would have to accept my

> special attitude, my special place in this scheme—otherwise I would have no place in any scheme. What was the most difficult was the fact that I was forced to admit something I had always hidden from myself, which the American Negro has always had to hide from himself as the price of his public progress: that I hated and feared white people. This did not mean that I loved black people; on the contrary, I despised them. . . .[9]

Phillis Wheatley, as a black, and especially as a black cut off from her racial fellows in a slave society, wrote verse permeated with this social ambivalence, by what Baldwin and others suggest is a self-hatred motivated by the factor of race.

The poem "To Maecenas," which opens the 1773 edition of her work and which Matson sees as an example of the flight-to-freedom strain in the poem is, for the attentive reader, an initiation into Wheatley's racial ambivalence. A glance at "To Maecenas" will show that the poem is meant to be a dedicatory piece in imitation of the standard Augustan enshrinement of the benefactor's many virtues as a patron of the arts. The reader is not surprised, then, when Phillis assumes the self-demeaning posture so characteristic of the style:

> Great Maro's strain in heavenly numbers flows,
> The Nine inspire, and all the bosom glows.
> O could I rival thine and Virgil's page,
> Or claim the Muses with the Mantuan Sage;
> Soon the same beauties should my mind adorn,
> And the same ardors in my soul should burn:
> Then should my song in bolder notes arise,
> And all my numbers pleasingly surprise;
> But here I sit, and mourn a grov'ling mind,
> That fain would mount and ride upon the wind.

However, she ties this sense of inadequacy to her being black, and in doing so goes beyond the demands of the convention. Her otherwise standard lament over her "grov'ling mind" is impossible to divorce from the specifically racial content of the fifth stanza:

> The happier Terence all the choir inspired,
> His soul replenish'd and his bosom fir'd;
> But say ye Muses, why this partial grace,
> To one alone of Afric's sable race;
> From age to age transmitting thus his name
> With the first glory in the rolls of fame?

She presents Terence, an African by birth, as having exhausted the poetic gifts available to Africans. Thus her "grov'ling mind" is the child of a lack of talent which she attributes to her being of the "sable race." The solution she seeks to this racial quandary is to turn to the master's patronage:

> I'll snatch a laurel from thine honor'd head,
> While you indulgent smile upon the deed.

While flattery of the patron is certainly commonplace within the convention, it is noteworthy here in the context of the racial character of her complaint: she as a black cannot expect to write well, and the best she can do is to hope that the master will be indulgent in her defense.

A different sort of poem, "To the University of Cambridge in New England," contains a dimension of Wheatley's demeaning of her blackness that goes beyond the "smug contentment at her own escape from Africa"[10] that James Weldon Johnson found in her poems. The poem is a moral admonition to the students at Harvard and is, for the most part, predictably Christian in its warning:

> Improve your privileges while they stay,
> Ye pupils, and each hour redeem, that bears
> Or good or bad report of you to heaven.
> Let sin, that baneful evil to the soul,
> By you be shunned, nor once remit your guard;
> Suppress the deadly serpent in its egg.

The significance of the poem in the context of the present discussion, though, lies not in the conventional moral statement but rather in the rationale used to justify such a warning. In the opening stanza she uses her African origins to establish her credibility as one who knows evil and who therefore feels impelled to warn others:

> While an intrinsic ardor prompts to write,
> The muses promise to assist my pen;
> 'Twas not long since I left my native shore
> The land of errors and Egyptian gloom:
> Father of mercy, 'twas thy gracious hand
> Brought me in safety from those dark abodes.

From this opening she makes no transition, but merely begins her admonition. She neither elaborates nor explains why Africa and her being from Africa have thus enabled her to warn, but implies that her having recently been brought from Africa is justification enough for her to speak on evil and its consequences. She also assumes that her readers will make the same association and equate her origin in the "dark abodes" of Africa with an intimate acquaintance with evil not available to the white American Harvard students that are her peers.

The third stanza makes it clear that the thrust of the opening carries beyond an identification of her African background with paganism to a rejection of Africa as not only the land of pagan error, but also of satanic evil. She indicates that in delivering her from Africa's "Egyptian gloom" the "gracious hand" of God did more than rescue her from the dimly remembered doctrinal deficiencies of pagan cults. The passage of warning quoted above concludes as follows:

> Supress the deadly serpent in its egg.
> Ye blooming plants of human race divine,

An Ethiop tells you 'tis your greatest foe;
Its transient sweetness turns to endless pain,
And immense perdition sinks the soul.

Once more, without elaboration or explanation, she assumes that her being an "Ethiop" is sufficient credential to speak familiarly of the "deadly serpent" and the state of a soul sunk in perdition. And finally, in identifying herself as an African, she implicitly excludes herself from the class "blooming plants of human race divine" whom she addresses, underscoring the assumed moral distinction she has made based on color. In doing so, she transforms an otherwise religious warning into an indictment of her color and her African heritage.

"On Being Brought from Africa to America" is similar to the "Cambridge" poem in its gratuitous alignment of blackness and evil. The first half of this short poem is another of Wheatley's predictable religious verses. The tone of her calling Africa a "Pagan land," and of her declaration of happiness at having come to know God and salvation in America, is matter of fact. The second half of the poem, though, is devastating in its assumptions about black people:

Some view our sable race with scornful eye,
"Their color is a diabolic die."
Remember, Christians, Negroes, black as Cain,
May be refined, and join th' angelic train.

On the surface, this might pass with the first four lines as a vote of confidence in the salvation of black men through the mercy of God's deliverance. It might even seem to be a rather presumptuous reminder to white people by an adolescent slave girl that they ought not judge blacks too harshly. But, significantly, Wheatley's reminder includes an implicit affirmation of the very indictment she seeks to refute. That is, she does not attempt to discredit the myth that the black man's color reflects a special moral inheritance from Cain the murderer, marked by God in *Genesis* as a sign of his fratricide (though no mention is made in the Biblical story of the skin marking being total pigmentation differentiation). On the contrary, she apparently accepts the myth, dubious as it is, and in doing so affirms that in its native state the "diabolic die" of black people reflects an essentially corrupt moral nature specifically related to the mere fact of blackness. These final four lines indicate that blacks have value not in their origins and in their humanity, but only in so far as they can be "refined" to fit into the "angelic train" of the white Christians she addresses—in other words, only to the degree to which they can reject their African origins and assume the moral values of the white Christians.

Another of her "address" poems, "To the Right Honorable William, Earl of Dartmouth, His Majesty's Principle Secretary of State for North America" proves, upon close inspection, to be unintentionally ironic and not, as Matson suggests, rebellious. The poem, largely a celebration of freedom, was written in anticipation of what the colonists hoped would be a vigorous effort by Dartmouth to work on their behalf. As such, it serves to illustrate how far removed from the issue of slavery and from her African origins Phillis had become by 1772.

In a letter accompanying the poem she requests that Dartmouth be indulgent in perusing the poem, an address by a presumptuous African, and she goes on in the poem to express her hopes that freedom might return to New England. There is no suggestion in the poem that the freedom of which she speaks is related to the issue of slavery. On the contrary, the remarks in the letter and in the poem indicate that the freedom of which she speaks is limited to an anticipated resolution of the political and economic conflicts between the colonists and the crown during the years preceding the revolution:

> No more, America, in mournful strain
> Of wrongs, and grievance unredress'd complain,
> No longer shalt thou dread the iron chain,
> Which wanton Tyranny with lawless hand
> Has made, and with it meant t' enslave the land.

Wheatley introduces the slavery question in the third stanza as a means of justifying her presuming to speak on the topic of freedom and tyranny. Clearly distinct from the plea for a return of liberties by King George to the colonists, her claim to authority in discussing tyrants is surprisingly empty of commentary on the question of freedom as it related to the slaves:

> Should you, my lord, while you peruse my song,
> Wonder from whence my love of Freedom sprung,
> Whence flow these wishes for the common good,
> By feeling hearts alone best understood,
> I, young in life, by seeming cruel fate,
> Was snatch'd from Afric's fancy'd happy seat:
> What pangs excruciating must molest,
> What sorrows labour in my parents' breast?
> Steel'd was that soul and by no misery mov'd
> That from a father seiz'd his babe belov'd:
> Such, such my case. And can I then but pray
> Others may never feel tyrannic sway?

She does not claim her authority to speak of freedom from her experience as a slave, nor does she draw on observations of the less comfortable lot of those slaves around her as one might expect her to. Rather, hers is a second-hand authority derived from her sorrow at imagining what her parents must have suffered at her loss. She implies that her own fate as a slave has not been cruel: Africa is only a "fancy'd happy" place;

moreover, her indication that it was a "seeming cruel fate" that snatched her away suggests that it was, indeed, a fortunate day that saw her sold into slavery and removed from her African heritage.

One might object that it was not the prerogative of the slave Phillis to criticize such institutions as slavery. However, in the same poem she does not shrink from criticizing the "wanton Tyranny," of the crown—statements which are, as she reminds us several times, presumptuous for a slave to make. The disregard for the issue of slavery which this inconsistency implies is very aptly described by Saunders Redding:

> If the degree to which she felt herself a Negro poet was slight, the extent to which she was attached spiritually and emotionally to the slaves is even slighter. By 1761 slavery was an important, almost daily topic. The Boston home of the Wheatley's, intelligent and alive as it was, could not have been deaf to the discussions of restricting the slave trade. . . . Not once, however, did she express either in word or action a thought on the enslavement of her race; not once did she utter a straightforward word for the freedom of the Negro. . . . It is this negative, bloodless, spirit-denying-the-flesh attitude that somehow cannot seem altogether real in one whose life should have made her sensitive to the thing she denies.[11]

The Dartmouth poem in particular, then, serves as one measure of how far removed from the reality of her blackness Phillis had become, at least intellectually, during the period in which she wrote. Matson's suggestion, tempting though it is, that Wheatley is protecting herself by her indirectness, seems to have an element of conjecture not really supported by biographical or textual evidence.

Besides the rather direct inferences treated thus far, there are less significant indications of Phillis Wheatley's racial ambivalence scattered throughout her other poems. Some of these will be noted briefly. In "A Hymn to Humanity," a poem similar to "To Maecenas" in its conventional tone of praise of a benefactor, she again asserts the specifically racial cause of her deficiencies as a poet. "Afric's muse" of the sixth stanza is the "languid muse of low degree" which she claims earlier on in the poem as her own. As in "To Maecenas," she is rescued by the white patron whom she lauds. Similar to the Harvard poem discussed earlier is "On the Death of the Rev. Mr. George Whitefield." In closing a catalogue of appeals which she uses to convey a sense of Whitefield's preaching voice, she writes:

> Take [Jesus] my dear Americans, he said,
> Be your complaints on his kind bosom laid:
> Take him, ye Africans, he longs for you,
> Impartial Saviour in his title due:
> Wash'd in the fountain of redeeming blood,
> You shall be sons, and kings, and priests to God.

The assumption is the same as that made in the Harvard poem: Americans—the white colonists—come to Jesus to air complaints, for a reason that is larger than the mere fact of their being Americans or human; the Africans come to Jesus, apparently, because they are Africans—no other reason is given. Wheatley once again infers an immediate relationship between being African and the moral evil which stands so gratuitously in need of washing.

As a sort of footnote to the discussion just concluded, it might be appropriate to comment on the possibility of racial undercurrents in the light/darkness images so pervasive in Phillis Wheatley's poetry. The validity of reading a racial significance in the use of images of light and dark in the poetry of one who was an admirer of Milton and who knew the scriptures is questionable indeed. However, in view of the more tenable indications of racial ambivalence on Wheatley's part already mentioned, it is not unreasonable to at least mention the possibility of a connection. That is, assuming that images derive their power from some referent in the experience of the author or of the reader of a given poem, the proliferation of images which ally light with the good, the intelligent, and the divine and dark with error, damnation, and chaotic evil might very well be significant in a racial context in the writings of one who was cut off from her black fellows, who was estranged from, who perhaps hated the blackness which separated her from the white world into which she was only partially impressed and toward which she apparently looked with admiration and gratitude. Psychoanalyst Joel Kovel and historian Winthrop Jordan have argued persuasively in, respectively, *White Racism: a Psychohistory* and *White over Black*[12] that in the American experience it is impossible to dissociate the respective value placed on black and white persons from the traditional associations of black-bad, dirty, dead and white-good, clean, alive. When such equations are reinforced by religious symbolism and by cultural and economic devaluation of black people in the institution of slavery and its heirs, the racial significance of a poetic vocabulary permeated by such equations might be credibly posited. The possibility of such a significance, at least, will be assumed in the discussion of Wheatley's religion which follows.

In a letter to Arbour Tanner, Wheatley indicates that the religion in which she believed was one area in which her attitude toward her blackness and her being of African origins played a significant role:

> Let us rejoice in and adore the wonders of God's infinite love in bringing us from a land semblent of darkness itself, and where the divine light of revelation (being obscured) is as darkness. Here the knowledge of the true God and eternal life are made manifest; but there, profound ignorance overshadows the land. Your observation is true, namely, that there was nothing in us to recommend us to God. . . . It gives me very great pleasure to hear of so many of my nation seeking with eagerness the way of true felicity.[13]

Her comment that there "was nothing in us to recommend us to God," a sentiment common to the New England protestantism in which she was formed, is especially significant in the racial context in which she was writing in that part of the letter. Her derogatory references to Africa are familiar from the ambivalence expressed in the poems. Here, though, the sense of the prose suggests that it was in their state of African ignorance that there was nothing to recommend them to God. The thrust of the passage, it seems, is one of seeing in religion an escape not from their condition of servitude but from the conditions of their Africanism—an escape they rejoice to see so many blacks accepting. Matson sees the escapist elements in the religious poems, in general, as having connotations of protest: the repeated assertion of escapist motifs being seen, "after a fashion," as protest against the condition of slavery.[14] Again one must, at least in part, disagree: the escape Wheatley envisions is one that will purify her of the evil she sees as intrinsic to her blackness and her African origins.

In discussing the religion of Phillis Wheatley in his classic study of black religion in literature, Benjamin Mays employs the term "compensatory." He describes the function of this compensatory religion in this way:

> Miss Wheatley's religion is one of sweetness and affection. Her ideas of God help one to endure suffering and to bear up under it. They are capabale of lending sweetness to life, giving it an elegant tone. . . . She is hardly concerned about transforming society. She is more interested in the individual and his soul's salvation.[15]

The evidence from the poetry substantiates Mays' observations. Two types of religious concern are found in Phillis Wheatley's poetry: the delineation of a cosmology in which the primary fact is God's providential management and the vision of a corrupt world from which Providence eventually will deliver the virtuous believer. Repeatedly, in the many poems written on the deaths of various persons, these two strains join with the matrix of light/dark imagery to create a pattern of imagery in which the conventional themes of man's insignificance and God's providential concern reflect as well Wheatley's ambivalence over and desire to escape from her own blackness. Perhaps most typical is "To a Lady on the Death of Three Relations":

> We trace the pow'r of Death from tomb to tomb,
> And his are all the ages yet to come.
> 'Tis his to call the planets from on high,
> To blacken Phoebus, and dissolve the sky;
> His too, when all in his dark realms are hurl'd,
> From its firm base to shake the solid world;
> His fatal sceptre rules the spacious whole,
> And trembling nature rocks from pole to pole.

From this sombre beginning the poem moves to hope, the mourner admonished to "smile on the tomb, and sooth the raging pain" in a vision of the ethereal world. Significant for our purpose is the typical alignment of imagery along the lines of the equation observed by Kovel and Jordan: death and perdition converge in the image of blackness. For Wheatley, the terms of religious escape and racial denial of the self are, here and elsewhere, the same. Traditional and familiar though the religious sentiments be, the existence of a racial significance in their expression is more than mildly suggested when viewed from the perspective of the demeaned blackness present in the poems discussed earlier.

No doubt Phillis Wheatley was a bright young lady—perhaps, as Matson properly suggests in her evaluation of the poetry, a genius. To master English in sixteen months at the age of eight years was and still is an admirable accomplishment. Moreover, to produce even second-rate poetry in a milieu in which most blacks were oppressed and illiterate was at least a social, if not exactly a literary, triumph. Only occasionally worth reading for its aesthetic value (like indeed most Colonial poetry), her poetry retains a cultural significance beyond its literary merit that will insure its perpetuation as a proper object of study in the cultural history of black people in America. Literary phenomenon though she might have been, Wheatley's true legacy is the testimony her poetry gives to the insidious, self-destroying nature of even the most subtle, most gentle of racially oppressive conditions. It is in this aspect, although entirely remote from her conscious aims as a poet, that her poetry has its rich and alarming educative value today.

Notes

1. "Phillis Wheatley—Soul Sister," *Phylon*, 33 (Fall, 1972), 222–230.

2. Julian D. Mason, ed., *The Poems of Phillis Wheatley* (Chapel Hill, University of North Carolina Press, 1966).

3. The persistence of the slave mentality is fully discussed in William H. Grier and Price M. Cobb, *Black Rage* (New York, Basic Books, 1968).

4. Biographical material compiled from Charles F. Heartman, *Phillis Wheatley: A Critical Attempt and a Bibliography of Her Writings* (New York, Privately published, 1915); Vernon Loggins, *The Negro Author* (Port Washington, Kennikat, 1964); Julian D. Mason, ed., *The Poems of Phillis Wheatley* (Chapel Hill, University of North Carolina Press, 1966); and Margaretta Matilda Odell, *Memoir and Poems of Phillis Wheatley* (Boston, Light & Horton, 1835).

5. Mason, *op. cit.*, p. 1.

6. Odell, *op. cit.*, p. 10.

7. J. Saunders Redding, *To Make a Poet Black* (College Park, Md., McGrath Publishing Co., 1968), p. 3.

8. J. Saunders Redding, "The Negro Writer and American Literature," in Herbert Hill, ed., *Anger and Beyond* (New York, Harper & Row, 1966), p. 1.

9. *Ibid.*, p. 2.

10. James Weldon Johnson, *The Book of American Negro Poetry* (New York, Harcourt, Brace, 1922), p. xxvii.

11. Redding, *To Make a Poet Black*, *op. cit.*, pp. 9–11.

12. (New York, Vintage Press, 1971): (Chapel Hill, University of North Carolina Press, 1968).

13. Mason, *op. cit.*, p. 104.

14. Mason, *op. cit.*, p. 223.

15. Benjamin E. Mays, *The Negro's God as Reflected in His Literature* (New York, 1938), pp. 105–06.

"Our Modern Egyptians": Phillis Wheatley And the Whig Campaign Against Slavery in Revolutionary Boston

Charles W. Akers*

One day in 1767, merchant John Wheatley of Boston entertained at his dinner table two gentlemen from Nantucket who had just narrowly escaped shipwreck in a fierce storm off Cape Cod. The small, frail black girl serving the table listened to their thrilling story and soon afterwards wrote a few lines of verse asking the purpose of the "Great Supreme" in such a miraculous deliverance. When this poem appeared in a Newport, Rhode Island, newspaper at the end of the year, it marked the first publication of Phillis Wheatley, Boston's celebrated black poet of the American Revolution.[1]

She was thirteen or fourteen at the time, though no one knew for certain. Six years before, when she had been imported from Africa, she appeared to be seven or eight. Offered for sale in Boston among a shipment of new slaves, Phillis was purchased by Wheatley as a servant for his wife. Between this precocious slave child and her mistress there quickly developed a warm relationship, and Phillis responded eagerly to the stimulating environment of the pious but sympathetic Wheatley household. In the words of her master: "Without any Assistance from School Education, and by only what she was taught in the Family, she, in sixteen Months Time from her Arrival, attained the English Language, to which she was an utter Stranger before, to such a Degree, as to read . . . the most difficult Parts of the Sacred Writings, to the great Astonishment of all who heard her."[2]

Early in her teens she began writing poetry for her own amusement, but by New England standards her verse proved too good to escape notice. At about the same time as her first published poem, she composed a poetic admonition for an "Ethiop" to Harvard students to make the most of the college education denied her because of sex and race. Soon afterwards she wrote similar warnings to religious freethinkers and atheists. Then in 1770, her "Elegiac Poem" about the death of the renowned evangelist, George Whitefield, was widely published throughout the American colonies.[3]

*Reprinted from *Journal of Negro History*, 60, No. 3 (July, 1975), 397–410. With permission of J. Rupert Picott of the Association for the Study of Negro Life and History, Inc.

Her growing reputation prompted a proposal to publish a collection of her poetry "as a reward to a very uncommon Genius." When too few Bostonians subscribed to this undertaking, Phillis' master arranged for publication in England under the patronage of the Countess of Huntingdon, a noblewoman noted for piety and opposition to slavery. While this volume was in the press, Phillis sailed for England with a member of the Wheatley family. Physicians had advised sea air for her "poor state of Health." She made her "Farewell to America" in a poem prominently displayed in the local newspapers. Writing to an English friend, a member of the American Board of Customs Commissioners noted the embarkation of this African girl who "is certainly an extraordinary instance of natural genius."[4]

In England she attracted sufficient attention to bring introductions to a number of notables, among them Benjamin Franklin and Lord Dartmouth, the colonial secretary whose coming to office Phillis had saluted in verse. She was promised an audience with George III, but the trip had to be cut short so that she could return to her mistress, who had been taken seriously ill. By leaving so unexpectedly she missed not only presentation to the monarch, but she also missed being on hand for the publication of her poetry in London. When she reached home in September 1773, the *Boston Gazette* hailed the return of "Phillis Wheatley, the extraordinary Poetical Genius."[5]

The appearance of *Poems on Various Subjects, Religious and Moral* climaxed the young poet's career just as she left her teens. This volume contained an attestation to "assure the World" that its thirty-nine verses were truly the work of "Phillis, a young Negro Girl, who was but a few Years since, brought an uncultivated Barbarian from Africa, and has ever since been, and now is, under the disadvantage of serving as a Slave in a Family in this Town." To quell all suspicions of a hoax, the original attestation, signed by the "most respectable Characters in Boston," might be seen at the publisher's London shop. It included the names of Thomas Hutchinson, the royal governor, and of John Hancock, the focus of Boston's resistance to British policies for the colonies. The *Poems* revealed Phillis to be an imitative poet whose work lacked qualities of greatness; but clearly she had written some of the most interesting verse of colonial America. Her triumph is well measured by the reprint of *Poems* twice in England and five or more times in the United States during the next quarter century.[6]

After the volume of 1773, she continued to write a quantity of verse and a series of revealing personal letters, which she was encouraged to publish even in an age when letter writing ranked as a leading literary pursuit. A subscription for a second volume, dedicated to Franklin and containing both poetry and letters, fell victim to the turmoil of the Revolution, and in time most of this material was unfortunately lost.[7]

Phillis enjoyed another moment of fame when in 1776, Washington took favorable notice of her poem celebrating his appointment as "Generalissimo of the armies of North America."[8] In spite of this, she experienced little but ill health and hardship for the remainder of her life. John Wheatley freed Phillis near the beginning of 1774, in response to his wife's deathbed wish.[9] He had retired from business in 1771, and all of the Wheatley family died by the end of the Revolution. Apparently seeking new security, Phillis married John Peters, who has typically been blamed for her subsequent troubles. But Peters was a free black man of considerable ability and personal charm who appears not to have deserved his reputation as a ne'er-do-well whose irresponsibilities contributed to his talented wife's untimely death. Among the scanty evidence is the record of his paying taxes in 1780, on a house in Boston of above average value. Whatever the truth concerning her husband, after an unsuccessful struggle to keep alive her three sickly children, Phillis was buried in an unmarked grave at the end of 1784. She was barely thirty.[10]

Wheatley's poetry has long been recognized as a landmark in the history of black literature. Such recognition, though, has often been accompanied with laments that she appeared to enjoy the fleeting rewards of a natural precocity at the price of a shameful indifference to the plight of less gifted and less fortunate fellow slaves. One of her short verses seems to offer compelling evidence that she accepted so completely the culture of her new homeland that she could believe slavery and racial prejudice to be of little consequence compared to the blessings of Christian civilization:

> 'Twas mercy brought me from my *Pagan* land,
> Taught my benighted soul to understand
> That there's a God, that there's a *Saviour* too;
> Once I redemption neither sought nor knew.
>
> Some view our sable race with scornful eye,
> "Their colour is a diabolic die."
> Remember, *Christians*, *Negroes*, black as *Cain*,
> May be refin'd, and join th' angelic train.[11]

Considered alone, these lines have naturally led students of Wheatley's writing to a conclusion that may be partially unjustified in the light of what is now known concerning her life and the society in which she lived. Until the last decade, her interpreters usually concentrated more on the poetry than on the poet. Consequently, they quoted or paraphrased each other's biographical sketches but did not search for additional evidence. No scholar appeared with the combination of interest in her life and the knowledge of Boston history necessary to trace her short career as reliably as possible from the meager sources. Shirley Graham's highly fictionalized children's biography remained the only popular account.[12] Even Julian D. Mason, Jr., made no biographical advancement in the introduction to his useful modern edition of Wheatley's writings published in 1966.

Phillis Wheatley's biographical image may be changing. Four new letters, adding a few details of her life, have been discovered in Scotland.[13] This essay introduces another letter, lost sight of since an excerpt was printed in two Boston newspapers of 1774; it provides the first major revelation of her private thoughts concerning slavery. Equally important, a fuller understanding of Revolutionary Boston's social structure and the place of slavery in it furnish a setting in which to place these and any future discoveries concerning her.

On the eve of the Revolution, Boston contained approximately six hundred slaves, mainly house servants like Phillis. The tax list of 1771, shows that ninety percent of the town's slave owners were assessed for either one or two "Servants for Life between 14 and 45 Years of Age." The other slave owners owned three or four, except one who was taxed for six. Heavily concentrated in the richer wards with the most elaborate homes, these house slaves served the local elite.[14] Americans brought up on the myth that Samuel Adams almost single-handedly led his townsmen into rebellion may have difficulty in picturing Boston as a city economically dependent on the commercial and shipping enterprise of the wealthiest one or two percent of the population. Excluding officials and those otherwise tied directly to royal government, the large majority of the socio-political elite constituted the solid base of resistance to British attempts to alter imperial relations. Though the demagoguery of Adams has occupied center stage in nearly all histories, the American Revolution in Boston was essentially an elitist movement backed by most of the town's wealthy citizens.[15]

Thus, in Boston as in Virginia, elitist patriots cried for the rights of man while they continued to enjoy the labor of their African slaves. In 1771, for example, John Hancock and James Bowdoin—the two wealthiest Whigs and perhaps the richest men in town—each paid taxes on two slaves, and the leading young Whig politician, Dr. Joseph Warren, on one.[16] Boston newspapers attacking the tyranny of the British ministry also announced slave auctions and advertised for sale scores of skilled and well-behaved slaves to be uprooted and subjected once more to the inhumanity of the market for no fault but "want of Employ." Unlike the plantation South, in urban Boston masters often regarded slave children as an unjustified expense. As a result, advertisement after advertisement contained such words as, "A Likely Negro Child of a good Breed to be given away. Inquire of the Printers."[17] The newspapers also carried frequent notices of rewards for the return of runaways, particularly for young male slaves seeking to escape by going to sea. One can document the presence of slavery in the pages of the *Boston Gazette*, the boldest

Whig newspaper, as easily as in those papers supporting the mother country.[18]

Yet almost from the beginning of their struggle against Britain, Massachusetts Whigs recognized the contradiction between their professed libertarian principles and the presence of chattel slavery. In his widely read pamphlet of 1764, *The Rights of the British Colonies Asserted and Proved*, James Otis bluntly asserted that all men are "by the law of nature freeborn" whether "white or black," and that "those who every day barter away other men's liberty will soon care little for their own."[19] While celebrating repeal of the Stamp Act, Boston instructed its representatives elected in 1766, to "move for a law, to prohibit the importation and purchasing of slaves for the future" with a view toward the "total abolishing of slavery from among us." Early the next year the printers of the *Gazette* issued a pamphlet forcefully outlining an anti-slavery case, stressing practical as well as religious and humanitarian arguments. In March 1767, the General Court debated, without reaching agreement, on several bills prohibiting or at least restricting the slave trade.[20]

As if to emphasize the seriousness of the legislature's inaction, the *Boston Post-Boy* published on the front page in December an account of a traveller who was shipwrecked off the coast of Africa and then rescued by "naked negroes," who "seemed to be some of the happiest creatures on earth." Their bliss was suddenly transformed into the worst misery with the arrival of slavers seeking a cargo for an English captain. The piece concluded by detailing the "distresses of these poor enslaved wretches" as they were transported to the West Indies and sold to cruel masters.[21]

The following year Charles Chauncy, the venerable pastor of the Boston First Church, lent his influence to the cause with a pamphlet asserting that "It is most horribly shameful, that so many of the human species, as good by nature as their masters, and that have as good a right to the freedom of men, should be bought and sold as though they were cattle: and dealt with as though they were an inferior order to dogs!" In his election sermon of 1770, Samuel Cooke forcefully declared, "We, the patrons of liberty, have dishonored the Christian name and degraded human nature nearly to a level with the beasts that perish." Others fell back of the jeremiad to bewail the present token of divine displeasure (British oppression) as God's rod to punish His covenanted people who had transgressed by becoming slavers.[22] In 1771, a bill prohibiting the importation of slaves passed the House and Council, but Governor Thomas Hutchinson refused to sign it without explicit instructions from the ministry. Hutchinson naturally distrusted the sincerity of the bill's Whig sponsors, and he saw little moral difference between binding a white servant for a fixed term of years and a black servant for life. In Massachusetts slaves were classified as "servants for life." They could institute civil suits in the courts and had not entirely lost their personal and property rights.

Thus, from the Tory perspective, the current anti-slavery drive could be viewed as no moral issue but only another attempt to weaken and embarrass royal authority.[23] Hutchinson seems to have agreed with the Englishman whose letter on slavery was reprinted in Boston in 1773:

> Upon the whole, therefore, it appears plainly, as well from the reason and nature of things as from well-known facts, that the negroes of the British colonies are much more happy and easy than the slaves to *necessity* in any part of the world; and much more so than the subjects of any arbitrary government in Europe; and that their slavery is little more than *nominal* in comparison of them, nor their labours by any means greater than what ninety-nine men out of a hundred *must* undergo for the support of life throughout the whole world, and even in the most free governments.[24]

While Phillis visited England during the summer of 1773, agitation against slavery mounted again, this time marked by five petitions to the General Court from slaves seeking their freedom. One petition from Boston slaves pleaded the cause of the "discreet, sober, honest, and industrious" among them who were embittered with "this most intolerable Reflection. That let their Behaviour be what it will, neither they, nor their Children to all Generations, shall ever be able to do, or to possess and enjoy any Thing, no, not even *Life itself*, but in a Manner as the *Beasts that perish*. We have no Property! We have no Wives! No Children! We have no City! No Country!" Nevertheless, the petitioners resolved to obey their heavenly father and their earthly masters while awaiting the relief which would be life to the dead.[25]

Those attending the Harvard Commencement of 1773, heard a debate on the legality of slavery, and the arguments soon appeared in a pamphlet.[26] That same year there appeared a Boston edition of Benjamin Rush's persuasive *Address to the Inhabitants of the British Settlements in America, upon Slave-Keeping*. An "African" patriot, writing in the *Massachusetts Spy* early in 1774, put the issue squarely before the Sons of Liberty: "You are taxed without your consent, because you are not represented in parliament (I grant that a grievance) and have petitioned for relief and cannot get any. Pray, Sir, what can you impute it to? Are the Britains' hearts harder than yours? Are not your hearts also hard, when you hold them in slavery who are intitled to liberty, by the law of nature, equal as yourselves? If it be so, pray, Sir, pull the beam out of thine eye."[27] The legislature responded in March 1774, with an act levying heavy fines for importing or purchasing slaves but dodging the issue of slavery itself.[28] Once more the measure died for want of the governor's signature. The *Boston Gazette* offered a benediction over the frustrated Whig attack on slavery with the epitaph of John Jack, published from outside the town during the siege of Boston:

GOD
Wills us free[;]
Man
Wills us slaves[;]
God's will be done[.]
Here lies the body of John Jack[,]
Native of Africa, who died March 1773[,]
Aged about sixty years.
Tho' born in a land of slaves[,]
He was born free.
Tho' he lived in a land of liberty[,]
He lived a slave,
'Till by his honest tho' stolen labour
He acquired the source of slavery[,]
Which gave him his freedom:
Tho' not long before[,]
Death the grand tyrant
gave him his final emancipation,
and put him on a footing with kings.
Tho' a slave to vice
He practiced those virtues
without which kings are but slaves.[29]

As far as the record shows, Phillis Wheatley publicly contributed to the Whig attack on slavery only once. In March 1774, the year after she had returned from England and had been granted her freedom, two Boston newspapers published an excerpt from a letter she had written to the noted Indian preacher, Samson Occom. Apparently unnoticed by past scholars, this eloquent letter affords a brief glimpse into her private thoughts concerning the institution that had torn her from the "Pagan land" of her birth and thrust her into Christian civilization. As a letter from a recently-freed slave to an outspoken Indian defender of his people against whites, it takes on added significance.

A graduate of Eleazar Wheelock's Indian school, Occom had been the main attraction on the school's fabulously successful fund-raising tour of Great Britain in 1766–1767. But after his return he found an Indian preacher in New England who was poverty stricken. He became even more embittered when Wheelock employed the money raised abroad to relocate the school, transform it into Dartmouth College, and began admitting many whites. His Alma Mater has turned herself into an "alba mater," he charged. Their interest in missions had led the Wheatleys to open their home to Occom during his Boston visits. Consequently, Phillis knew him well, and they had corresponded occasionally. Occom had once suggested to Mrs. Wheatley that Phillis should be returned to Africa as a "Female Preacher to her kindred."[30] The Indian preacher and the black poet had discussed the plight of their respective peoples before; in any case, when Occom wrote Phillis in February 1774, concerning the natural rights of Negroes, she hastened to reply the same day:

> I have this Day received your obliging kind Epistle, and am greatly satisfied with your Reasons respecting the Negroes, and think highly reasonable what you offer in Vindication of their natural Rights; Those that invade them cannot be insensible that the divine Light is chasing away the thick Darkness which broods over the Land of Africa; and the Chaos which has reigned so long, is converting into beautiful Order, and reveals more and more clearly, the glorious Dispensation of civil and religious Liberty, which are so inseparably united, that there is little or no Enjoyment of one without the other: Otherwise, perhaps, the Israelites had been less solicitous for their Freedom from Egyptian Slavery; I do not say they would have been contented without it, by no Means, for in every human Breast, God has implanted a Principle, which we call Love of Freedom; it is impatient of Oppression, and pants for Deliverance; and by the Leave of our Modern Egyptians I will assert, that the same Principle lives in us. God grant Deliverance in his own way and Time, and get him honor upon all those whose Avarice impels them to countenance and help forward the Calamities of their Fellow Creatures. This I desire not for their Hurt, but to convince them of the strange Absurdity of their Conduct whose Words and Actions are so diametrically opposite. How well the Cry for Liberty, and the reverse Disposition for the Exercise of oppressive Power over others agree,—I humbly think it does not require the Penetration of a Philosopher to determine.[31]

The devout Christian and loyal Whig spoke in this letter, but so did the African slave who yearned for deliverance from "oppressive Power." By acknowledging that the slave's humanity could be asserted only "by the Leave of our Modern Egyptians," Phillis revealed her understanding of the essential weakness in the protracted local campaign against slavery.

Despite their rhetorical and legislative endeavors, the Whigs indictment of slavery remained theoretical and lacked urgency. The most patriotic newspapers continued to carry advertisements offering blacks for sale and posting rewards for the capture and return of runaway slaves. Bostonians valued their "good" slaves like Phillis Wheatley, who, outwardly at least, yielded readily to the inculcation of a culture in which pious, submissive blacks found security—too often only temporarily—in positions of service to the white elite. One advertisement in the *Gazette* expressed this truth succinctly by offering for sale "A healthy, tractable Negro Girl, about 18 Years of Age," for whom her master no longer had employment.[32] Today the evidence that Boston merchants did not deserve their later reputation as great slavers is conclusive.[33] Still, with their networks of trade connections, merchants could quickly sell to the West Indies those blacks who proved intractable, while retaining the docile house slave, who became euphemistically a "servant," attended church and partook of the sacraments with the family, and often received his freedom as a reward for faithful service and good behavior. The extreme price demanded from a Black who adjusted to the New England culture is illustrated by the case of Benjamin Chase, a mulatto living in Danvers. During a long and exemplary Christian life, he refused to marry because he wanted neither to degrade himself by taking a black wife nor to debase any white woman worthy of his respect and affection.[34]

The Boston slave could hope for no better lot than that of Cato, favorite servant of the Hancocks. He received his freedom at age thirty, married, and baptized his children at the prestigious Brattle Street Church, all the while continuing to serve the town's leading family. The will of John Hancock's Aunt Lydia freed her two slaves and left small sums to these as well as Cato, who had been earlier emancipated by her husband's will. Like Hancock, many of the Whig elite had been brought up in households with a faithful and beloved black servant. Stories of slave cleverness in manipulating whites and folk tales reputed to be of African origin regaled the highest social circles and unconsciously confirmed the cultural prejudice that the best of the black race, Christianized and civilized, should gratefully accept the favor of serving kindly white masters. Thus slave or free, meek or defiant, stupid or gifted, saintly or sinful, the Boston Black could never fully escape, even on the church records, the stigma of what Phillis Wheatley described as the "diabolic die."[35]

There were other limitations to the Whig attack on slavery. A fear of slave revolt had spread from the southern colonies as far north as Massachusetts. In Boston the threat to domestic security posed by unruly, vengeful slaves imparted a somewhat self-seeking tone to the ideological case against slavery. Stories of slaves setting fire to their masters' houses troubled many townsmen.[36] Whig ambivalence on the Black came to the surface when the British troops arrived in 1768. After watching soldiers being disciplined on the Common by lashes administered at the hands of black musicians, a writer in the "Journal of the Times"—the "syndicated" Whig newspaper column published throughout the colonies—commented that "to behold Britons scourged by Negro drummers, was a new and very disagreeable spectacle." Later the "Journal" complained of soldiers promising freedom to slaves who would cut their masters' throats, "asserting that now the soldiers are come, the Negroes shall be free, and the Liberty Boys slaves." When the British regiments in Boston finally reached full strength, the "Journal" sarcastically noted, "It is to be hoped that the arrival of these troops will lead some officers to conclude that the aid and countenance of our Negro gentry may now be dispensed with." In 1769, the selectmen ordered the Boston Watch to restrict the movements of Negroes after nine o'clock at night. Those Whigs intent on obtaining convictions in the Massacre trials criticized the admission of testimony from Negroes in favor of the accused. In defending the soldiers, John Adams sought to absolve the town of blame for the mob in King Street by describing it as a "motley rabble of saucy boys, negroes and mulattoes, Irish teagues, and outlandish jack tarrs," in contrast to the "good people of the town."[37]

Amid the many attacks on slavery, there appeared an occasional defense of the institution based not on an assertion of black inferiority but on a comparison of the lot of slaves in the colonies with that of Europeans under arbitrary rulers and on the economic importance of slave labor to the colonies.[38] Yet most Boston Whigs remained half-heartedly hostile to the slave trade while acquiescing in the local institution with its relative benevolence. They were, nevertheless, psychologically unprepared to grant actual equality to any Black or to appreciate the impatience of the slave's cry for freedom.

A case in point is the relationship of Phillis Wheatley to Dr. Samuel Cooper, the silver-tongued pastor of the Brattle Street Church in which the town's mercantile wealth was heavily concentrated. Cooper's grandfather, Samuel Sewall, had left his grandson a strong anti-slavery heritage, including publication in 1700, of *The Selling of Joseph*, one of the first significant public protests against slavery in the colonies. Phillis revered Cooper, who had baptized her in 1771, while he substituted in the pulpit of the Old South Church. In the last year of her life she wrote an *Elegy* on the death of this "Great Divine" whose rhetorical power she admired. Yet there is not the slightest record that this influential preacher-politician, a major leader of resistance to England, ever raised his voice against the nefarious institution his grandfather had fought so vigorously. As far as can be determined, Cooper remained unmoved by the black quest for freedom. His complacency reflected the prevailing attitude of the mercantile congregation that he served.[39]

Phillis Wheatley's attitude toward slavery, contained three elements. First, as a devout, sincere Christian, she could take comfort in the belief that she "should willingly submit to servitude to be free in Christ," that she should give thanks for God's mercy in providing slavery as the means of her rescue from paganism.[40] As a loyal Whig and patriot, she celebrated the Revolution in verse and saw hope for the Afro-American in the libertarian ideology giving birth to the United States. But at the same time, she could never forget that she was an African who had felt "oppressive Power" and that white patriots still daily exercised such power. Read in this light, some of her poetry can be seen to contain all three elements, but nowhere as clearly as in her letter to Samson Occom.[41] A fuller insight may be found in the discovery of new sources; but it seems probable that the more we learn of her life, the more she will emerge as black woman deeply conscious of her origins and of the plight of the black race in the New World.

As a result of legal actions under the constitution of 1780, slavery gradually disappeared in Massachusetts after the Revolution, though leaving largely intact the white view of the African which had troubled even the gentle soul of Phillis Wheatley. Despite the suffering of her last years, she greeted the end of the War for Independence with *Liberty and Peace*, a poem celebrating the victory of "Columbia's Cause" over "great Britannia." This small pamphlet concluded with lines voicing her prayer for the spread of "Heavenly *Freedom*" throughout the new nation. An untimely death spared her the painful knowledge of what the "Modern Egyptians" had in store for her people.[42]

Notes

1. Carl Bridenbaugh, "The Earliest-Published Poem of Phillis Wheatley," *New England Quarterly*, XLII (December 1969), 583–584.

2. John Wheatley's biographical statement concerning Phillis in the preface to her *Poems on Various Subjects, Religious and Moral* (London, 1773) is reproduced in Julian D. Mason, Jr., *The Poems of Phillis Wheatley* (Chapel Hill, 1966); see also p. 107. In *Sibley's Harvard Graduates*, IX (Boston, 1956), 8–9, Clifford E. Shipton quotes the advertisement from the *Boston Evening Post*, August 3, 1761, which he maintains offered Phillis for sale among a group of "small Negroes." But I have been unable to locate such an advertisement as cited, or in any Boston newspaper for this period.

3. All of her extant verse is in Mason, *Poems*, except for the poem edited by Bridenbaugh and the four in Robert C. Kuncio, "Some Unpublished Poems of Phillis Wheatley," *New England Quarterly*, XLIII (June 1970), 287–297. Her poem on Whitefield was advertised for sale in the Boston newspapers beginning October 13, 1770, and was published in a Boston and several other American editions. According to the "Proposals" for printing her first volume, she had written poetry as early as 1765; *Censor* (Boston), February 29, 1772, p. 2/2.

4. *Censor*, February 29, 1772, p. 2/2. Sara Dunlap Jackson, "Letters of Phillis Wheatley and Susanna Wheatley," *Journal of Negro History*, LVII (April 1972), 214. Wallace Brown, "An Englishman Views the American Revolution: The Letters of Henry Hulton, 1769–1776," *Huntington Library Quarterly*, XXXVI (1972–1973), 140. "Farewell to America" appeared in the *Boston Post-Boy*, May 10, 1773, p. 3/1, and was widely copied by other newspapers.

5. Mason, *Poems*, p. 106. Albert Henry Smyth, ed. *The Writings of Benjamin Franklin*, 10 vols. (New York, 1907), VI, 96. Jackson, "Letters," pp. 214–215, *Boston Gazette*, September 20, 1773, p. 2/1.

6. The attestation is reproduced in Mason, *Poems*. For discussion of the quality of her poetry, see Mason, pp. xviii–xiviii; and Sidney Kaplan, *The Black Presence in the Era of the American Revolution* (Washington, 1973), p. 158.

7. Mason, *Poems*, pp. 111–113.

8. John C. Fitzpatrick, ed., *The Writings of George Washington*, 39 vols. (Washington, 1931–1944), IV 360–361. Mason, *Poems*, pp. 87–90.

9. Kenneth Silverman, "Four New Letters by Phillis Wheatley," *Early American Literature*, VIII (1974), 268.

10. For bibliographical items on the Wheatley family, see *Boston Gazette*, February 4, 1771, p. 3/1; July 15, 1771, p. 1/3; March 7, 1774, p. 3/2. Details of her life after 1773 are difficult to document. The best accounts are Benjamin Brawley, *The Negro in Literature and Art in the United States*, 3rd ed. (New York, 1929), pp. 15–37; and Kaplan, *Black Presence*, pp. 150–170. There is no full biography written from original sources. Phillis is not mentioned in John Wheatley's will (Suffolk County, Mass., Probate Records, vol. 77, 359–360). In 1780 "John Peters Negro" paid taxes in Boston on real estate assessed at an annual rental value of 150 pounds ("Assessors' 'Taking Books' of the Town of Boston, 1780," *Bostonian Society*

Publication, IX, 1912, 35). When compared to other assessments, this figure would seem to indicate that Peters owned a house of above average value.

11. "On Being Brought from Africa to America," Mason, *Poems*, p. 7.

12. Shirley Graham, *The Story of Phillis Wheatley*, 12th printing (New York, 1969).

13. Silverman, "Four New Letters." These four letters, belonging to the Earl of Leven, were written by Phillis to John Thornton, an English merchant and philanthropist to Christian missions. The letter of October 30, 1770 [1774] provides the first evidence as to when Phillis was freed.

14. Massachusetts Archives, CXXXII, 92–147. The 1771 tax valuation list gives a total of 407 slaves between 14 and 45 years of age. By estimating the number not included in this age bracket and the untaxed slaves of ministers, the total of 600 was reached. The black population of Boston fluctuated from year to year, but it seems safe to assume that there were nearly 1,000 in Boston on the eve of the Revolution. Thus one can speak roughly of Boston's population containing 6 to 8 percent blacks, nearly as many free as slave. See appendices to Lorenzo Johnston Greene, *The Negro in Colonial New England* (1942; rpt. New York, 1968), and the 1765 census returns for Boston in J. H. Benton, Jr., *Early Census Making in Massachusetts, 1643–1765* (Boston, 1905).

15. I present the case for this interpretation of Revolutionary Boston in a book still in manuscript.

16. Massachusetts Archives, CXXXII, 92–147. Since 20 percent of the individual valuations are missing, it is not always possible to know how many slaves were held by individual Whigs.

17. *Boston Gazette*, April 2, 1770, 3/3.

18. This section is based on a file of slave advertisements from the Boston newspapers.

19. Bernard Bailyn, ed., *Pamphlets of the American Revolution*, I (Cambridge, Mass., 1965), 439–440.

20. *A Report of the Record Commissioners of the City of Boston, Containing the Boston Town Records, 1758 to 1769* (Boston, 1886), p. 183. [Nathaniel Appleton, Jr.] *Considerations on Slavery in a Letter to a Friend* (Boston, 1767). *Journal of the . . . House of Representatives of . . . Massachusetts Bay*, 1766 session, pp. 353, 358, 387, 390, 393, 408, 409–410, 411, 420. George H. Moore. *Notes on the History of Slavery in Massachusetts* (New York, 1866), pp. 126–128.

21. December 7, 1767, pp. 1–2. See also *Boston Gazette*, March 30, 1767, p. 3/1.

22. Charles Chauncy, *The Appeal to the Public Answered* (Boston, 1768), p. 117. A. W. Plumstead, ed., *The Wall and the Garden* (Minneapolis, 1968), pp. 343–344. *Boston News-Letter*, June 1, 1769, p. 1/2.

23. Moore, *Slavery in Massachusetts*, pp. 133–143. Bernard Bailyn, *The Ordeal of Thomas Hutchinson* (Cambridge, Mass., 1974), p. 378.

24. *Boston Post-Boy*, January 14, 1773, p. 4/1–2.

25. *The Appendix, Or, Some Observations on the Expediency of the Petition of the Africans Living in Boston* . . . (Boston, 1773), pp. 9–11. See also, Herbert Aptheker, ed., *A Documentary History of the Negro People in the United States*, 5th paperbound ed. (New York, 1968), I. 6–9; and Kaplan, *Black Presence*, pp. 11–14.

26. *A Forensic Dispute on the Legality of enslaving the Africans* . . . (Boston, 1773).

27. *Massachusetts Spy*, February 10, 1774, p. 3/1–2.

28. *Journal of the . . . House of Representatives of . . . Massachusetts Bay*, January–March 1774 session, pp. 221, 224, 241–243.

29. *Boston Gazette*, October 9, 1775, p. 4/2.

30. On Occom, see Harold Blodgett, *Samson Occom* (Hanover, N.H., 1935), p. 122 and passim; and Leon Burr Richardson, *An Indian Preacher in England* (Hanover, N.H., 1933).

Occom had resided in the Wheatley home when preaching in Boston the year before this letter was written (Jackson, "Letters," p. 213). See also Silverman, "Four New Letters," pp. 266–267.

31. *Boston Post-Boy (Massachusetts Gazette)*, March 21, 1774, p. 3/2; *Boston News-Letter (Massachusetts Gazette)*, March 24, 1774, p. 1/3. There seems no reason to doubt the authenticity of a letter published where Phillis was certain to see it in print, but nothing is known concerning the course by which the letter found its way into these newspapers. Because this excerpt was published in the two newspapers most friendly to royal government, its appearance might be interpreted as an attempt to embarrass the Whigs, except that the Tories had an even worse record on slavery. I have not attempted to analyze how the slavery issue was affected by the Whig-Tory political struggles.

32. *Boston Gazette*, November 2, 1767, p. 2/1.

33. For an introduction to the new evidence, see Gilman M. Ostrander, "The Making of the Triangular Trade Myth," *William and Mary Quarterly*, XXX (October, 1973), 635–644.

34. This paragraph is based on a study of Boston church records and newspaper advertisements concerning slaves. For slavery of Benjamin Chase, see *The Diary of William Bentley*, 4 vols. (1907–1914; rpt. Gloucester, 1962), IV, 227–228.

35. *Records of the Church in Brattle Square* (Boston, 1902), pp. 184, 185, 187, 189. Suffolk County; Mass. Probate Records, vol. 76, 512–516. Examples of stories told concerning slaves are in L. H. Butterfield, ed., *Diary and Autobiography of John Adams*, 4 vols. (Cambridge, Mass., 1961), II, 13–14; and William Tudor, *The Life of James Otis* (Boston, 1823), pp. 449–450n.

36. In his *Considerations on Slavery*, Nathaniel Appleton, Jr. argued against slavery on the ground, among others, of the threat to domestic security (p. 13).

37. Oliver M. Dickerson, ed., *Boston under Military Rule (1768–1769) as Revealed in a Journal of the Times* (Boston, 1936), pp. 3, 6, 16, 17, 18, 21. *A Report of the Record Commissioners of the City of Boston, containing the Selectmen's Minutes from 1769 Through April 1775* (Boston, 1893), pp. 45. Hiller B. Zobel, *The Boston Massacre* (New York, 1970), pp. 258, 284, 292–293.

38. For examples of defenses of slavery, see *Boston Evening Post*, March 28, 1774, p. 1/1; and *Boston Post-Boy*, January 4, 1773, p. 4/1–2. Some evidence that the condition of the black in Boston was improving in the decade before the Revolution is possibly provided by the comparative mortality figures for whites and blacks given in *First Report of the Record Commissioners of the City of Boston*, 2nd ed. (Boston, 1881), pp. 11–12; but it is difficult to be certain without more reliable estimates of the number of blacks living in Boston during each year.

39. For the baptism, see *Records of the Church in Brattle Square*, p. 187. Contrary to the common assertions, Cooper and not Joseph Sewall baptized Phillis, and there was nothing unusual about a slave being admitted to full communion in a Boston Congregational church, *Sibley's Harvard Graduates*, XI (Boston, 1960), 192–213, provides the best sketch of Cooper in print. I have found no concern for slavery in his manuscripts or printed works. For the *Elegy* on Cooper's death, see Mason, *Poems*, pp. 90–92.

40. Silverman, "Four New Letters by Phillis Wheatley," p. 268.

41. For an attempt to analyze the racial aspects of her poetry, see Arthur P. Davis, "Personnel Elements in the Poetry of Phillis Wheatley," *Phylon*, XIII (1953), 191–198.

42. Mason, *Poems*, pp. 93–95.

SELECTED ORIGINAL ESSAYS

The Influence of Alexander Pope on the Writing Style of Phillis Wheatley

Albertha Sistrunk*

During the Colonial period in America few blacks received recognition for either their talents or for their contributions to the life of the Colonies. This phenomenon existed in part because the institution of slavery and its imposed restrictions conspired to stifle the creative ambitions and talents of blacks. Some few fortunates among the slaves, however, escaped the imposed restrictions. Historians have unveiled the achievements of several early black poets: Lucy Terry, Frances Harper, Jupiter Hammon, and Phillis Wheatley attracted favorable attention throughout the Colonies. Their contributions are quite remarkable when one realizes the limitations under which they struggled to transcend their predestined black fate—the fate of every child born behind the veil.

Phillis Wheatley, who, like many other slaves, was kidnapped from her home in Africa and brought to Boston, stands out as the foremost black of the Colonial period. Upon her arrival, she attracted the attention of John Wheatley, who bought her as a servant for his family. Brawley stated, "The Wheatley's daughter observed the ease with which she assimilated knowledge and began to teach Phillis, giving special attention to instruction in the scriptures and morals. Within sixteen months from the time of her arrival in Boston, Phillis was able to read fluently the most difficult parts of the Bible. . . ."[1]

Phillis's tutelage by the Wheatleys' daughter commenced at age seven or eight. It consisted of some ancient and modern geography, a little ancient history, and a fundamental acquaintance with the most important Latin classics. The type of teaching she received during these formative years, the time when social scientists say a child is most susceptible to his immediate environment, aided considerably in the molding of her personality and in the shaping of her career as a poet.

Phillis Wheatley, a woman of unusual piety and culture, felt and internalized the influence of her family environment. Any eighteenth-century slave who lived with an aristocratic family in Boston, "the reputed cradle of all that is refined in American manners and letters," the cradle of liberalism, was bound to be affected by this immediate environ-

*Published with the permission of the author.

ment. Another measure of the influence of her environment was the type of limitations imposed on her: limited in the sense that she was living with a family whose social stratification recognized only certain literary works as "good"; limited in the sense that she was a young slave girl who had to read what was thoughtfully handed down to her by the great "white massa"; limited also in the sense that eighteenth-century America failed to produce a single outstanding poet who might serve as a model for the aspiring poet. As Chas. F. Heartman, author of *Poems and Letters*, an anthology of Wheatley's works, has observed:

> Phillis Wheatley's first poem was published in 1770, five years before the dawn of the American Revolution, and the birth of German Idealism. . . . Phillis wrote before the mighty outburst of the human spirit which gave rise to Geothe, Schiller, and Heine in Germany, and Wordsworth, Byron, Keats and Shelley in England.[2]

Regardless of these limitations, Phillis produced poetry that would compare favorably with the other American poetry of her period.

Alexander Pope, along with Thomas Gray, reigned supreme during the eighteenth-century American literary period. Pope was not considered by some as a poet; however he was conceded to be the best substitute for one that an age of prose could produce. Therefore, it is of little consequence to expect that Phillis, an avid reader, did not share the opinion of the populace about the significance of Pope and Gray. Brawley reported that "she read Pope at an early age, that his translation of Homer was her favorite classic, and before long she too began to make verses."[3] Whether she was influenced by Alexander Pope is not a debatable issue, but to what extent he influenced her style of writing makes for an interesting investigation—the focus for this discussion.

Aside from the most obvious dissimilarities between these two poets—white English male/black slave girl—master/prodigy—there are disparities that are worthy of attention to aid in understanding Pope's influence. Pope's personality was scrutinized by his critics, who characterized him as envious, conniving, spiteful, and a dishonest hunchback. Also, Pope tended to use his writings to openly attack and often criticize his enemies and friends. He very seldom portrayed his characters as virtuous; Parkin surmised thus:

> . . . everyday realism prevented him from depicting any human being as faultless. Even his eulogy on Martha in "Moral Essay II" is amusingly undercut. She is the best of women, but still a woman, and as such only the "fairest of the spotted kind."[4]

Although Pope was not afraid to present vices and follies in his writings, religious principles were invariably at the bottom of his approach to correctable evil.

In contrast, piety was the ruling sentiment in Phillis Wheatley's character. She bore only love and gratitude for her slave family: she obviously harbored no feelings of revenge and hatred against anyone for her own "lowly" state in life. Only once—in her poem "To the Right Honorable William, Earl of Dartmouth . . ."—did she envision the "American Dream":

> No More, America, in mournful strain
> Of wrongs and grievances unredress'd complain
> No longer shalt thou dread the iron chain,
> Which wanton Tyranny with lawless hand
> Had made, and with it mean t'enslave the land.[5]

Pope's ideas on writing warrant consideration in order to understand the extent to which he influenced Wheatley's writing style. For Pope, writing in any historical established genre was, in a broad way, imitation—he believed wholeheartedly in imitation and translation. Therefore, Phillis's imitation of Pope was the suggested course for writers of the eighteenth century.

Second, Pope was greatly concerned with an exact representation of values. Similarly, Wheatley's objectivity is a readily discernible characteristic of her poetry; she seems to have been acutely concerned with both sides of any situation that she presented. In "Liberty and Peace" she welcomed freedom, but she also recognized the aftermaths of war: death of loved ones, despoilment of property, and lingering feelings of bitterness and hostility against the foe.

Third, "Pope's poetry dealt with two kinds of experiences which from the standpoint of the individual may be called evil: cosmic evil, about which man can do nothing except submit; and man-made evil, which is correctable by human endeavors."[6] Wheatley's apparent acceptance of her black fate might be attributed in part to a similar belief; consequently, she saw slavery as a necessary man-made evil that would be eventually abolished by collective human endeavors. Interestingly, slavery was abolished because it was thought to be politically expedient at the time; the use of militant protest tactics—fiery sermons and speeches, revolts, insurrections, whippings, and lynchings of men—were the real human endeavors, but they alone did not correct this evil.

Last, Pope thought that the aim of character analysis should be the discovery of the "ruling passion," be it good or bad. He felt that the conception of moderation was first of all implicit in the genre, which forbade extremes of any kind; therefore, passion had to be muted. In his "Moral Essay I," he discusses the ruling passion:

> And you brave Cobham, the latest breath
> Shall feel your ruling passion strong in death
> Such in those moments as in all the past,
> "Oh, save my country, Heav'n" shall be your last.[7]

He is suggesting that Cobham's love of country was his ruling passion even at death; such a passion has rational aims and it brings rewards of virtue. In "On Virtue," Phillis hailed virtue as a "bright jewel" for which she was aiming. She undoubtedly internalized a similar philosophy about an undying love for country; her patriotism for America was so overwhelming that she frequently referred to Africa, her homeland, as that "dark abode":

> 'Twas not long since I left my native shore
> The land of errors, and the Egyptian gloom
> Father of mercy, 'twas thy gracious hand
> Brought me in safety from those dark abodes.[8]

In "On Being Brought from Africa to America," she sings a similar tune; she is rejoicing because she was kidnapped from Africa and brought to America, where she learned there was a God and a Savior. Conclusively, the Wheatleys' daughter's tutelage as well as Pope's philosophy on writing did influence young Phillis Wheatley's thinking, ideas, attitude, and subsequently her writing style.

The extent to which Pope influenced Wheatley's writing style can best be shown by examining closely their literary works for minor and major commonalities. The most obvious similarities that exist between these two poets are as follows.

THEIR WRITINGS SHOW A DIRECT ACQUAINTANCE WITH MYTHOLOGY AND THE LATIN CLASSICS

Pope's poetry and prose show his keen appreciation of and indebtedness to Homer, Virgil, and Horace. In his "Essay on Criticism," he cautioned successful imitators to follow nature. What he meant is clear from his account of Virgil:

> When first young Maro in his boundless mind
> A work t' outlast Immortal Rome design'd,
> Perhaps he seem'd above the Critick's Law
> And but from Nature's Fountains scorn'd to draw:
> But when t' examine ev'ry Part he came,
> Nature and Homer were, he found, the same.[9]

In the same "Essay" he describes Horace, whom most critics suggest he was imitating throughout the poem. Pope's translation of Homer's *Iliad* also attests to classical influence.

Brawley suggested that Wheatley gained precision from her acquaintance with greater Latin authors. In her poems there are numerous examples of classical allusions; she commenced "On Recollection" with an invocation to the muses:

Mneme begin. Inspire, ye sacred nine,
Your vent'rous Afric in her great design.
Mneme, immortal pow'r. I trace the spring:
Assist my strains, while I thy glories sing.[10]

In addition, in "To Maecenas" she alluded to Homer, Patroclus, Achilles, Pelides, Virgil, and Maro. She used the section entitled "Niobe in Distress for her Children" from Ovid's *Metamorphosis*, book 6 as a frame in which to provide a view of the painting by Richard Wilson. Conclusively, Phillis's poems were replete with invocations to the Greek and Roman gods, fairies, fates, and muses.

POPE AND WHEATLEY TENDED TO DEDICATE THEIR WORKS TO REAL PERSONS

Pope enlivened his poems with well-defined pictures of types of individuals; his character sketches, however, were often critical rather than complimentary. In "Epistles to Several Persons" ("Moral Essay I"), Pope undercuts by satire his friend Cobham, the viscount to whom the poem was dedicated (cited above):

And you! brave Cobham, to the latest breath
Shall feel your ruling passion strong in death:
Such in those moments as in all the past,
"Oh, save my country, Heav'n!" shall be your last.

Similarly, Wheatley tended to dedicate her works to people she admired; she has been accredited as the first to hail General Washington, the great leader during the period, in a dedicatory poem:

Thee, *first in peace and honours*,—we demand
The grace and glory of the martial band.
Fam'd for thy valour, for thy virtues more,
Hear every tongue thy guardian aid implore![11]

She also dedicated poems to bereaved friends who had lost loved ones.

POPE AND WHEATLEY WERE AKIN IN THEIR CHOICE OF SUBJECT MATTER

In "Essay on Man," Pope considered man in "the abstract, his nature and state"; he attempted to vindicate the ways of God to man. Wheatley also referred to actual people and everyday happenings vis-à-vis her poem to General Washington for his role in ending the war, and her poems to those who were struggling to understand the inevitable fate of all mankind—death.

Both Pope and Wheatley preferred pastoral poetry to genuine lyrics.

This preference can be discerned by examining two passages that are strikingly similar in structure and in subject matter:

> Soon as the Flock shook off the mighty Dews
> Two Swains, whom Love kept wakeful, and the muse,
> Pour'd o'er the whitening Vale their fleecy Care,
> Fresh as the Morn, and as seasons fair.[12]
>
> Soon as the sun foresook the eastern main
> The pealing thunder shook the heav'nly plain;
> Majestic grandeur! From the Zephyr's wing.
> Exhales the incense of the blooming Spring.[13]

Pope wrote a discourse on pastoral poetry before he wrote his poems on the four seasons, from which the first excerpt was taken—"Discourse of Pastoral Poetry: Spring"; he firmly believed that true wit and nature were one. Wheatley also loved to write pastoral poetry; she did not write one genuine lyric. She elected to describe the parts of the day: morning and evening instead of the seasons; the second excerpt above comes from her "An Hymn to the Evening"—which clearly shows the extent to which she was indebted to Alexander Pope.

Pope and Wheatley seemingly preferred to write elegies instead of genuine lyrics. Pope in his "Elegy to the Memory of an Unfortunate Lady" provides a typical example of elegiac irony:

> So Peaceful rests, without a stone, a name
> What once had beauty, titles, wealth, and fame.
> How lov'd, how honour'd once, avails thee not.
> To whom related, or by whom begot;
> A heap of dust alone remains of thee;
> Tis' all thou art, and all proud shall be.[14]

In contrast, Wheatley wrote with less mockery; she expressed in her elegies the Christian idea that death is the beginning of a new phase of life—eternal life after death. She echoes this belief:

> But though arrested by the hand of death,
> Whitefield no more exerts his lab'ring breath,
> Yet let us view him in th' eternal skies,
> Let ev'ry heart to this bright vision rise;
> Till life divine re-animates his dust.[15]

It is also fitting to note that both poets used religious themes in their poems: Pope's Salpedon's speeches reflected a serious use of religion, and Wheatley's poems are replete with her unfaltering religious convictions.

BOTH PRODUCED AN ARTISTIC HEROIC COUPLET

During the eighteenth century, style was a mere matter of ornament; a writer's artistic ability attested to his skill in employing literary devices. It was Pope's mechanical skill in manipulating the couplet that won him literary acclaim. The basic features of Pope's couplet are balanced antithesis and parallelism, rhyme, closure, and sentence form. The following selected excerpts focus on a few of the *isolated* features of his couplet: however, in most instances, features work together to establish a couplet norm.

Balanced Antithesis and Rhyme

"Pope frequently rhymes words whose effect depends upon some clever or shocking disparity in meaning. The alogical relation creates simultaneously an ironic resemblance of difference between the rhyme words."[16] In essence, Pope used rhyme as an attention-getting device:

> Whether the nymph shall break Diana's law
> Or some frail china jaw receive a flaw.

"The ease with which Phillis Wheatley was able to chisel the heroic couplet when no more than sixteen or eighteen years of age, was amazing."[17] Therein she employed rhymes quite artistically:

> Now here, now there, the roving Fancy flies
> Till some lov'd object strikes her wandering eyes.
> From star to star the mental optics rove
> Measure the skies, and range the realms above.

Sometimes the resemblance of sound plus the contrast or difference of meaning is emphasized by the poet's use of different parts of speech to achieve rhyme (the first two lines are Pope's):

> Thus critics, of less Judgment than *Caprice*
> Curious, not knowing, not exact but *nice.*
>
> Come let us with the same vigor *rise*
> And take a prospect of the blissful *skies*.
>
> or
>
> And may each clime with equal gladness *see*
> A monarch's smile can set his subject *free.*

Parallelism and Sentence Form

In "Discourse on Pastoral Poetry: Spring," every speech of Daphnis corresponds exactly in length and sense to every speech of Strephon. "When Strephon invokes in four lines the aid of the gods and promises a sacrifice if successful—

> Inspire me, Phoebus, in my Delia's Praise
> With Waller's Strains, or Granville's moving Lays!
> A Milk-white Bull shall at your Altars stand,
> That threats a Fight, and spurns the rising Sand.

then Daphnis immediately does the same in the same number of lines":[18]

> Oh Love! for Sylvia let me gain the Prize
> And make my tongue victorious as her Eyes;
> No Lambs or Sheep for Victims I'll impart,
> The Victime, Love, shall be the Shepherd's Heart.[19]

Similarly, in "A Rebus by J. B.,"[20] Wheatley presented three stanzas of six lines; she provided in each stanza a clue to aid in solving the riddle:

I

> A *bird*, delicious to the taste
> On which an army once did feast
> Sent by an hand unseen; (What?)
> A creature of the horned race,
> Which Britain's royal standards grace;
> A gem of vivid green

II

> A *town* of gaiety and sport,
> Where beaux and beauteous nymphs resort,
> And gallantry doth reign: (Which?)
> A Darden hero fam'd of old
> For youth and beauty, as we're told
> And by a monarch slain.

III

> A *peer* of popular applause
> Who doth our violated laws,
> And grievance proclaim. (Who?)
> Th' initials show a vanquished town
> That adds fresh glory and renown
> To old Britannia's fame.[21]

Wheatley used the first line of each stanza to identify and describe the major subject as underlined; the second and third lines of each stanza, except the first one, provide historical data that place the subject in ancient time.

Closure and Openness

"The following lines are composed, despite Pope's punctuation, of one sentence, and after the subject 'He' in the first line, the lines, as merely a series of verb phrases which are predicates":[22]

He gathers Health from Herbs and Forest yields,
And of their fragrant Physick spoils the Fields:
With Chymic art exalts the Min'ral Pow'rs.
And draws the Aromatick Souls of Flow'rs.
Now marks the Course of rolling orbs on high;
O'er figur'd Worlds now travels with his Eye.[23]

Wheatley in "To a Clergyman on the Death of his Lady" strings along four adverbial clauses that all commence with "where," and she does not provide the subject of these clauses until the fifth line:

Where contemplation finds her sacred spring,
Where heav'nly music makes the arches sing,
Where virtue reigns unsully'd and divine,
Where wisdom throned, and all the graces shine,
There sits thy *spouse* amidst the radiant throng,
While praise eternal warbles from her tongue.[24]

Parallel Sentence Structure

Pope's identical sentence structure and ordered lines helped to create a vivid impression. In "Windsor-Forest," he listed the kinds of fishes that this place yielded:

Our Plenteous Streams a various Race supply:
The bright-ey'd Perch with Fins of Tyrian Dyes,
The Silver Eel in shining Volumes roll'd
The Yellow Carp, in Scale bedrop'd with Gold,
Swift Trouts, diversif'd with Crimson Strains,
And Pykes, the Tyrants of the watry Plains.[25]

The last excerpt from Wheatley above shows that she also made use of identical sentence patterns. In the excerpt below she strings along three infinitive phrases that explain the part recollection might play for bereaved persons:

Let Recollection bear a tender part
To sooth and calm the tortures of your heart;
To still the tempest of tumultuous grief;
To give the heav'nly Nectar of relief;
Ah! cease, no more her unknown bliss bemoan!
Suspend the sigh, and check the rising groan.[26]

Also, in "A Funeral Poem on the Death of C. E. . . ." Wheatley not only uses related sentence patterns, but very artistically sets up a counterpoint and states the responses of the dead babes:

Then, smiling thus: "To this divine abode,
"The seat of saints, or seraphs, and of God,
"Thrice welcome thou" The raptur'd babe replies,
"Thanks to my God, who snatch'd me to the skies,
"E'er vice triumphant hand possess'd my heart,
"E'er yet the tempter had beguil'd my heart,
"E'er yet on sin's base actions I was bent
"E'er yet I knew temptations dire intent;
"E'er yet the lash for horrid crimes I felt,
"E'er vanity had led my way to guilt,
"But, soon arrived at my celestial goal
Full glories rush on my expanding soul."[27]

POPE OCCASIONALLY USED EVERYDAY WORDS

Pope, but not Wheatley, frequently used familiar phrases and colloquial expressions in his poetry. Wheatley's diction tended to be more formal than Pope's. The following couplets (Pope's preceding Wheatley's) show their use of diction: (1) use of homely words:

All fools have still an *itching* to decide,
And fain would be upon the laughing side.

She leaves her *earthly mansion for the skies*
Where new creations feast her won'dring eyes.

(2) use of contractions, omissions, and colloquial exaggerations:

To tell 'em, would a hundred require,
Or one vain wit's, that might a hundred tire.

To heav'n's high mandate cheerfully resign'd
She mounts, she flies, and leaves the rolling Globe behind.

(3) use of names and actual persons and places:

Might he return, and bless once more our eye,
New Blackmores and New Milbourne must arise.

The loss of thee on Tyler's soul returns,
And Boston for her dear physician mourns.

Even though the two poets show a preference for short, unpretentious words, Pope also writes with a more elevated style:

Such late was Walsh—the Muse's judge and friend,
Who justly knew to blame or to commend;
To failings mild, but zealous for desert;
The clearest head, and the sincerest heart.
This humble praise, lamented shade! receive
This praise at least a grateful Muse May give:

The Muse, whose early voice you taught to sing,
Prescribed her heights, and pruned her tender wing.[28]

The diction in the excerpt above is more general, more poetic.

Wheatley is often hailed for her diction that belonged to the pseudoclassic tradition—"fleecy care," "tuneful nine," and "feather'd vengeance,"[29] Her poem "To University of Cambridge . . ." shows Wheatley's use of a more elevated style; she has selected her diction in keeping with her audience and her subject matter:

Students, to you 'tis giv'n to scan the heights
Above, to traverse the ethereal space,
And mark the system of revolving worlds.
Still more, ye sons of science, ye receive
The blissful news by messenger from heav'n
How Jesus' blood for your redemption flows.[30]

In "An Hymn to the Morning," Phillis's diction is more poetic:

Aurora hail, and all the thousand dyes,
Which deck thy progress through the vaulted skies;
The morn awakes, and wide extends her rays,
On ev'ry leaf the gentle Zephyr plays;
Harmonious lays the feather'd race resume,
Dart the bright eye, and shake the painted plume.[31]

It is evident from analyzing their poems that Wheatley borrowed from Pope several trite and repetitious words, phrases, and names. Also, both poets tended to frequent use of the colon and semicolon as internal punctuation marks.

THE FUNCTION OF THE IMPLIED DRAMATIC SPEAKER AFFECTED THE DICTION AND TONE OF THEIR POETRY

An understanding of the diction and tone of the poetry of Pope and Wheatley is best gained by examining their use of the implied dramatic speaker. This device is present in all poetry; however, poets may vary their use from poem to poem. In his "Pastoral," Pope carefully maintains a distance between himself and his subject. Parkin concluded that "an important function of Pope's speakers is precisely to secure that depersonalization and objectivity which to the neo-classical mind seemed the only basis for a sane, well-rounded view of man and the universe."[32] However, in "Eloisa to Abelard," this distance between subject and speaker is nonexistent; the speaker is herself the letter writer. She has several implied audiences: Abelard, herself, Heaven, and literary Posterity. She speaks to Abelard thus:

Thou, Abelard! the last sad office pay,
And smooth passage to the realms of day:

See my lips tremble, and my eye-ball roll,
Suck my last breath, and catch my flying soul!
Ah no—in sacred vestment mays't thou stand.
The hallow'd taper trembling in thy hand,
Present the cross before my lifted eye,
Teach me at once, and learn of me to die.[33]

An analysis of this poem in its entirety reveals two interesting points: Eloisa varies her tone as she directs herself to the various implied audiences; she is more tense when she directs herself to Posterity.

Another measure of Pope's effective use of the dramatic speaker is the storytelling quality—a narrative element in his poetry which can be attributed, in part, to the fact that he, unlike Wheatley, was a poetry as well as a prose writer; he is often recognized and credited as just the latter.

The dramatic speakers in Wheatley's poems are often restrained. They are indeed like Wheatley herself, persons who never obtrude directly into the action and the emotion of the poem. In her zeal for objectivity, Phillis quite often omitted the personal note. In essence, she revealed very little about herself: her past as a slave, the institution of slavery under which she labored, and her reactions to the racial problems during the eighteenth century were not often evidenced in her poetry. For this dispassion—this distancing herself from her subject—she has been attacked by contemporary critics who have apparently overlooked the fact that depersonalization and objectivity were the overriding concerns during the eighteenth century.

However, in "Isaiah LXII: 1–8," through the effective use of rhetorical questions, she has captured Isaiah's prophetic tidings from God. Then too, the implied dramatic speaker in "To the Right Honourable William, Earl of Dartmouth . . ." is undoubtedly the inner voice of the poet who is rejoicing over her independence/freedom. She cries:

Hail, happy day, when smiling like the morn,
Fair Freedom rose, New England to adorn:
The northern clime beneath her genial ray,
Dartmouth, congratulates thy blissful sway:
Elate with hope her race no longer mourns
Each soul expands, each grateful bosom burns,
While in thine hand with pleasure we behold
The silken reins, and Freedom's charms unfold.[34]

The overriding tone of this poem is one of conciliation/jubilation—oh happy day!

Finally, apart from the major literary devices discussed in this essay, the two poets made effective use of irony, humor, and repetition; their use of these was interspersed in the overall discussion. Furthermore, figurative devices such as similes, metaphors, alliterations, personifications, symbolism, and imagery were not explicitly discussed, but it is evident from the passages quoted that Wheatley was also indebted to Pope as a model for the effective use of them. The influence of Pope on her use of symbolism and imagery alone would make for an interesting study.

Conclusively, Alexander Pope's influence on Phillis Wheatley's writing style was significant enough to warrant this investigation. Since Wheatley's poetry is presently being revisited by contemporary critics, it is befitting that such an analysis be made to understand and appreciate the literary worth of this young black poet. One cannot overemphasize the importance of applying the literary theory of historicity when trying to criticize the poems of Wheatley. The primary concern is that her poetry should be judged in relationship to the poetry of the eighteenth century, the social and political conditions of the age she lived and wrote in, the limitations of her immediate environment (the home of the aristocratic Wheatleys), and her personal limitations as a black female, rather than by the standards used to judge twentieth-century black poets. If the latter criteria are used, she will inevitably appear in a less favorable light. She needs not to be heaped with golden garlands, but she deserves more credit than she has received—she deserves to be acclaimed along with Paul Laurence Dunbar as one of the early black poets of unusual literary distinction.

Notes

1. Benjamin Brawley, *Early Negro American Writers* (1935; rpt. New York: Books for Libraries Press, 1968), p. 31; a selection with biographical and critical introductions.

2. Chas. E. Heartman, ed., *Phillis Wheatley (Phillis Peters) Poems and Letters: First Collected Edition* (1915; rpt. Miami: Mnemosyne, 1969), p. 18.

3. Brawley, p. 31.

4. Rebecca P. Parkin, *The Poetic Workmanship of Alexander Pope* (Minneapolis: Univ. of Minnesota Press, 1955), p. 217.

5. Heartman, p. 13, ll. 15–19.

6. Parkin, p. 211.

7. Aubrey Williams, ed., *Poetry and Prose of Alexander Pope* (Boston: Houghton Mifflin, 1969), p. 166, ll. 262–65.

8. Heartman, p. 33, ll. 3–6.

9. Williams, pp. 41–42, ll. 130–35.

10. Heartman, p. 80, ll. 1–4.

11. Heartman, p. 33, ll. 25–28.

12. Williams, p. 8, ll. 17–20.

13. Heartman, p. 83, ll. 1–4.

14. Williams, pp. 115–16, ll. 69–74.

15. Heartman, p. 37.

16. John H. Jones, *Pope's Couplet Art* (Athens: Ohio Univ. Press, 1969), p. 6.

17. Brawley, pp. 33–34.

18. Parkin, p. 69.

19. Williams, p. 9, ll. 45–52.

20. "Rebus": a mode of expressing words and phrases by pictures of objects whose names resemble those words or the syllables of which they are composed.

21. Heartman, pp. 92–93.

22. Jones, p. 207.

23. Williams, p. 71, ll. 241–46.

24. Heartman, p. 84, ll. 1–6.

25. Williams, p. 69, ll. 141–46.

26. Heartman, p. 59, ll. 5–10.

27. Heartman, p. 75, ll. 11–22.

28. Williams, p. 57, ll. 729–36.

29. Brawley, p. 34.

30. Heartman, p. 33, ll. 7–12.

31. Heartman, p. 83.

32. Parkin, p. 12.

33. Williams, p. 112, ll. 321–28.

34. Heartman, p. 73, ll. 1–8.

Phillis Wheatley and the Sublime

John C. Shields*

Wheatley's literary imagination shows her familiarity with one of the major aesthetic ideas of the eighteenth century, but her use of the sublime indicates knowledge of another. The sublime in literature constitutes the expression of the enthusiastic passions: these passions are most powerfully and successfully conveyed in compressed and immediate images. In their poetry, both Mather Byles and Wheatley express ideas about the sublime. While Byles uses the word "sublime," however, merely to describe the quality of height, Wheatley makes use of the sublime as a principle of artistic creation. In "An Hymn to Humanity" the word "Graces" suggests her familiarity with the early eighteenth-century notion of the sublime as "a grace beyond the reach of art." Rejecting the pastoral tradition of "green enbow'ring woods," she chooses the grand style that allows her to mount "sublime above inferior things." Her depiction of Apollo's anger in "Niobe in Distress . . ." indicates what John Dennis calls the most forceful image of the sublime.

Sometimes she produces poems which illustrate what David Morris calls "the religious sublime," that is, the expression of the enthusiastic passions in predominantly Christian language and images. But more often her interpretation parallels the theories expressed by several of the sublime's eighteenth-century commentators, such as John Dennis, Joseph Addison, Edmund Burke, and Henry Home, Lord Kames. In some respects, Wheatley even anticipates Immanuel Kant's "Analytic of the Sublime." Samuel Holt Monk insists that the sublime, the interest in which was stimulated first by Boileau's translation of Longinus' *Peri Hupsous* was "on every one's tongue."[1] The four Englishmen named above are hardly the exclusive commentators upon this popular idea. David Morris, author of *The Religious Sublime*, writes "Almost no critic could resist explaining what Longinus had meant by the sublime."[2] Dennis, Addison, Burke, and Kames were, however, four of the best known of the eighteenth-century commentators on the subject. Their own popularity, combined with their treatment of an idea which enjoyed something of a

*Published with permission of the author.

vogue,[3] increases the possibility that their ideas about the sublime might have extended to Wheatley's Boston.

Joseph Addison, whose *Spectator* was the most widely read of the gentlemen's magazines of eighteenth-century England, expressed in language designed to edify English gentlemen some of the most lofty but clearly stated ideas about the sublime, or what he called "grandeur" or "greatness."[4] In *Spectator* 412 Addison writes:

> Our Imagination loves to be filled with an Object, or to grasp at any thing that is too big for its Capacity. We are flung into a pleasing Astonishment at such unbounded Views, and feel a delightful Stillness and Amazement in the Soul at the Apprehension of them.[5]

This passage identifies the devotional imagination as the mental faculty of one who desires intensely to grasp the ineffable. The consequent failure yields wonder and awe. Monk maintains that what Addison describes here is "essentially the sublime experience from Addison to Kant."[6] Wheatley's "On Imagination" suggests the power Addison describes, but with a significant difference:

> From star to star the mental optics rove,
> Measure the skies, and range the realms above.
> There in one view we grasp the mighty whole,
> Or with new worlds amaze the unbounded soul. (30)†

Like Addison, Wheatley specifies a limitless vision, but she adds the idea of "new worlds." Addison's description speaks of views in created nature; Wheatley's "new worlds," however, introduces the poet's own conception of myth, this latter notion anticipating the apocalyptic romantics.

In the next *Spectator* (413) Addison maintains that God supersedes the imagination. The cause of our pleasure "in any thing that is great" must, therefore, come with contemplation of "The Supreme Author of our Being."[7] God then raises within those human beings who "contemplate his Nature" "the highest pitch of Astonishment and Devotion . . . that is neither circumscribed by Time nor Place, nor to be comprehended by the largest capacity of a Created Being."[8] As for Addison, Wheatley's "Great God," the central subject of her poetics of ascension, is finally "incomprehensible, unknown" (8).

In his extremely popular *Philosophical Enquiry into the Origin of Our Ideas of the Sublime and Beautiful* (1757), Edmund Burke does not appear to be so concerned with the religious significance of the sublime as are Wheatley and Addison. Rather, Burke is more interested in a sensationalist view (which holds that all knowledge originates in sensation) of the psychology of the sublime.[9] He does, however, relate the deity to the feeling of the sublime, at least as first cause,

†Numerals in parentheses refer to the pagination of Phillis Wheatley's volume of *Poems* as reprinted in Julian D. Mason, ed., *Phillis Wheatley's Poems* (Chapel Hill, 1966).

> Whenever the wisdom of our Creator intended that we should be affected with any thing, he did not confide the execution of his design to the languid and precarious operation of our reason; but he endued it with powers and properties that prevent [precede] the understanding, and even the will, which seizing upon the senses and imagination, captivate the soul before the understanding is ready either to join with them or to oppose them.[10]

Although Wheatley advances reason (not distinct from imagination) as an ordering principle, hardly "languid and precarious," the language she uses to describe the movement of the imagination parallels that of Burke's passage cited above. In "On Imagination" she pictures the mind's eye as seizing upon "some lov'd object" which then "all the senses binds, / And soft captivity involves the mind" (30).

Wheatley's idea of pain does not correspond precisely to Burke's. He, rather, bases his theory of the sublime upon

> Whatever is fitted in any sort to excite the ideas of pain, and danger, that is to say, whatever is in any sort terrible, or is conversant about terrible objects, or operates in a manner analogous to terror.[11]

Here for the first time, Burke clearly articulates the antithesis of pleasure, source of the beautiful, and pain which paved the way for Kant's "Analytic of the Sublime"[12] as well as Keats's oxymoronic figures of "sad joy." Wheatley derives the emotions of pain and danger which evoke the sublime from three sources: first, from the desire to escape temporal "woes, a painful endless train" (97); second, from the depiction of the wrath of an angry god as in "Goliath" and "Niobe"; and third, from an aching reluctance to surrender her poetic world.

In his *Elements of Criticism* (1762), Kames is not concerned with the antithesis of pain and pleasure.[13] He considers instead the pleasure received from imaginative literature. Having identified Addison's grandeur or greatness as the sublime, he asserts that the enthusiastic passions "commonly signify the quality or circumstance in objects by which the emotions of grandeur and sublimity are produced; sometimes the emotions themselves."[14] In this last phrase Kames foreshadows Kant, who insists that the sublime does not reside "in any of the things of nature, but only in our own mind."[15] To Kant the feeling of the sublime never occurs "in objects" but always results from a mental response to their contemplation. Like Kant, Wheatley considers the sublime as a mental response and thereby avoids Kames's tendency to confuse object and response.

In examining the sublime, Kames emphasizes height; but he carefully avoids identifying the sublime as an elevated distance above the contemplating person. He does maintain that "Ascent is pleasant because it elevates us"[16] and that "an expression or sentiment that raises the mind" is "great or elevated."[17] "The effect of motion and force *in conjunction* [emphasis mine] provokes the most sublime response, which the image of the planetary system most successfully stimulates:

> . . . if we could comprehend the whole system at one view, the activity and irresistible force of these immense bodies would fill us with amazement: nature cannot furnish another scene so grand."[18]

Three lines from Wheatley's "Thoughts on the Works of Providence" display Kames's combined motion and force:

> Ador'd the God that whirls surrounding spheres,
> Which first ordain'd that mighty *Sol* should reign
> The peerless monarch of th' ethereal train. (20)

In "On Imagination" Wheatley "comprehend[s] the whole system at one view":

> From star to star the mental optics rove,
> Measure the skies, and range the realms above,
> There in one view we grasp the mighty whole. . . . (30)

In Kames the blending of force and motion in one image causes pleasurable amazement; but in Wheatley, this combination identifies God as ultimate Creator. The contemplation which engages the mind of her persona gives the persona more than a pleasing self-awareness; it gives her knowledge of God, her ultimate end of contemplation.

This mode of contemplation which seeks knowledge of God most clearly places many of her poems in the tradition of the religious sublime, begun by John Dennis. In the fourth chapter of *The Grounds of Criticism* (1704), "What the Greater Poetry Is, What Enthusiasm Is," Dennis identifies the "Enthusiastick Passions" as those emotions which great poetry excites. Contemplation and meditation give rise to these emotions,[19] the strongest of which "must be rais'd by religious Ideas; that is, by Ideas which either shew the Attributes of the Divinity or relate to his Worship."[20]

Dennis anticipates Burke when identifying "Enthusiastic Terror" as the most powerful of the passionate disturbances of the mind. But he departs from Burke when insisting that this terror "must needs be deriv'd from Religious Ideas" and when naming the "Idea of an angry God" as the most appropriate stimulus of this "Terror."[21] Dennis defines the imagination as the mental faculty which creates this intensity:

> From the Spirits being set in a violent Emotion, and the Imagination being fir'd by that Agitation; and the Brain being deeply penetrated by those Impressions, the very Objects themselves are set as it were before us, and consequently we are sensible of the same Passion that we should feel from the things themselves.[22]

Dennis also believed that the Bible was the most exalted source of sublime poetry[23] which could itself provoke powerful feeling.

Wheatley's Jehovah in "Goliath" not only satisfies Dennis's "Idea of an angry God" as one who "grasps the thunder and . . . wings the storm"

(17) but agrees with his recommendation of the Bible as a source. Her explanation of the imagination as a faculty of the mind which fastens upon "some lov'd object" and then causes excited passions "through the glowing veins to . . . dart" (30) demonstrates a similar theory. At the end of one poem, the stark image of Niobe's clasping to her breast the last of her fourteen children illustrates a powerful anxiety which the reader vicariously shares: "in vain she begs, the Fates her suit deny, / In her embrace she sees her daughter die" (53). Dennis and Wheatley employ the same metaphor, the sun, as the central stimulus to religious contemplation. In Dennis's words,

> . . . the Sun mention'd in ordinary Conversation, gives the Idea of a round flat shining Body, of about two foot diameter. But the Sun occuring to us in Meditation gives the Idea of a vast and glorious Body, and the top of all the visible Creation, and the brightest material Image of the Divinity.[24]

Many of her poems suit the tradition of the religious sublime established by Dennis. Like him, she agrees that the greatest sublimity originates in religious ideas; her wrathful Jehovah and Apollo embody "the Idea of an angry God" which Dennis demands as the primary "Enthusiastic Terror"; her biblical paraphrase, "Goliath of Gath," shows the Bible as a source for sublimity. And she clearly uses the imagination as a vehicle of passion in her ascent to God.

David Morris in the *Religious Sublime* adds to Dennis's set of criteria the eighteenth-century celebration of Milton's epic style as demonstrated in *Paradise Lost.* Although few succeeded, many poets tried to emulate Milton's emotional power and high sublimity; this attitude partly explains Wheatley's interest in the epyllion or short epic. Pope's *Iliad* and *Odyssey* were not her only sources for the epic style. Although she never names Pope in her poems and letters, she calls Milton Britain's Homer (86). Concerning the religious sublime, Morris generalizes that, even though Dennis is the only theorist who "constructs an entire theory of poetry" around this idea,[25] it "was in the air"[26] and "did not require the superstructure of a supporting system."[27] Poets such as Addison Thomson, Young, the elder Thomas Warton, and Christopher Smart wrote poems in the tradition of the religious sublime. According to Morris, four poetic forms suited this tradition: the biblical paraphrase, already by the beginning of the eighteenth century an established literary fashion; the eschatological poem expressing desire for God in an afterlife; poems on the attributes of God; and finally poems which celebrate imaginative devotion.

Morris maintains that a biblical paraphrase composed in the tradition of the religious sublime can be "either an original poem which relies strongly upon scripture for imagery, style, situation, or subject . . . or a reasonable close reworking of specific biblical passages."[28] The full title of Wheatley's poem about David and the giant, "Goliath of Gath. I Sam.

Chap. XVII," suggests that this piece falls under Morris's second category. But discussion of "Goliath" has shown that Wheatley exceeds a mere reworking, first by construing the poem as an epyllion or short epic and second by incorporating into her text several interpolations of her own design, one of which extends to thirty lines. Despite its strong reliance upon scripture, this piece is original.

Her second and last biblical paraphrase, "Isaiah LXII. 1–8," represents her most concerted effort to create highly compressed and elevated verse. Her choice of scripture is of great consequence. One of the principal editors of *The Interpreter's Bible,* James Muilenburn, observes about this biblical passage:

> Church fathers like Tertullian, Origen, Jerome and their successors have interpreted it [63:1–8] messianically. Theology and poetry have joined in recasting and reinterpreting the thought in ways which, while foreign to the original meaning, have nevertheless done some justice to its sublimity.[29]

Wheatley's own interpretation falls into the same pattern established by these church fathers. The poem opens with a syncretistic invocation:[30] "Say, heav'nly muse, what king, or mighty God, / That moves sublime from *Idumea's* road?" (27). While this stranger in the King James version is "glorious in his apparel, travelling in the greatness of his strength," Wheatley describes him as a "king" or "mighty God" who "moves sublime." He does not simply walk as an ordinary man; he moves not along but "from" the road. The motion, "moves sublime from Idumea's road," suggests a tension between human movement which is horizontal, and semidivine movement which is vertical or ascending. This image prepares the reader for the poet's interpretation of this stranger in the remainder of the poem as the son of God, "th' Almighty savior."

Her "Savior" appears in complete battle array:

> . . . with martial glories join'd,
> His purple vesture waves upon the wind.
> Why thus enrob'd delights he to appear
> In the dread image of the Pow'r of war? (27)

The biblical version mentions nothing about war per se, although there the traveler's statement implies battle: "the day of vengeance is in mine heart." In both versions the well-known metaphor of the winepress follows. The people who have sinned against God become like grapes which the traveler treads down in his fury. This metaphor occurs in the biblical text within the traveler's speech which extends through the remaining six verses of Isaiah 63:1–8. These six verses Wheatley contracts into a single couplet: "Compress'd in wrath the swelling wine press groun'd, / It bled, and pour'd the gushing purple round" (27). The language of the first line closely resembles that of Revelation 14:19, "the great winepress of the wrath of God," which typologists often suggest Isaiah 63:3 foretells.

Whether Wheatley had Revelation 14:19 in mind when composing "Compress'd in wrath the swelling wine press groan'd" is less important than the sublimity she creates by condensing six biblical verses into one couplet. Then after the poem's first eight lines, a twenty-two-line typological commentary follows in which the poet dramatizes the "savior" named in Isaiah 63:8 as Christ speaking from the cross. Wheatley thus compresses thirty-two lines of scripture into the first eight of her poem. In the process, she creates one of her most powerful images of the religious sublime. Concerning biblical paraphrases of the eighteenth century, David Morris thinks that "nearly all proved unequal to the spirit of the original."[31] Wheatley's performance in "Isaiah LXIII. 1–8," however, captures the sublimity of the original; indeed it surpasses its biblical source in compression and immediacy. The fervor that Wheatley shows in her eschatological poems, those expressing intense desire for God and heaven, matches her artistic enthusiasm.

The eschatological poem, Morris asserts, treats the few final things: death, judgment, heaven, and hell.[32] Wheatley's heaven is a realm of "Life without death, and glory without end" (6). In her poetic world, death represents a release from mundane existence, metaphysical slavery, into heavenly freedom. Wheatley rarely treats the last judgment and hell. However, in "An Elegy, to Miss Mary Moorhead, on the Death of Her Father, the Rev. Mr. John Moorhead," her first published poem after the appearance of her 1773 volume, she writes of the horrors which "the final Judgment brings" to "the Sinner's Mind" (80). She depicts "Jehovah's wrath" which rains fiercely down upon the unrighteous man:

> The winged Hours, the final Judgment brings,
> Decides his fate, and that of Gods and Kings;
> Tremendous Doom! And Dreadful to be told,
> To dwell in Tophet 'stead of shines of Gold.
> "Gods! Ye shall die like Men," the Herald cries,
> "And stil'd no more the Children of the Skies." (80)

The Tophet which she uses as a synonym for hell probably derives from Isaiah 30:33 where a place by this name is described: "the pile thereof is fire and much wood; the breath of the Lord, like a stream of brimstone, doth kindle it." In this passage, she achieves the ultimate in sublime terror by projecting the image of the last day as one in which even the hierarchy of deities is destroyed, all save Jehovah. This cosmic devastation comes from her mythic henotheism; otherwise it has little meaning, except to serve as a metaphor for those sinners who think themselves God's coequals—Lucifer and his rebels. God's Adversary and his band, however, are never "stil'd . . . Children of the Skies." Hence in these lines, she once again makes use of henotheistic myth.

Although she rarely depicts hell and the last judgment, the one time she does speak of "Tremendous Doom!" she creates powerful sublimity which isolation intensifies. With much greater frequency, she celebrates attributes of God, who is angry only in "Goliath of Gath" and "Niobe in Distress . . . ," as well as in the elegy examined above. In "Thoughts on the Works of Providence," she presents Him as essentially forgiving. After celebrating His wisdom and goodness, her persona speaks hopefully:

How merciful our God who thus imparts
O'erflowing tides of joy to human hearts,
When wants and woes might be our righteous lot,
Our God forgetting, by our God forgot! (22)

In this same passage, she also presents her most imaginative devotion. Addison, whom Morris identifies as a primary theorist of imaginative devotion, writes in *Spectator* 465, "Faith and Devotion naturally grow in the Mind of every reasonable Man, who sees the Impressions of Divine Power and Wisdom in every Object on which he casts his Eye."[33] In *Spectator* 489, he expands this view:

> I must confess, it is impossible for me to survey this World of fluid Matter, without thinking on the Hand that first poured it out, and made a proper Channel for its Reception. Such an Object naturally raises in my Thoughts the Idea of an Almighty Being, and convinces me of his Existence, as much as a Metaphysical Demonstration. The Imagination prompts the Understanding, and by the Greatness of the sensible Object, produces in it the Idea of a Being who is neither circumscribed by Time or Space.[34]

Clearly in each citation the operative faculty, that instrument of Addison's "Understanding," is imagination. Morris observes that eighteenth-century poets grasped fully Addison's analysis of the role of the imagination in the service of religious feeling."[35]

Wheatley expresses precisely this grasp in these lines about her vehicle of ascent:

Imagination! who can sing thy force?
Or who describe the swiftness of thy course?
Soaring through air to find the bright abode,
Th' empyreal palace of the thund'ring God. (30)

This same power mediates between the persona and God in the devotional piece "Thoughts on the Works of Providence." But in "Thoughts" she calls the imagination reason: "As reason's pow'rs by day our God disclose, / So we may trace him in the night's respose" (22). Whereas in the other poem she calls the imagination the mental power which soars "through the air to find the bright abode" of the "thund'ring God," in "Thoughts" the "reason's pow'rs" discover God. As she construes them, the faculties of imagination and reason are virtually synonymous. What follows her identification in "Thoughts" of the "imagination-reason" as the power which enables one to find God is a description of the fancy's roving "Licentious and unbounded" through the land of dreams. Her persona defines sleep as a time "When action ceases and ideas range," and when the fancy "in giddy triumph reigns" (22). Here, Wheatley departs from Addison's theory of the imagination and looks ahead to Coleridge. Addison maintains that the words fancy and imagination are virtually synonymous. She identifies fancy, however, as a largely passive faculty of the mind, a power of association subordinate to the imagination—not its equivalent. The "imagination-reason" is the principle of action. But both Wheatley and Addison identify the imagination as a principle of meditative devotion. The imagination acts for both as that mental faculty which enables one to perceive sublimity.

Within Wheatley's canon, one can find excellent examples of each type which Morris sets apart as constituting the tradition of the religious sublime: there are two fine biblical paraphrases, "Isaiah LXIII. 1–8," and the epyllion "Goliath of Gath"; eschatological poems, many of which enumerate the attributes of God; and finally still others (including some in the first three categories) which display imaginative devotion. Her use of the sublime, however, is not confined to the religious but points directly towards Kant's "Analytic of the Sublime" (in the *Critique of Judgment,* 1790). Kant's "Analytic," which represents the most systematic treatment of the subject, sanctioned the enthusiastic passions for nineteenth-century romanticism.

Unlike Wheatley, Kant distinguishes in the "Analytic" between imagination and reason. To him, imagination mediates between the world of sensibility (perception) and that of understanding (abstract conceptualization) and reason. Reason, Kant maintains, enables one to conceive a priori the ideas of noumena or theoretical objects or powers (totalities such as absolute mass, space, or truth) which at last transcend human experience. Whereas the beautiful can be perceived in experience because the object of that perception is finite, the sublime cannot be grasped as a whole because it is finally infinite and ineffable. Consequently, man enjoys the beautiful as a positive pleasure, but he experiences the sublime as an incomplete, negative pleasure. Although Wheatley confuses the faculties of reason and imagination, she represents her most powerful mode of ascent in the negative pleasure of sublimity.

Both in Kant and in Wheatley, the inexorable attempt of the human mind to grasp totalities and the equally inexorable failure to do so incites the feeling of the sublime.[36] Kant describes the sublime feeling as "a mental movement combined with an estimate of the object" which "has to be estimated as subjectively final (since the sublime pleases)."[37] Kant means that before any object can please it must suggest a totality. In the case of judging the beautiful, the mental process is based upon perceivable finite objects. But in the case of the sublime, judgment is not based upon sensory experience, since it allows only for a subjective idea of totality. The faculty which grasps both the beautiful and the sublime is imagination, which is passive with the beautiful and active or "set in motion"[38] with the sublime.

Wheatley's theory of the imagination as principle of action parallels Kant's analysis of that faculty which sets into motion the response to the sublime object. In "On Imagination," she writes that "we see, / . . . Thy wond'rous acts in beauteous order stand" (29) and that "We on thy pinions can surpass the wind, / And leave the rolling universe behind" (30). The imagination encourages and sustains ascent toward her "Great God, incomprehensible, unknown / By sense" (8). Her "Great God" is no necessary hypothesis of absolute totality as in Kant; He is an actual Being having both finite and infinite existence. Poet and philosopher, nevertheless, have conceived a totality that is finally "knowable" only through subjective and nonsensuous intuition.

In his "Analytic," Kant maintains that the mental movement which a stimulus provokes as the sublime feeling passes through the imagination (like Wheatley's vehicle) either as a contemplative thought process or as a desire, is an exercise of the conscious will. But Kant carefully separates the feeling of the sublime from the realm of belief and assigns it to the aesthetic judgment; the sublime response results only from cognition and desire, "apart from end or interest." Whereas an apparently infinite quantity, the universe for example, solicits the cognitive sublime, which Kant finally calls "mathematical," a theoretical conception of some numenal totality calls up the "dynamic" sublime seated in desire. In Wheatley, this desire, is of course, for God. The mathematical sublime is then quantitative while the dynamic is theoretical. Here the "object" which provokes the sublime response, whether mathematical or dynamic, is never the actual object in nature. Rather the response of sublimity always occurs within the mind.[39] In his commentary upon Kant, Frederick Copleston clarifies this premise in Kant's thought: "We must never forget that for Kant the object must conform to the mind rather than the other way about."[40]

Kant defines the sublime as ". . . the mere capacity of thinking which evidences a faculty of mind transcending every standard of sense."[41] One condition of thought which can lead one to the sublime response is the mathematical or the quantitative (my word, not Kant's), that which enables one to estimate "*how great* any thing is."[42] Natural objects which evoke the sublime feeling or convey the idea of infinity confirm "the inadequacy of even the greatest effort of our imagination"[43] to estimate their magnitude. The sublime response to a great quantity is, then, a negative pleasure. That is, the mind aspires to grasp the infinite whole, and in its certain failure is satisfied by the pleasure of partial comprehension. Like Kames, and Wheatley, Kant finds that contemplation of the cosmos most powerfully induces the feeling of the mathematical sublime: "Now in the aesthetic estimate of such an immeasurable whole, the sublime does not lie so much in the greatness of the number, as in the fact that in our onward advance we always arrive at proportionately greater units."[44] By contemplating first the earth, next the sun as well as the planets, and finally the stars, one progresses to greater and greater quantities. Such contemplation "represents our imagination in all its boundlessness, and with it nature, sinking into insignificance before the ideas of reason, once their adequate presentation in poetry, e.g. is attempted."[45]

Opening with an image of ascent, Wheatley's poem "Thoughts on the Works of Providence" depicts Kant's mathematical sublime: "Arise, my soul, on wings enraptur'd rise" (19). The destination here is "the monarch of the earth and skies" (19) named in the second line. Wheatley's objective is to contemplate Almighty God symbolized in her mandala image of the sun; but the means of attainment is imaginative meditation upon the cosmos, "the earth and skies." In her depiction of the cosmic image, she does not confine herself merely to space. This "monarch" "round its centre moves the rolling year." Wheatley's quantitative sublime is one of time as well as space. The poet carefully focuses upon "the God unseen," the ultimate objective of her contemplation, as the power "Which round the sun revolves this vast machine" (20) and "whirls surrounding spheres" (20).

She continues to concentrate upon the sun, "peerless monarch of th' ethereal train," by enumerating the vast distance between it and her contemplating persona: "of miles twice forty millions is his height" (20). In establishing this distance (even though inaccurately), the poet has swiftly shifted the center of focus eighty million miles from "mighty Sol" to the persona and her world on earth:

> And yet his radiance dazzles mortal sight
> So far beneath—from him th' extended earth
> Vigour derives, and ev'ry flow'ry birth. (20).

The enjambment of the last three lines contributes to the image of speed traveled over a great distance and emphasizes the energy of this mental movement. Then Wheatley abruptly shifts the focus back to the cosmos:

> Vast though her orb she [the earth] moves with easy grace,
> Around her Phoebus in unbounded space.
> True to her course th' impetuous storm derides,
> Triumphant o'er the winds, and surging tides. (20)

Once again the imagination of the reader soars with the persona's. The pattern established here resembles Kant's illustration of the mind "set in motion in the representation of the sublime in nature." "This movement," Kant writes, "especially in its inception, may be compared with a vibration, i.e. with a rapidly alternating repulsion and attraction produced by one and the same Object."[46] Herein lies the negative pleasure of the sublime. When the imagination is raised high, it can sustain itself only briefly before falling into failure. Wheatley's energetic illustration of this alternate rise and fall depicts Kant's "vibration."

Having represented the boundless imagination, she devotes the remainder of "Thoughts" to a tabulation of God's goodness and wisdom as they affect the immediate world of man and nature. "Thoughts" concludes with a philosophical dialectic between Reason and Love in which the reason discovers the solution to the question " 'What most the image of th' Eternal shows?' " (22). She resolves the problem of her dialectic by asserting that "infinite *Love*" appears "wher'er we turn our eyes" (23). The persona's contemplation of the deity has taught her to discover a benevolent totality and design in "Great God, incomprehensible, unknown / By sense." Contemplating the sublimity of the universe causes "our imagination in all its boundlessness, and with it nature," to sink "into insignificance before the ideas of reason, once their adequate presentation is attempted." In other words, Wheatley has represented Kant's mathematical sublime.

She equally expresses Kant's dynamic sublime in her intense desire for union with God. Kant makes several observations about the dynamic sublime which apply directly to Wheatley's poetics of ascent. The dynamic sublime, Kant insists, "must be represented as a source of fear,"[47] which awe and astonishment create. He maintains, however, that such fear can incite the feeling of sublimity only in the most moral: "the righteous man fears God without being afraid of Him, because he regards the case of his wishing to resist God and His commandments as one which need cause *him* [*sic*] no anxiety."[48] This last statement implies an idea needing explanation. Whereas God was the implicit goal of the mathematical sublime (echoing Addison's incitement to devotion), He is the explicit end of the dynamic sublime. Such is surely the case of Wheatley's poetics of ascent. In her elegies, she agrees with Kant; for only the virtuous and exemplary receive the reward of union with God. Kant maintains that the righteous man fears God's overwhelming might and simultaneously enjoys that fear as imaginative or poetic. He explains:

> . . . it is only under presupposition of this idea [the feeling of the sublime] within us, and in relation to it, that we are capable of attaining to the idea of the sublimity of that Being which inspires deep respect in us, not by the mere display of its might in nature, but more by the faculty which is planted in us of estimating that might without fear, and of regarding our estate as exalted above it [i.e., fear].[49]

In the concluding section of the "Analytic of the Sublime," Kant restates this necessary precondition of moral consciousness: "As a matter of fact, a feeling for the sublime in nature is hardly thinkable unless in association with an attitude of mind resembling the moral."[50] The moral man, says Kant, is capable of the affection of "*astonishment* amounting almost to terror, the awe and thrill of devote feeling, that takes hold of one when gazing upon the prospect of mountains ascending to heaven, deep ravines and torrents raging there, and deep-shadowed solitudes that invite to brooding melancholy."[51] The spirits of *Sturm* and *Drang* and nineteenth-century romanticism gather here. Kant closes by reminding the reader that "the sublime must in every case have reference to our *way of thinking*, i.e. to maxims directed to giving the intellectual side of our nature and the ideas or reason supremacy over sensibility."[52] Kant then reiterates the importance of the instrument of reason:

> . . . though the imagination, no doubt, finds nothing beyond the sensible world to which it can lay hold, still this thrusting aside of the sensible barriers gives it a feeling of being unbounded; and that removal is thus a presentation of the infinite. As such it can never be anything more than a negative presentation—but still it expands the soul.[53]

Kant's dynamic sublime describes Wheatley's poetics of ascent in its most exalted achievement—freedom. Kant concedes that freedom is the final end of the sublime: "*The inscrutability of the idea of freedom* precludes all positive presentation."[54] So artists like Wheatley must be content with negative representations. Here one may recall her letter to the Indian evangelist Samson Occum in which she writes that all men, including her enslaved black brethren, possess an intense "Love of Freedom" which "is impatient of Oppression and pants for Deliverance."[55] Her "Love of Freedom" moves beyond that of the political freedom hoped for in "Liberty and Peace" and "To His Excellency General Washington"; rather she most fervently and most consistently seeks the "beautitude beyond the skies" (40). This quest for divine knowledge exceeds mere enjoyment and resembles Kant's dynamic sublime.

"An Elegy . . . on the Death of . . . John Moorhead" demonstrates this resemblance. Here the persona describes the confessed sinner's contemplation of the sun as being symbolic not simply of God's benevolence but also of his anger: "Jehovah's Wrath revolving, he [the confessed sinner] surveys, / The Fancy's terror, and the Soul's amaze" (80). Like Kant's righteous man, Wheatley's confessed "sinner" fears the potential anger of Jehovah, as seen in the fancy's association of the sun with God's might. But at the same time this image of power transcends the sensible world and "expands the soul." Such expansion, "the Soul's amaze," instills a feeling of the sublime—fear and courage or what Kant terms astonishment. This "representation" of divine wrath is mental and not finally dependent upon images of sense. The sublime image of the sun, "Jehovah's Wrath revolving," replete with might of potential destruction, lifts the mind from the ordinary to metaphysical contemplation.

This feeling of the sublime, Kant insists, embraces resignation:

> Even humility, taking the form of an uncompromising judgement upon his short-comings, which, with the consciousness of good intentions, might readily be glossed over on the ground of the frailty of human nature, is a sublime temper of the mind voluntarily to undergo the pain of remorse as a means of more and more effectually eradicating its cause.[56]

In his *Elements*, Lord Kames had expressed a similar notion of the sublime feeling much earlier in this century: ". . . but then every one must be sensible, that the emotion [the sublime feeling] is merely a flash, which, vanishing instantaneously, gives way to humility and veneration."[57] This feeling of humility induced by the sublime accounts for the recurrent self-depreciation Wheatley's personae make throughout her work. In "To Maecenas" her persona says that she "fain would mount, and ride upon the wind" but is prevented by "a grov'ling mind" (3). In "On Imagination," however, she asserts that "We on thy [Imagination's] pinions can surpass the wind" (30). Anticipating Wordsworth's "winds that will be howling at all hours," this wind imagery assumes a force of sublimity.

Wheatley's most piquant expression of humility comes when painful reality intrudes upon her world. Foreshadowing Keats, this painful surrender appears in the conclusion of "On Imagination." Following a warm description of a mythical realm, its "mountains tipt with radiant gold" (recall Kant's "prospect of mountains ascending to heaven"), her persona remarks "But I reluctant leave the pleasing views" because "Winter austere forbids me to aspire, / And northern tempests damp the rising fire" (31). Having resigned the cooling of poetic afflatus to the reality of the encroaching "northern tempests" of gelid winter, the persona exclaims, "Cease then, my song, cease the unequal lay" (31). The "lay" ends not because the poet is less competent than any other good one, but because no person can indefinitely sustain a mythical world. Wheatley has once more attempted to ascend toward the sublime notion of deity—to seek momentary release from the temporal world "Oppress'd with woes." She has consequently endured again Kant's "pain of remorse."

Although Phillis Wheatley's aesthetic of the sublime parallels many theories expressed by major eighteenth-century figures who preceded her including John Dennis, Joseph Addison, Edmund Burke, and Lord Kames, it shows marked similarities to the "Analytic" of Immanuel Kant whose work followed her death by six years. Like the German philosopher, she identifies the imagination as the means toward grasping partial knowledge of the deity; she employs imagery of the solar system as the most exalted symbol of God in nature, illustrating the mathematical sublime; her passionate desire to ascend toward heavenly and absolute freedom represents the dynamic sublime; and finally, her demonstration of humility epitomizes the sublime as a negative pleasure. Such a comparative study invites two conclusions about this young black American poet. Her use of the sublime as the primary manifestation of her poetics of ascent indicates that she was a serious poet. But focus upon the sublime as it appears in her poetry suggests that Wheatley's work falls into a tradition which foreshadows the "romanticism" (an inadequate term) of the nineteenth century.

Notes

1. (1935; rpt. Ann Arbor: Univ. of Michigan Press, 1970), p. 24—hereafter cited as *The Sublime.*

2. David B. Morris, *The Religious Sublime: Christian Poetry and Critical Tradition in 18th Century England* (Lexington: Univ. of Kentucky Press, 1972), p. 99—hereafter cited as Morris.

3. *The Sublime*, p. 24.

4. Monk writes in *The Sublime* that for Addison "Greatness is identical with sublimity, but Addison prefers not to use the latter term, probably because of its association with rhetoric and purely critical writing" (p. 57).

5. *The Spectator*, ed. Donald F. Bond (London: Oxford Univ. Press, 1965), III, 540—hereafter cited as Bond.

6. *The Sublime*, p. 58.

7. Bond, III, 545.

8. Bond, III, 545.

9. In the introduction to his edition of Burke's *Enquiry*, J. T. Boulton distinguishes between Addison's claim that "the delight afforded by 'Greatness' was divinely ordained to lead to contemplation of the nature and power of God" and Burke's sensationist explanation in the *Enquiry* that stimulus to the sublime operates upon the mind's power to associate previously recorded sensations and to produce affections of awe and wonder, the most powerful stimulus being that of terror (p. 1).

10. Edited by J. T. Boulton (New York: Columbia Univ. Press, 1958), p. 107—hereafter cited as Burke. Although Burke sprinkles throughout his treatise such phrases as "the infinitely wise and good creator," his center of interest is directed not toward God and devotion but toward the analytical psychology of response.

11. Burke, p. 39.

12. See Monk's discussion on p. 91 of *The Sublime* where he concludes: ". . . in introducing pain as the basis of sublimity, he [Burke] opens the way for the inclusion of ideas and images in art that had hitherto been considered as lying properly outside the sphere of aesthetic pleasure."

13. J. T. Boulton, editor of Burke's *Enquiry*, deduces that "Kames's *Elements of Criticism*, though not published until 1761, was partly written and possibly wholly planned before Burke's work could have exerted any influence" (p. lxxxiii).

14. 6th ed. (1785; rpt. New York: Garland Publishing, 1973), I, 211—hereafter cited as Kames.

15. Immanuel Kant, *Critique of Aesthetic Judgement*, trans. and ed. James C. Meredith (Oxford: Clarendon Press, 1911), p. 114—hereafter cited as Kant.

16. Kames, p. 220.

17. Kames, p. 223.

18. Kames, p. 256.

19. *The Critical Works of John Dennis*, ed. Edward N. Hooker (Baltimore: Johns Hopkins Press, 1939), I, 338—hereafter cited as Dennis.

20. Dennis, p. 339.

21. Dennis, p. 356.

22. Dennis, p. 363.

23. See volume one of Dennis' *Critical Works,* especially pp. 271, 325–26, 363–73, for Dennis' own testimony to this position and Morris's *The Religious Sublime,* p. 63, which corroborates this assertion.

24. Dennis, p. 339.

25. Morris, p. 98.

26. Morris, p. 103.

27. Morris, p. 99.

28. Morris, pp. 107–08.

29. *The Interpreter's Bible,* ed. George A. Buttrick (Nashville: Abingdon Press, 1956), V, 726.

30. The reader should be reminded that this sort of invocation, although much in vogue throughout the eighteenth century, in Wheatley indicates a fusion of pagan classicism with Protestant Christianity.

31. Morris, p. 114.

32. Morris, p. 114.

33. Bond, IV, 114.

34. Bond, IV, 234.

35. Morris, p. 134.

36. It should be remarked that Kant does not, of course, confine this idea of noumena to the feeling of the sublime. The idea of noumena arises in Kant's analysis of the practical reason as describing objects or powers which transcend experience but whose existence must be postulated in order to explain the possibility of "inscrutable freedom." Kant sets up the pure reason as the faculty of conceptualization based upon sensory experience.

37. Kant, p. 94.

38. Kant, p. 107.

39. Kant, p. 94.

40. *A History of Philosophy*, VI, *Modern Philosophy*, Pt. II, *Kant* (Garden City, N.Y.: Doubleday, 1970), II, 51.

41. Kant, p. 98.

42. Kant, p. 98.

43. Kant, p. 103.

44. Kant, p. 105.

45. Kant, p. 105. Such contemplation precedes Wheatley, Kames, and Kant by some 3,000 years. At least from Pythagoras' time and his musical harmony of the spheres, man has looked at the stars as a macrocosm of universal harmony. He has thought himself to be a microcosm of that harmony. For further information see *The Dictionary of the History of Ideas*, especially Gretchen L. Finney, "Harmony or Rapture in Music" (II, 388–95) and George Boas, "Macrocosm and Microcosm" (III, 126–31).

46. Kant, p. 107.

47. Kant, p. 109.

48. Kant, p. 110.

49. Kant, p. 114.

50. Kant, p. 120.

51. Kant, pp. 120–21.

52. Kant, p. 127.

53. Kant, p. 127.

54. Kant, p. 128.

55. From the letter to Occum quoted in Charles W. Aker's " 'Our Modern Egyptians': Phillis Wheatley and the Whig Campaign Against Slavery in Revolutionary Boston," *Journal of Negro History*, 60 (1975), 406.

56. Kant, p. 114.

57. Kames, pp. 242–43.

Phillis

Naomi Long Madgett*

I hardly remember my mother's face now,
But I still feel
At my bosom a chill wind
Stirring strange longings for the sturdy back
I used to lean against for warmth and comfort
When I had grown too tall to ride.

And I am blinded by
The glint of sunlight
Striking golden fire from the flint
Of seafoamed rocks below me
On some island not too far from home.

After that, the only light I saw
Was a few wayward chinks of day
That somehow slanted into the airless tomb
Where chains confined me motionless to a dank wall.

Then the sun died and time went out completely.
In that new putrid helltrap of the dead
And dying, the stench
Of vomit, sweat, and feces
Mingled with the queasy motion
Of the ship until my senses failed me. . . .

I do not know how many weeks or months
I neither thought nor felt, but I awoke
One night—or day, perhaps—
Revived by consciousness of sound.
I heard
The pounding of the waves against the shipside
And made believe its rhythm

*Reprinted with the permission of the author.

Was the speech of tribal drums
Summoning in acute need the spirit
Of my ancestors. I dreamed I saw
Their carven images arrayed
In ceremonial austerity. I thought I heard
Their voices thundering an answer
To my supplication: "Hold fast.
Sur/vive sur/vive sur/*vive!*"
And then I slept again.

Once more the sunlight came, but not the same
As I remembered it. Now it sat silver-cold
Upon the indifferent New England coast. Still
It was good to see the sun at all.
And it was something
To find myself the bright dark mascot
Of a blind but well-intentioned host—
A toy, a curiosity, a child
Taking delight in anyone's attention
After so long a death.

As I grew older, it was not enough.
The native lifesong once again burst free,
Spilled over sands of my acquired rituals—
Urged me to match the tribal rhythms
That had so long sustained me, that must
Sustain me still. I learned to sing
A dual song:

My fathers will forgive me if I lie
For they instructed me to live, not die.
"Grief cannot compensate for what is lost,"
They told me. "Win, and never mind the cost.
Show to the world the face the world would see;
Be slave, be pet, conceal your Self—but be."

Lurking behind the docile Christian lamb,
Unconquered lioness asserts: "I am!"

Phillis Wheatley and the Elegiac Mode

Mukhtar Ali Isani*

Phillis Wheatley not only gained her initial fame with an elegy, the celebrated poem on George Whitefield's death in 1770, but over the remaining years of her life retained her place in the public eye in no small part because of her facility with the elegy. A third of her compositions in *Poems on Various Subjects, Religious and Moral* (1773) are elegies. Elegies appear in like proportion among the poems she tried in vain to publish as her second collection, in 1779. She receives little recognition as an elegist, but these poems have merit. They make effective use of the mix of elegiac traditions prevailing in the poet's time. While they are comparatively numerous, they are genuine effusions of a feeling heart. While they appear to be composed with rapidity and sometimes even in haste, they are generally the result of careful planning and thoughtful revision. Their faults are obvious but their strengths must also be noted. Certainly, these poems lent her much of her contemporaneous fame.

In New England of Wheatley's day, the elegy not only bore the approval of the past but could also claim the favor of a considerable segment of the reading public of the time. It received its share of space in the colonial newspapers and was welcome fare in the magazines. With proper appreciation of the power of "sympathy," a typical editor encouraged another young lady who showed signs of talent in this mode and announced: "We are ready to indulge the 'luxury of grief' whenever she shall think proper to 'attune our soul to woe.' " This was an age of sentiment, conducive to the flow of the elegy.

Wheatley's elegy on Whitefield was, of course, one of many written about the divine. But her poem was recognized as "extraordinary." Both the age and status of the author and the quality of the verse were matters for comment. One advertiser went so far as to declare: "This excellent Piece ought to be preserved for two good Reasons, first, in Remembrance of that great and good Man, Mr. Whitefield, and second on Account of its being wrote by a Native of Africa, and yet would have done Honor to a Pope or Shakespere."[1]

*Published with the permission of the author.

One can only guess how much Wheatley knew of the background of the elegy. She must have had some knowledge of the neoclassic effort and a lesser awareness of the earlier use of the genre—for example, by Ovid, with whom she shows familiarity. She was equally heir to the elegiac tradition of Puritan America, and in many ways her poems hark back to the popular usage of the century before.

The poet may have had no knowledge of Greek poetics, but she understood the primacy of the *anagnorisis* or "revelation" in the elegy. Her elegy is basically a didactic poem which has as its climax a comforting revelation, both philosophic and religious. In its Aristotelian sense, the *anagnorisis* is significantly "a transition from ignorance to knowledge."[2] The metaphors of light and darkness, common to the elegy, she found especially useful. Light had been used freely in the seventeenth and eighteenth centuries as a symbol of love, profane and holy. In Wheatley's elegiac verse, it is generally used to depict the transition to the immortal state. It depicts love, purity, and true knowledge, but also faith and hope, and is placed in opposition to the dark. "On the Death of the Rev. Dr. Sewell" paints a heavenward rising Sewall with a "brighter lustre than the sun." In the Whitefield elegy, the poet appeals to the moon and the "stars of light" to present testimony on behalf of the departed evangelist. Repeatedly in her verse, she describes the passage from the "vale of night" to the "hills of light." The "light divine," symbolized by the refulgence of the sun, is the light without which would prevail "the reign of endless night." Light, reminds the poet, is "the first fair product of th' omnific God" (22).[3] Those mourning "beneath the cypress-shade," are reminded of "the fair sunshine of celestial day" (46–47). Death brings only a temporary darkening. Thus, the virtues of Mrs. Thankfull Leonard, shining with "rays divinely bright," are clouded briefly with the "shades of night" but soon expand into "unbounded Love" (78).

More than personal piety is responsible for the religious flavor of Wheatley's poems. The influence of the tradition of the New England funeral elegy is especially evident.[4] By Wheatley's time, the funeral elegy, once the prerogative of the clerics, was almost entirely the work of laymen, including those with no special call to letters. Broadsides remained in vogue, but increasingly such verse was appearing through the cheaper media of newspapers and magazines. The didactic emphasis and the use of mortuary detail continued, but the latter was declining. Wheatley's use of pentameter couplets and emphatic mortuary reminders is in the tradition of New England funerary verse. Current practice was responsible for encouraging the use of the stock image and phrase. The recurring personification of Death, the frequent return to "the mansions of the dead," the visions of spirits, and the sounds of angelic choirs had the sanction of the time. Occasionally, the poet can be accused of sentimentalism, but the neoclassic restraint which was changing the tone of the Puritan elegy was also an influence on Wheatley's poetry.

In its choice of elements and in its emphasis, Wheatley's elegiac verse bears a stamp of its own. The poet set up a pattern and, unfortunately, often repeated herself. Her typical elegy is not principally a song of sorrow. It is a poem of solace through praise. It often relies on dialogue to achieve *anagnorisis*. Its setting is not in this world but in the next, and its comfort is based on the pious philosophy that the world to come is a happier place than man's terrestrial home.

There are only two movements in Wheatley's elegy: the lament and the consolation, with the consolation outweighing the lament in emphasis. Viewing the elegy as a poem of comfort, Wheatley vocalizes the grief of those closest to the deceased. The poet seldom appears in the elegiac image; she speaks with an authorial omniscience. As the titles suggest, the poems were written for the bereaved. With few exceptions, such as the elegy on Whitefield, the humanistic pondering in the general on the loss to mankind is either secondary or absent. Fully half the elegies in *Poems on Various Subjects* are addressed to specific individuals directly in the titles and nearly all subsequent elegies are addressed in like manner.

The elegies of Wheatley also express her own sense of loss. They are not artificial exercises in a long popular mode. Though suggestions have been made to the contrary, there is no evidence that they were written on request. When the subject of an elegy is identifiable, it is clear that the poet wrote about people she knew and thus did not make a gesture devoid of feeling or calculated to enhance her fame. Of the fourteen elegies in *Poems on Various Subjects*, the first is on her pastor, the Reverend Joseph Sewall of Boston's Old South Church, and one whose death she had already anticipated with grief in August, 1765. The second is on the evangelist Whitefield, a man she saw as a saint and knew through personal acquaintance. There is one on Dr. Samuel Marshall, a Boston physician she appears to have known through his wife Lucy, admitted to membership in the Old South Church on the day of Wheatley's admission. Two notables who signed the introductory attestation in her book, Thomas Hubbard and Lieutenant-Governor Andrew Oliver, had poems addressed to them, as did Hubbard's daughter on the death of her husband. There is an elegy addressed to the Reverend Timothy Pitkin of Farmington, Connecticut, brother-in-law of a benefactor of Wheatley, David Wooster, who later became the subject of an elegy himself.[5] The poet's practice of using partial names and dashes to assure privacy creates problems for identification of names, but there are suggestions of familiarity, and research will continue to prove the assertion that the elegies express genuine emotion.

Wheatley's poems are poems of solace, but though she would have disagreed, the lamentation and not the Christian consolation is often poetically the stronger part of her elegy. There is a fair variety of method. The entry into the poem is swift and effective, and the apotheosis may come at the beginning rather than near the climax. In her initial elegy, the very first line places Whitefield on his "immortal throne." The second line of the Sewall elegy lets the reader find the pastor "number'd with the happy dead." The poet commences with a vision of the mourner or the mourned, or with general thoughts on "Death's domain." Images such as those of Lucy Marshall rending "the graceful tresses from her head" or Mary Moorhead finding that "various Anguish rocks her Soul by turns" once served to provide recognition of their bereavement; they still quickly establish the personal touch in these poems which are almost formulaic in pattern. The apostrophe to Death or the melancholy rumination on his power are of course typical stylistic devices of Wheatley's time, and the poet uses them to advantage. In one poem he is called "All conquering." In another, his "awful" power is traced "from tomb to tomb" and we are reminded, more imaginatively, that

> "His too, when all in his dark realms are hurl'd,
> From its firm base to shake the solid world;
> His fatal sceptre rules the spacious whole,
> And trembling nature rocks from pole to pole. (23)

Elsewhere she goes on to rhetorically demand, "Dost thou go on incessant to destroy / Our griefs to double, and lay waste our joy?" (12). Such passages provide a necessary broadening of focus and check the poet's tendency toward excess of piety.

The consolation suffers from its limited imagery. The poet is drawn to stock images (upward rising souls, "heav'ns high palaces," heavenly choirs, and the like) and the repeated recommendation to focus on the lasting joys of the world to come. The dialogue of solace between the dead and the living is not common in the poetry of the time. Wheatley's fairly extensive use of this device may have aroused no comment, but the method does not elicit approval in the modern age. It proved effective as a means of providing comfort for the bereaved but appears a weakening force to those of another day inclined to read her compositions principally as works of art.

As an occasional poem, the elegy had to be written relatively quickly. Wheatley's artistic concern is evident in the variant versions available, showing how painstakingly she developed the poems and the care with which she returned to the elegies even after original publication. Her changes range from the alteration of a few words to the addition of enough matter to almost double the original length. Of the original sixty lines in the manuscript version of the Sewall elegy, only six remain unchanged. "On the Death of J. C. an Infant" had only twenty-three lines in manuscript; Wheatley added nineteen more.[6] The difference between broadside versions and the later book versions is less dramatic but still significant. The poet could not always stand back and survey the work of passion with complete objectivity, but she was undeniably persevering in the service of the craft. Both thought and feeling blend in her elegies, though feeling has the edge.

The purpose of Wheatley's elegies was, in most cases, the provision of emotional support. "Permit the Muse that healing to impart," she implores the Reverend Pitkin. "Let Recollection bear a tender part / To sooth and calm the tortures of your heart," she advises Thomas Hubbard. If only the poet could see the happiness of the dead, she wishes in another poem. Then

> What heav'nly grandeur should exalt her strain!
> What holy raptures in her numbers reign!
> To sooth the troubles of the mind to peace,
> To still the tumult of life's tossing seas,
> To ease the anguish of the parents heart,
> What shall my sympathizing verse impart? (12)

Even among the more critical, it is only in the aggregate that the elegies fail to find favor. There are several good elegies. When the poet's feelings are strongest, the poems are generally strongest. When a close personal relationship is involved, the poem succeeds in presenting both pathos and art. But often Wheatley writes of an anguish which is only indirectly hers. The poems on children, some merely infants, lessen the sum total of her achievement in the elegy. To a degree, she felt their parents' pain, but the deeper sense of bereavement that gave weight to the poems on Whitefield, Marshall, and Cooper could not be there; the pain was once removed. The resulting heavy resort to pious but conventional images weakens the verse.

The better elegies owe much of their strength to the sense of personal loss and to a substantial discussion of the attributes of the deceased. In the elegy on Samuel Cooper, another notable who signed the attestation bound in her book, a maturer poet emphasizes her bereavement, picking from long-shared experience and observation, and mourning "a BROTHER with a BROTHER's heart." The image of the lingering fragrance of the wilted rose is far more effective than the stock images she uses elsewhere. Likewise, the brief elegy on Dr. Marshall gains from Wheatley's relationship with Lucy Marshall and the knowledge of "The babe unborn [who] in the dark womb is tost, / And seems in anguish for its father lost." It is not the vision of an "Æsculapius" which stays with the reader, but that of a father:

> Gone is *Apollo* from his house of earth,
> But leaves the sweet memorials of his worth:
> The common parent, whom we all deplore,
> From yonder world unseen must come no more,
> Yet 'midst our woes immortal hopes attend
> The spouse, the sire, the universal friend. (41)

While Wheatley studiously keeps the focus of the elegy on the deceased and the mourning kin, occasionally she projects herself into the poem. In the final lines of the poem to the Reverend Pitkin, she describes herself as the healer. In the elegy to Lieutenant-Governor Oliver, the unusual origin of the poet is identified to strengthen the religious testimony, for these are "heav'nly tidings from the *Afric* muse." She joins John Moorhead's congregation with the plural "we" and "us" in "An Elegy to Miss Mary Moorhead." In the elegy on the Samuel Cooper, we have principally a lament, and as one of the bereaved, Wheatley enters deliberately to record her grief:

> The hapless Muse, her loss in COOPER mourns,
> And as she sits, she writes, and weeps, by turns;
> A Friend sincere, whose mild indulgent grace
> Encourag'd oft, and oft approv'd her lays." (92)

While feeling fully a part of the multitudes united in Christ, Wheatley nevertheless remembered the separate identity and different fortunes of her race. In her poem on Whitefield, as she offers the divine to the various categories of mankind, she presents him also to the "Africans," for "Impartial SAVIOUR, is his title due." Those who follow his path, she declares, "shall be sons, and kings, and priests to God," a promise changed in the English broadside to "He'll make you free, and Kings, and Priests to God," explicitly including a higher freedom for her fettered people. In the yet uncollected poem, "On the Death of General Wooster," primarily an expression of patriotism and of gratitude to one who had shown interest in the fortunes of the poet and in the welfare of her race, Wheatley makes an abrupt switch from the praise of the Americans' struggle for freedom to the irony of the same people denying liberty to their African slaves. As the dying hero, facing heaven, prays for the success of "Columbia's" arms against the British, he interjects:

> But how, presumptuous shall we hope to find
> Divine acceptance with th' Almighty mind—
> While yet (O deed Ungenerous!) they disgrace
> And hold in bondage Afric's blameless race?[7]

For a poet who generally effaces herself in her elegies, the inclusion of such an interjection shows the strength of feelings she did not often express. Artificial as some of the methods may appear, these are poems from the heart.

The elegies of Wheatley are not her finest poems, but both the poet and her age saw much merit in them. They make effective use of practices accepted in her time. They are serious poetic efforts, flawed for a later age by the resort to convention and the freedom given to personal habit but strong in their sincerity and the spontaneity of utterance from a feeling heart. The stricter classicism of masters like Pope plays no major part in these elegies. Like Thompson, Gray, Goldsmith, and her countryman Freneau, Wheatley too was widening the range of eighteenth-century sensibility while working within the basic tradition of the age.

Notes

1. *New Hampshire Gazette,* October 19, 1770, p. 3, col. 2.

2. An excellent discussion of the classical background of elegiac poetry is available in Abbie Findlay Potts, *The Elegiac Mode: Poetic Form in Wordsworth and Other Elegists* (Ithaca: Cornell Univ. Press, 1967), pp. 36–66.

3. Page numbers given within parentheses in the text of this essay refer to *The Poems of Phillis Wheatley,* ed. Julian D. Mason, Jr. (Chapel Hill: Univ. of North Carolina Press, 1966). When the title or other adequate reference is given, the page numbers are omitted.

4. For a discussion of the funeral elegy in Colonial America, see John W. Draper, *The Funeral Elegy and the Rise of English Romanticism* (New York: Phaeton Press, 1967), pp. 155–77.

5. The Reverend Timothy Pitkin (1727–1812) was married to Temperance, the daughter of Thomas Clap. Mary, the sister of Temperance, was married to David Wooster, later to become a Revolutionary War general and the subject of Wheatley's elegy, "On the Death of General Wooster." See Franklin B. Dexter, *Biographical Sketches of the Graduates of Yale College* (New York: Henry Holt, 1896), II, 129–32; John Langdon Sibley, *Biographical Sketches of Those Who Attended Harvard College* (Boston: Massachusetts Historical Society, 1945), VIII, 48; William B. Sprague, *Annals of the American Pulpit* (New York: Robert Carter, 1859), I, 347n.

6. The early version was eventually published in Philadelphia. For the text, see *Methodist Magazine,* 1 (September, 1797), 431–32; reprinted in *Early American Literature,* 14 (Fall, 1979), 154.

7. Mukhtar Ali Isani, " 'On the Death of General Wooster': An Unpublished Poem by Phillis Wheatley," *Modern Philology,* 77 (February, 1980), 308.

[Phillis Wheatley and the Nature of the Negro]

Henry Louis Gates, Jr.*

There never was a civilized nation of any complexion than white, nor even any individual eminent in action or speculation. No ingenious manufacturers amongst them, no art, no sciences. On the other hand, the most rude and barbarous of the whites, such as the antient Germans, or the present Tartars, have still something eminent about them. In their valour, form of government, or some other particular. Such a uniform and constant difference could not happen, in so many countries and ages, if nature had not made an original distinction betwixt these breeds of men.

—David Hume

I

The matter of the nature of the Negro was one of intense speculation and enthusiastic surmise during and after "the case of James Sommersett, a Negro."[1] Samuel Estwick, the assistant agent for the Island of Barbados,[2] was so enraged by Lord Mansfield's judgment in the case that he, by his own admission, dashed off an impassioned, open reply near the end of 1772.[3] He significantly expanded a second edition so that his argument might be a more cogent one. Estwick's anonymous first edition was meant essentially to rebut Lord Mansfield's verdict in favor of the Negro by demonstrating that Negro slavery was an innovation in the history of human institutions, one unknown to common law, and "totally different" from ancient villeinage. His second edition, however, contained this argument but rather expanded to address what he now decided was to be the crux of Hargray's argument.[4]

In what must stand as one of the most peculiar assortments of popular and philosophical speculation on the matter, Samuel Estwick, by way of Saome Jenyns, John Locke, David Hume, and Pope, among others, structures a carefully considered affront on the nature of the Negro. Estwick's tract reveals tellingly the peculiar fashion in which romance, myth, and metaphor, coupled with rather imaginative

*Excerpted and abridged from the manuscript of *The Idea of Blackness in Western Discourse* (New York: Oxford University Press, 1982). With the permission of the author.

anatomical and philosophical disquisitions, meet in the vulgar practical application of the metaphor of a chain of being as a rigid construct of nature, which somehow, is held to exist in fact.

The urge to draw distinctions, Estwick argues, is perhaps the fundamental urge of modern science, uniting human reason and imagination in a grand synthesis as noble and as old as Aristotle. Nevertheless, modern man somehow flinches when confronted with the awful truth about his own condition. Why should that same principle found in nature, which allows man to separate both "vegetable and mineral kingdoms of this world" into "systems morally perfect," comprised of hundreds of subdivisions, not hold true for the varieties of man? The suggestion that mankind is above the principles of nature, profoundly uniform and "democratic" in every particular, can be folly, Estwick concludes, or else a species of hubris resoundingly aberrant.

Not only is this supposition an affront to reason, it defies that Divine sanction accorded the "great chain" itself.

> Does this not seem to break in upon and unlink that great chain of Heaven, which in due gradation joins and unites the whole with all its parts? May it not be more perfective of the system to say, that human nature is a class, comprehending an order of beings, of which man is the genus, divided into distinct and separate species of man? All other species of the animal kingdom have their marks of distinction: why should man be universally indiscriminate one to the other?[5]

The crux of the issue at hand, Estwick argues, is with what measure philosophy should determine that elusive "characteristic difference" between man and man? That which makes man a distinct creature from beasts, according to "the great Mr. Locke," is the exercise of reason. The measure, Estwick suggests, must not be reason, since Locke suggests that beasts to some degree share in the exercise of reason; it is, rather, the existence of a "moral sense." Estwick reasons that the single "faculty of the human mind," shared by all manner of the varieties of men, is "the capacity of perceiving moral relations." Further, and quite crucially, the "compound ratio of its exercise" must stand as nature's own way for men to draw distinctions among men. Where the faculty of reason serves "to raise [man] from the tenth to the ten thousandth link of the chain," so too does the "compound ratio" of the exertion of moral sense mark man from man. These differences are nature's, Estwick maintains, and signify a "purpose" for which the varieties of man must be best suited, just as surely as nature has signified distinct inherent functions for the elephant and the flea.

The disquisition proceeds by citing Hume's theory of tropical degeneration of the human mind. The tropical climate leaves the mind "utterly incapable of all the higher attainments. ' Moreover, Hume maintains, "there are four or five different *kinds* of men," by which he meant species.[7] The idea of multiple human species of men proved compelling to Estwick, but, perhaps surprisingly, only because he found it hyperbolic. "In order to have different *species* of men," Estwick comments on Hume's suggestion, it did not seem to him to be "at all necessary to have four or five different *kinds*."[8] There is, "but one" genus or "kind," that is, "mankind," comprised of "sorts" or "species" of men.[9] Then, citing Hume fully on the metonymic relation between "white" and "civilization"—"no arts, no sciences"—Estwick contrasts that by which Hume "marks the difference betwixt the several species of men," and that by which Estwick does.[10] Hume, as did Locke, distinguished man one from another "by their natural capacity or incapacity of exerting in degree the rational powers, or faculties of understanding. . . ."

Such was the distinction Locke employed to distinguish "between man and brutes."[11] Estwick, on the other hand, draws his boundaries with "the moral sense or moral powers. . . ." The exercise of reason, called for as a privileged category by Locke and Hume, was an unsatisfactory one because blacks could obviously read and write, skills learned through imitation and repetition

> . . . nor have I been able to find one author, by whom I could discover that there was any sort of plan or system of morality conceived by these tribes of Africa, or practised among them. Their barbarity to their children debases their nature even below that of brutes. Their cruelty to their aged parents is a kin to this. They have a religion, it is true; but it is a religion, [not] in *kind*, but in *species;* and verifying that unerring truth of Mr. Pope, that
>
> "Order is heaven's first law; and this contest,
> Some are, and must be, greater than the rest. . . .[12]

In sum, Estwick concludes, these physical and metaphysical "insuperable barriers" demonstrate conclusively that the Negro is a man apart from "the inhabitants of Europe" and destined to remain so. His proper place in European society is to serve "as articles of its trade and commerce only." The African, therefore, was consigned a slave by nature.

That Estwick's *Consideration on the Negro Cause* is emblematic of shared concerns of European and American philosophers wrestling with the unreconcilable contradictions of human enslavement, can be gleaned from a reading of the "pamphlet debate" over African mental capacity which raged in Philadelphia later in that same year, and especially in the curious history of Phillis, Negro servant to John Wheatley of Boston, and the curious history of the critical reception to her slim volume of *Poems on Various Subjects, Religious and Moral.*

Perhaps it is appropriately ironic that Phillis Wheatley—who contained so painstakingly her poetic concerns within highly contrived and classically structured decasyllabic lines of closed heroic couplets, which seem in retrospect to have been about the direct imitation of neoclassical poetic models rather than the imitation of nature or the fanciful invention of peculiarly American forms—would be judged by critics whose poetics seemed to be grounded not in the praise of imitation and artifice, but in the praise of a supposed unmediated relation between genius and nature. A major shift in the first principles of neoclassical poetics involved a fundamental reorientation of emphasis from what was, in the most general and inclusive terms, called "art" to its equally abstract and inclusive "opposite," "nature."[13] In Sir William Temple's essays "Upon Poetry" and "Upon Ancient and Modern Learning" (1690), Dryden's "Origin and Progress of Satire" (1693), key passages in Pope's *Essay on Criticism,* Voltaire's *Essay Upon Epic Poetry* (1727), Thomas Blackwell's *Enquiry into the Life and Writings of Homer* (1735), Johnson's "Prefaces to Shakespeare" (1765), Vico's *Princippi d'una scienza nuova* (1744), and Herder's "Briefweschsel uber Ossian und die lieder alter Volker" (1773), "neoclassical" historians and critics

> began increasingly to examine the special rhetorical circumstances, environmental causes, and historical setting of the author's production—his gifts, education, life, audience, geographic location, climate, nationality, language, and the spirit or condition of his age—thus providing, in general, a variety of explanations and justifications of the peculiar forms and qualities of the works of poets in different social conditions, ages, and nations.[14]

A second profound shift of emphasis, which occurred concomitantly with a shift from the concern with art to nature, involved a marked concern for the "nature" of the poet which often entailed attempted correlations between untutored, natural "genius" and "imagination," on the one hand,[15] and the effects of temperature, geography, and race, on the other. This direct relation between environment and "genius" had been made in English neoclassical criticism as early as 1690. Sir William Temple's "theory about the connection between the variable English weather and the odd humor of Englishmen was one of the earliest instances of the explanation of literature by climatic conditions."[16] Joseph Warton, in his *Essay on Pope,* published in 1756, formalized this relation into a maxim; the proper critic could "never completely relish, or adequately understand, any author, especially any ancient, except we constantly keep in our eye, his climate, his country, and his age."[17] Three years later, Oliver Goldsmith, writing in his *Enquiry into the Present State of Polite Learning,* argued adamantly that criticism must "understand the nature of the climate and country &c. before it gives rules to direct taste. In other words, every country should have a national system of criticism."[18] But both Hume and Lord Kames (the former in 1748 in his essay "Of National Characters,"[19] and Kames in 1774 in his *Sketches of a History of Man)*[20] expressed skepticism of the role of climate or geographical conditions as the paramount variable in the forging of "genius." Robert Wood's *An Essay on the Original Genius and Writing of Homer*, published in 1769,[21] related his study of the topography of the site of Troy to Homer's depictions. Robert Lowth, in *De sacra poesi Hebraeorum*,[22] published in 1753, attempted much the same thing by comparing the character of Hebrew poetry with the Palestinian landscape as well as the imagery of the Old Testament. These late eighteenth-century neoclassical impulses, combined with a dramatically increased degree of speculation by "Americans" on the effects of "environment" on political, religious, and cultural institutions, determined the character of the critical response to the writing of African slaves between 1773 and 1831.[23]

Locke's denial of the existence of innate ideas, along with the discovery first by explorers and then by anatomists that the human species existed in a number of variations, "necessitated the assumption that variations within the species derived from some less august sponsorship" than from God's design.[24] The variability of man arose, then, of necessity, from variations in man's environment. Rather than the soul of man, the environment of man could be and need be transformed to usher in either the inner or, more importantly, the outer drama of "salvation." Human nature, however, as Benjamin Rush put it so bluntly in 1773, is everywhere "the same."

The assertions of the "sameness" of human nature presupposed not only that the distinctions between men were circumstantial and arbitrary but also that these distinctions could well be changed. "This postulation of quintessential human nature," Winthrop Jordan maintains, "formed the critical point of contact between environmentalist thinking and the political ideology of the Revolution."[25]The idea of "natural" rights, then, was one which had as a corollary the idea that men were everywhere in essence the same although their environments might make them appear to be different somehow, and were entitled by this very fact to all of the attendant "natural" rights of mankind. As early as 1764, James Otis's *The Rights of the British Colonies Asserted and Proved* declared boldly that "the Colonists are by the law of nature free born, as indeed all men are, white or black."[26] Thus, John Wesley could declare in 1774 that the suspected "stupidity" of the African was a result of an imposed condition. "Their stupidity therefore in our plantations is not natural; otherwise than it is the natural effect of their condition."[27] Similarly, Levi Hart could in the same atmosphere denounce racial slavery as "a flagrant violation of the law of nature, of the natural rights of mankind,"[28] rather than as a violation of some unwritten covenant between God and man. The ramifications of environmentalism and the natural rights of man are outlined sharply in the Quaker David Cooper's summation of the larger implications of the continued existence of slavery and the colonists' declaration of certain "self-evident" truths:

> If these solemn truths, uttered at such an awful crisis, are self-evident: unless we can shew that the African race are not men, words can hardly express the amazement which naturally arises on reflecting, that the very people who make these pompous declarations are slave-holders, and, by their legislative conduct, tell us, that these blessings were only meant to be the rights of *white-men* not of all men. . . .[29]

By the publication of Phillis Wheatley's *Poems* in September, 1773, discussions over "innate" and "acquired" mental and moral qualities of man had become the subject of an impassioned and bitter controversy which reached the public in the form of a pamphlet debate carried along by argument and rebuttal in Philadelphia.

In an anonymously published pamplet, printed at least four times in 1773 under the title of *An Address to the Inhabitants of the British Settlement in America, Upon Slave-Keeping,* Benjamin Rush, a noted Philadelphia physician, not only served to focus the philosophical problems of racial slavery in the British settlements of America on the matter of the nature of the African, but he also became the first "antislavery" advocate to cite the poetry of Phillis Wheatley as an irrefutable proof of the African's mental equality with the European and of the African's fundamentally human nature. Rush's argument not only intends to refute David Hume's "Of National Characters," but it also serves as a powerful summation of the philosophy of natural rights which had, notwithstanding James Otis and the implacable Anthony Benezet, been wanting a solid context for its application. If Estwick's hurriedly revised second edition had been a sign of a profound recasting of the terms of the debate against slavery, then Rush's modest essay would determine the contours of a debate which would involve Richard Nisbet and Edward Long, Thomas Jefferson and the Abbé Grégoire, Voltaire and Benjamin Franklin, Henri Christophe and Ralph Waldo Emerson. It is a debate, glibly described journalistically today, in the coded terms of "nature" versus "nurture," but which had its origin in the complex quandary of the supposed composition of "human nature," and the suggested "scales" by which this "commodity" would be "measured."

Rush situates his argument in Africa initially, then accounts for any "debasement" from the European ideal as being "occasioned by climate," and any debasement from the African "ideal" as being the result of the institution of slavery.

> And here I need hardly say anything in favor of the intellects of the Negroes, or of their capacities for virtue and happiness, although these have been supposed by some to be inferior to those of the inhabitants of Europe. The accounts which travellers give us of their ingenuity, humanity, and strong attachment to their parents, relations, friends, and country, show us that they are equal to the Europeans, when we allow for the diversity of temper and genius which is occasioned by climate.[30]

To allow for "the diversity of temper and genius," which is virtually determined by "climate," was an unusually liberal and sophisticated rebuttal of the idea of an absolute system of aesthetics, such as had been espoused in early neoclassical poetics. Rush's thesis is a seminal one, based as it is on a quasi-aesthetic "relativity" and its corollary "environmentalism."

Citing the *Spectator*[31] as his reference, Rush maintains that already "We have many well attested anecdotes of as sublime and disinterested virtue among them as ever adorned a Roman or Christian character." Again, in a footnote, he cites as evidence the example of "a free Negro Girl":

> There is now in the town of Boston a free Negro Girl, about eighteen years of age, who has been but nine years in the country, whose singular genius and accomplishments are such as not only do honour to her sex, but to human nature. Several of her poems have been printed, and read with pleasure by the public.[32]

Well before her book of verse was to appear, Phillis, "a free Negro Girl," had been called upon as a living refutation of the charge of innate Negro inferiority and, concomitantly, as an ideal example of the miraculous effects of a shift in environment. Not only was Phillis a "Negro," but a "Girl" as well, whose "singular genius" did "honour to her sex." As the "free Negro Girl" in Boston demonstrates, even the Africans brought to the British settlements expressly for slavery can transcend their condition within an ideal environment. Rush's solution to the problem of the fate of the slaves, once manumitted, reflects his concern for this crucial role of environment in shaping character. The matter will be resolved through literacy. The functions of literacy, and the role of the arts, are meant to be essential to the ascertaining of the nature of the African's "civilization" and, therefore, of the nature of the African. Too rooted in eternal verities to be labeled "romantic," Benjamin Rush nevertheless epitomizes a major reorientation of values in early American aesthetic theory, which in turn reflects the increased demand for the protection of "natural" rights as well as the marked secularization of the "equality" of man.

Perhaps because of the refreshingly novel terms in which Benjamin Rush had cast his brief against the enslavement of human beings, there is no little irony in the fact that a passing remark about the sanction by scripture of slavery[33] should have become the premise for a strident rebuttal of Rush's pamphlet. Richard Nisbet, "an emotionally unstable West Indian living in Pennsylvania who later turned to the Negro's defense and closed his life in tragic insanity,"[34] undertook "a defense of the West-Indian Planters" in a pamphlet published as a direct response to Rush's *Address*.

Published anonymously, *Slavery Not Forbidden by Scripture: Or, a Defense of the West Indian Planters*,[35] struck hard. After citing the Old Testament chapter and verse to reveal the scriptural sanction of slavery, Nisbet addresses Rush's contentions of innate African mental capacity.

In a remark, which he employs rhetorically to introduce in a long footnote David Hume's estimation of the national character of the blacks, Nisbet explicitly concedes Rush's suggestion that environment could affect "intellect."

> It is impossible to determine, with accuracy, whether their intellects or ours are superior, as individuals, no doubt, have not the same opportunities of improving as we have: However, on the whole, it seems probable, that they are a much inferior race of men to the whites, in every respect.[36]

Individual differences can be accounted for, Nisbet confesses, by "the same opportunities of improving." Yet, individual exceptions do not alter the balance: "on the whole," the Africans "are a much inferior race of men to the whites."

The debate, Nisbet proceeds, must be settled in terms of the "general character" of their "genius." Only here can it be ascertained fairly if their enslavement runs counter to "natural" law, since a biblical sanction is evident. The problem is one of exception and the rule:

> A few instances may be found, of African negroes possessing virtues and becoming ingenious; but still, what I have said, with regard to their general character, I dare say, most people acquainted with them, will agree. [Referring the reader to a footnote, in much the same manner and at the identical place in his argument as had Rush, Nisbet concludes that the author of the address gives a single example of a Negro girl writing a few silly poems to prove that the blacks are not inferior to whites in understanding.][37]

The blacks, unlike the remainder of the world's people of color, have, alone, failed to cut "a figure in history." Not only had the Africans failed visibly to make "a figure in history," they indeed had no history and, the "few silly poems" of a Negro girl in Boston notwithstanding, "no arts." The Africans' "natural rights," Nisbet concludes in a flourish, center on their place on the scale of nature, a place determined by their lack of "genius."

Nisbet's pamphlet demanded a rebuttal. Rush's *A Vindication of the Address, To the Inhabitants of the British Settlements, on the Slavery of the Negroes in America, In Answer to a Pamphlet,* appeared just as anonymously as had his and Nisbet's earlier essays.[38] Premise by premise, Rush redresses Nisbet's argument with traveler's accounts, eyewitness testimony of slave brutality, and even the direct quotation of the clergy. The subjective biases of European travelers, along with certain blatant barriers to the meaningful exchange of knowledge, make our knowledge of the Africans little more than a motley array of rumor and hearsay.

Despite the role of the observer in the recording of the "nature" of African civilizations, however, Rush outlines, in a brilliant summation, the fundamental premise on which all natural rights philosophy was based, as well as those elements by which the distinctions among men could be explained.

> Human nature is the same in all Ages and Countries; and all the difference we perceive in its Characters in respect to Virtue and Vice, Knowledge and Ignorance, may be accounted for from Climate, Country, Degrees of Civilization, form of Government, or other accidental causes.[39]

In a rather rhetorical flourish, Rush concludes his rebuttal of the "African Genius" by devoting four pages to exemplify the subjectivity of judgment and the relativity of meaning and value. His argument turns on the idea of an absolute and constant "human nature," one infinitely adaptable and plastic. Echoing Beattie's *Essay*, Rush contends that were we able to free ourselves of the prejudices of our point in history, then we would be free of the illusion of unbridgeable human differences and "distinctions" which are merely veiled appearances.

Rush's position on the exigencies of interpretation, on the role of the interpreter in the determination of meaning, was an unprecedented one in the American discourses on African aesthetics. His was a position rooted in the biological sciences, but rooted as well in the theory of those "rights" which were "natural" to man. For these "rights" to exist, they must be applicable to all varieties of man. To place the blacks "below" the whites because of "color" or "custom" was to abnegate the very concept of natural rights. The idea of hierarchy, in this sense, Rush implied, reflected the fiction of an unchanging universe, in which no demands were made of the past, and no more demands could be made against the prevailing order of society.[40] As the anonymous author of *Personal Slavery Established* attested on his title page, in a famous epigraph from Pope, "Whatever is, is right."[41]

Profoundly, Rush suggests that that which passes for visible indications of an uncommon humanity between the African and the European is merely a distinct relation each bears to "nature" and to "art." "Where is the difference," he asks, "between the African savage, whose scanty wants are supplied by Nature; and the European Nobleman, whose numerous wants are supplied by Art?"[42] Importantly, Rush viciously attacks the idea of using "genius" or "the arts" to measure man's place in nature; it is this which constitutes the ultimate hubris, because it is a crime against nature itself. Nisbet's hubris, Rush concludes with great passion, was "the Attack you have made upon the Rights of Mankind."[43]

Impassioned and detailed biblical exegeses, which for two and a half centuries had tried to fit the rapidly proliferating kinds of men into an order ordained by God; the wildly speculative natural philosophy which clung, rather perilously, to the metaphor of the chain; the bemused arrangements, by cranial capacity, of the "progressively" larger skulls of ape and man; the creative and imaginative descriptions of black humanity repeated with such enthusiasms by the European discoverers of Africa; and a received metaphorical system which had consistently made analogous the color black with the shade of evil—all these complex matters lay buried beneath the debate over the "natural rights" of the African and his fitness for enslavement. As surely as the temporalization of the chain of being had led eventually to its demise as a valid construct by which philosophy could account for the order of things, so, too, had the American colonists' fundamental belief in a quantity they could call "the rights of man" led them to declare a belief in the determining power of environment on the reshaping of "a" human nature which had to be, by definition, "everywhere the same."[44]

As crucial as the year 1773 proved to be to the American colonist's struggle for independence from the crown, it also proved to be the determining year for speculation of the Negro's place in nature as well as for the manner in which "the arts" were to figure in the debate over slavery, a debate no longer seriously thought to be resolvable by scripture. It is ironic that Phillis Wheatley, who so painstakingly located her poetry within a larger and peculiarly Puritan tradition of Christian piety, would have her slim volume of verse utilized as prima facie evidence in a fundamentally secular debate over the rights of man.

II

For reasons as various as they are complex, it would appear that, had Phillis Wheatley not published, another African slave's poetry would have served equally well as a refutation of certain commonly repeated assumptions of the nature of the Negro. Although the word would reappear in the reviews of Phillis's *Poems*, "genius" was not her province to occupy. The formal gap between Milton, Pope, Gray, Addison, Watts, and Wheatley would appear to be a profound gap, although she rather self-consciously assumed these as her models.[45]

Although viewers seem to have found much in her verse that is genuinely "poetic," her verse, "criticized" rarely, seems to have been "read" primarily in nonliterary terms and for other than literary purposes. The nature of the function Wheatley served between 1773 and 1831 can be described usefully but analogously by two tropes. Phillis and her *Poems* bore a relation of metaphor and metonymy in the language of the criticism her verse elicited. Metaphors of her "blackness"—a blackness both spiritual and physical—punctuate her critics' essays as they do her own poetry, as in "To Maecenas," for example, and in "On Being Brought From Africa to America,"[46] which was often quoted in the earliest reviews of her book.[47] When Bernard Romans,[48] writing about the "capacity" of the Africans to be other than slaves, terms Phillis a mere exception, the figure he utilizes to characterize her is that of "a Phaenix of her race," which bears a certain resonance to Phillis's own lines on the mutability of blackness:

> 'Twas mercy brought me from my *Pagan* land,
> Taught my benighted soul to understand

> That there's a God, that there's a *Saviour* too:
> Once I redemption neither sought nor knew.
> Some view our race with scornful eye,
> "Their Colour is a diabolic die."
> Remember, *Christians, Negroes,* black as *Cain,*
> May be refin'd, and join th'Angelic train.[49]

After 1831, however, the metaphorical functions Phillis is made to serve shift somewhat.[50]

Metonymically, however, her relation to the potential of other black people to assume "cultivation" remained consistent in critical writings well into the twentieth century, in part because of Jefferson's use of her as the written record of the sum total of the African's potential for "civilization," followed by the manifestly felt need of blacks and their sympathizers to refute Mr. Jefferson's claims.[51] Metonymically, Phillis bears a relation to "Africa" and to the mental capacity of all other African people in a manner remarkably similar to that which Aristotle and Alexander, Milton, and Newton bear to "the white race" in the tropes frequently repeated in the practical criticism of her work, and in numerous disquisitions on the "nature" of the Negro.[52] It would not be incorrect to characterize the relation of Phillis Wheatley to "the black race" and the relation of her *Poems* to "black art" as a relation of synechdoche.[53] Because the history of the criticism of the poetry of slaves and ex-slaves, published in English between 1773 and 1831, is in large part the history of the critical reception of Phillis Wheatley, a short reading of her poetry could be of sufficient relevance to sustain a digression from an explication of her critics' judgments.

That Phillis Wheatley's verse could become cited so frequently as "the" example of the mental and aesthetic "capacity" of the African slave can be explained somewhat by the curious circumstances of her enslavement in Africa as well as by the condition of her servitude to Mr. and Mrs. John Wheatley of Boston.[54] Perhaps because of the extensive citations of her achievement and her poetry by both ardent supporters and opponents of racial slavery, the Wheatley scholarship is rather extensive, although her biographical "facts" are more highly refined than is the criticism of her verse.[55]

After 1770, Phillis's own history, except for accounts of her trip to London in 1773,[56] her tragic marriage to John Peters in 1778, and her untimely death in 1784,[57] has been the history of her publications, a history as curious as her biography. In 1770, Phillis published a broadside in Boston called *An Elegiac Poem, on the Death of that Celebrated Divine, and eminent Servant of Jesus Christ, the late Reverend, and pious George Whitefield, Chaplain to the Right Honourable the Countess of Huntingdon.* The poem was published in the *Massachusetts Spy* on October 11, 1770, and was republished in 1770—once in Newport, four times again in Boston, once in New York, and once in Philadelphia.[58] Phillis's broadside was appended the following year to Ebenezer Pemberton's *Heaven the Residence of Saints.*[59] As Mason rightly concludes, the *Elegiac Poem's* "several reprintings gave Phillis her first fame as a poet."[60]

A recurrent suggestion has been that Wheatley remained aloof from matters that were in any sense "racial," or, more correctly, "positively" racial.[61] Although much of the misreading[62] of Wheatley must certainly arise from a blatant unfamiliarity with the conventions of neoclassical verse as well as with the various forms of the elegy she used, there is another reason Phillis's verse has suffered sophisticated critical neglect. As William H. Robinson demonstrates rather passionately, there exists no edition of her "complete" works; further, "until 1935 perhaps no more than 12 or 14 of Phillis's poems had been anthologized in excerpted and complete versions,"[63] a remarkable statistic considering the extensive amount of "criticism" devoted to Wheatley since 1773. Although variants of her *Poems* have been reprinted frequently, they remain incomplete and inconsistent, as in the reprinting of her signature piece, "On the Death of the Rev. Mr. George Whitefield," in the 1770 Boston broadside and in the 1773 American edition of the *Poems.* The 1770 broadside contains sixty-two lines, the 1773 American edition, found in *Poems,* contains forty-seven lines. Another broadside version, likely published in London in 1771, contains sixty-four lines, including the otherwise deleted word "free" in reference to the relations between the "Impartial Saviour" and "ye Africans":

> Take him, ye Wretched, for your only Good;
> Take him, ye hungry Souls, to be your Food;
> Take him, ye Thirsty, for your cooling Stream;
> Ye Preachers, take him for your joyful Theme;
> Take him, my dear *Americans,* he said,
> Be your Complaints in his kind Bosom laid;
> Take him, ye *Africans,* he longs for you,
> Impartial Saviour is his Title due.
> If you will walk in Grace's heavenly Road,
> He'll make you free, and Kings, and Priests to God.[64]

In addition to errors of this sort, in the sixty published poems and twenty-two extant letters, there exist a number of apparently overlooked poems and letters in which Phillis Wheatley discusses the horrors of racial slavery and reveals, to a surprising degree, the quality of concern she felt for "Africans," which certainly cannot be said to be diminished by her affiliation to the idea of Christian beneficience and, always for Phillis, its concomitant, the "way of true felicity."[65] These poems include "To the University of Cambridge, in New England" [1767], "An Address to the Deist"—[1767], "America" [1768–1770][66] and especially "To Maecenas," the first title in her *Poems.* Here Phillis queries the Muse about the relation of the poet and poetry to "*Afric's* sable race":

Not you, my Friend, these plaintive strains become,
Not you, whose bosom is the *Muses* home;
When they from tow'ring *Helicon* retire,
They fan in you the bright immortal fire,
But less happy, cannot raise the song,
The fault-ring music dies upon my tongue.
The happier *Terence* all the choir inspir'd,
His soul replenished, and his bosom fir'd;
But say, ye Muses, why this partial grace,
To one alone of *Afric's* sable race;
From age to age transmitting thus his name
With the first glory in the rolls of fame?[67]

Similarly, her "Reply" to "The Answer" to Phillis's poem, "To a Gentleman in the Navy,"[68] demonstrates an uncommon amount of emotion for her "Afric's blissful plain":

In fair description are thy powers displayed
In artless grottos, and the sylvan shade;
Charm'd with thy painting, how my bosom burns!
And pleasing Gambia on my soul returns,
With native grace in spring's luxuriant reign,
Smiles the gay mead, and Eden blooms again,
The various bower, the tuneful flowing stream,
The soft retreats, the lovers golden dream,
Her soil spontaneous, yields exhaustless stores;
For phoebus revels on her verdant shores.
Whose flowery births, a fragrant train appear,
And crown the youth throughout the smiling year,
There, as in Britain's favour'd isle, behold
The bending harvest ripen into gold!
Just are thy views of Afric's blissful plain,
On the warm limits of the land and main.
Pleas'd with the theme, see sportive fancy play,
In realms devoted to the God of day![69]

Phillis Wheatley shared her antislavery sentiment in a compelling letter to Samuel Occom, the famous Mohegan Indian Presbyterian preacher,[70] who that same year published *A Choice Collection of Hymns and Spiritual Songs*. This letter was written to Occom in Boston on February 11, 1774, and published in *The Massachusetts Spy* on March 24, 1774, the *Boston Post Boy* on March 21, 1774, the *Providence, Rhode Island Gazette*, on March 26, 1774, and the *Connecticut Journal* on April 1, 1774.[71] A headnote from the editors attest that they "are desired to insert [the letter] as a Specimen of her Ingenuity."[72] The letter is a subtle and controlled but passionate and eloquent address on the sheer evil of racial slavery:

> I have this Day received your obliging kind Epistle, and am greatly satisfied with your Reasons respecting the Negroes, and think highly reasonable what you offer in Vindication of their Natural Rights: Those that invade them cannot be insensible that the divine Light is chasing away the thick Darkness which broods over the Land of Africa; and the Chaos which has reign'd so long, is converting into beautiful Order, and reveals more and more clearly, the glorious Dispensation of civil and religious Liberty, which are so inseperably united, that there is little or no Enjoyment of one without the other: Otherwise, perhaps the Israelites had been less solicitous for their Freedom from Egyptian Slavery; I don't say they would have been contented without it, by no means, for in every human Breast God has implanted a Principle, which we call the love of Freedom; it is impatient of Oppresion, and pants for Deliverance; and by the Leave of our modern Egyptians I will assert that the same Principle lives in us. God grant Deliverance in his own Way and Time, and get him honor upon all those whose Avarice impels them to countenance and help forward the Calamities of their fellow Creatures. This I desire not for their Hurt, but to convince them of the strange Absurdity of their Conduct whose Words and Actions are so diametrically opposite. How well the cry for Liberty, and the reverse Disposition for the exercise of oppressive Power over others agree,—I humbly think it does not require the Penetration of a Philosopher to determine.

For "what" reasonable being, Phillis asks, could hold in mind any doubt that slavery is evil incarnate: the matter is as simple as that.

The letter to Occom, and a few others,[73] when considered with the poems in which Wheatley does address "Africa" or "Africans," suggests strongly that the nature of Wheatley's poetry remains to be ascertained, as does her role in Afro-American literary history, and even her "nonrole" as a poet of "racial sentiment."

Imitating Pope in rhythm and meter Phillis wrote in decasyllabic lines of closed heroic couplets. There is much use of invocation, hyperbole, inflated ornamentation, and an overemphasis of personification all of which characterize neoclassical poetry.

Seventeen or one third of her extant poems are elegies, fourteen of which appeared in the first edition of *Poems on Various Subjects, Religious and Moral,* five of which have been revised from earlier published elegies. In one of the few close readings of Phillis Wheatley's verse, Gregory Rigsby[74] demonstrates conclusively that Phillis's elegies are a creative variation of the "English Elegy" and the "Puritan Elegy."[75] Wheatley's elegies are threnodic, after the fashion of the "Renaissance Elegy," in that they are meant "to praise the subject, to lament the death, and to comfort the bereaved."[76] Yet, they are "Medieval" rather than "Elizabethan"[77] insofar as they prefer a sublime resignation to an unrestrained death-force, and seem to avoid the protest against it.[78] The medieval resignation toward death, coupled with the function of the "Renaissance Elegy,"[79] and the form of the threnody as it developed in

Elizabethan poetry, were fused together in the "Puritan Funeral Elegy," a form peculiar to colonial America.

The Puritan funeral elegy, in turn, derived its specific shape and tone from the early American funeral sermon, based as it was on energetic exhortation.[80] But, as Rigsby argues, Wheatley utilized the triple function of the Renaissance elegy within "her own elegiac structure and established more elaborate conventions."[81] Rigsby then identifies these elements to be the underlying "structure of a Wheatley elegy": (1) the deceased in Heaven; (2) the deceased "winging" his way to Heaven: (3) an appreciation of the deceased's work on earth; (4) seraphic strains of heavenly bliss; (5) consolation of the living; (6) exhortation.[82] The identification of the conventions of her elegies indicates that Wheatley was an "imaginative" artist to a degree largely unrecognized in critical literature. Although her remaining occasional verse lacks the irony, the contrast, and the balance of Pope's poetry, which she cited as her conscious model, her critical reception since the eighteenth century has failed in a remarkably consistent way to read her verse in comparison with the various literary traditions which she so obviously attempted to imitate and by which she just as obviously sought to measure herself. Curiously, all of her extant poems, except five, utilize the heroic couplet.[83] Vernon Loggins traces, albeit vaguely, the influence of Milton in her hymns to morning and evening,[84] as well as in her poem to General Lee,[85] as he does Gray's influence on her elegy to Whitefield and Addison and Watt's presence in "Ode to Neptune" and "Hymn to Humanity."[86] But these, again, are suggestions of influence rather than practical criticism.

As William Cairns recognized as early as 1912, the criticism of Phillis Wheatley's poetry has been a matter centered primarily around exactly what the existence of the poeisis faculty signifies about a far more problematical inquiry. Phillis Wheatley's verses, Cairns writes,

> are good conventional work in the forms then popular, devoid of originality, but really remarkable considering the history of the author. That they have been remembered is partly due, however, to the fact that in the days of the abolitionists they were often cited to prove the intellectual capability of the negro.[87]

The peculiar history of the author's reception by critics has, ironically enough, largely determined the theory of the criticism of the creative writings of Afro-Americans from the eighteenth century to the present time.

Notes

1. *Daily Advertiser,* January 18, 1773, p. 1.

2. Samuel Estwick, *Considerations on the Negro Cause, Commonly So Called* (London: J. Dodsley, 1772), p. 1.

3. *Daily Advertiser,* January 18, 1773, p. 1.

4. Samuel Estwick, *Consideration on the Negro Cause Commonly So Called, Addressed to the Right Honourable Lord Mansfield, Chief Justice of the Court of King's Bench;* 2nd. ed. (London: J. Dodsley, 1773); subsequent references will be to this edition.

5. Estwick.

6. David Hume, cited in Estwick, p. 77.

7. Estwick.

8. Estwick, p. 78.

9. Estwick.

10. Estwick.

11. Estwick.

12. Estwick, pp. 80–81.

13. See esp. R. S. Crane, "English neo-classical criticism," in *Dictionary of World Literature,* ed. J. T. Shipley (N.Y.: Philosophical 1943); R. S. Crane, ed., *Critics and Criticism, Ancient and Modern* (Chicago: Univ. of Chicago Press, 1952); R. S. Crane, "On Writing the History of English Criticism, 1650–1800," *University of Toronto Quarterly,* 22 (1953), 376–91.

14. Robert Marsh, "Neo-classical Poetics," in *Princeton Encyclopedia of Poetry and Poetics,* ed. Alex Preminger (Princeton: Princeton Univ. Press, 1974), p. 560; cf. Crane, "On Writing the History of English Criticism, 1650–1800," pp. 380–82.

15. See William Temple, "Upon Poetry," in *Critical Essays of the Seventeenth Century,* ed. J. E. Spingarn (Oxford: Oxford Univ. Press, 1908–09), III, 104–05.

16. Rene Wellek, *A History of Modern Criticism: 1750–1950* (London: Jonathan Cape, 1970), pp. 124–25. Temple's correction is to be found in his essay "Upon Poetry" written in 1690; see note 15.

17. Joseph Wharton, *Essay on the Writings and Genius of Pope* (London, 1756), I, 5.

18. Oliver Goldsmith, *An Enquiry into the Present State of Polite Learning* (London: R. & J. Dodsley, 1759), p. 95. In subsequent editions, Goldsmith deleted the whole of this chapter (7). Cf. his article in the *Critical Review*, 9 (1760), 10–19.

19. David Hume, *Essays: Moral, Political, and Literary,* ed. T. H. Green and T. H. Gross, 2 vols. (London: Longmans, 1875), I, 252.

20. Henry Home Kames, *Sketches of a History of Man* (Edinburgh: Creech, 1774), I, 12.

21. Robert Wood, *An Essays on the Original Genius and Writings of Homer* (London: T. Payne & E. Elmsly, 1775), p. 15.

22. Robert Lowth, *De Sacra poesi Hebraeorum* (Oxford: E. Typographeo Clarendoniano, 1753); an English translation appeared in 1787.

23. Cf. Winthrop Jordan's discussion of "Environmentalism and Revolutionary Ideology" in *White Over Black: American Attitudes Towards the Negro*, 1550–1812 (Chapel Hill: Univ. of North Carolina Press, 1968), pp. 287–94.

24. Jordan, p. 288.

25. Jordan, p. 289.

26. James Otis, *The Rights of the British Colonies Asserted and Proved* (Boston: Edes & Gill, 1764), p. 29.

27. John Wesley, *Thoughts Upon Slavery* (Philadelphia: Joseph Cruckshank, 1774), p. 47.

28. Levi Hart, *Liberty Described and Recommended* (Hartford: Eben Watson, 1775), p. 16.

26. [David Cooper], *A Serious Address to the Rulers of America, on the Inconsistency of Their Conduct Respecting Slavery* (Trenton: J. Phillips, 1783), pp. 12–13.

30. Rush here cites "le Poivre," referring obviously to [Pierre Le Poivre], *Travels of a Philosopher: Or, Observation on the Manners and Arts of Various Nations in Africa and Asia . . . Translated from the French of M. Le Poivre* (London: T. Becket, 1769).

31. *The Spectator,* Vol. 1, no. 11, contains a summary, from Lign's *Account of Barbados,* of the legendary "History of Inkle and Yarico," pp. 49–51.

32. Rush, *An Address,* p. 4.

33. Rush, *An Address,* p. 10.

34. Winthrop Jordan, *White Over Black*, p. 306. On Nisbet's mental health, see Samuel Coates, *Notebook on Cases on Insanity,* Medical Library of the Pennsylvania Hospital, Philadelphia; *The Autobiography of Benjamin Rush,* ed. George Corner (Princeton: Princeton Univ. Press, 1948), p. 83n.

35. [Richard Nisbet], *Slavery Not Forbidden by Scripture; Or, a Defence of the West India Planters, By a West Indian* (Philadelphia: John Dunlap, 1773).

36. [Nisbet], only p. 21.

37. [Nisbet], p. 23.

38. [Benjamin Rush], *A Vindication of the Address, To the Inhabitants of the British Settlements, on the Slavery of Negroes in America in answer to a Pamphlet entitled, "Slavery Not Forbidden by Scripture; Or a Defence of the West-India Planters from the Aspersions thrown against them by the author of the Address." By a Pennsylvanian* (Philadelphia: John Dunlap, 1773).

39. [Rush], *A Vindication,* pp. 24–25.

40. Cf. Loren Eisley, "Race: the reflections of a biological historian," in *Science and the Concept of Race,* ed. Margaret Mead (New York: Columbia Univ. Press, 1968), p. 84.

41. *Personal Slavery Established, By the Suffrages of Custom and Right Reason. Being a Full Answer to the gloomy and visonary Reveries, of all the fantical and enthusiastical Writers on that Subject* (Philadelphia: John Dunlap, 1773), title page.

42. [Rush], *A Vindication,* p. 31.

43. [Rush], *A Vindication,* p. 53.

44. Cf. Anthony Benezet, letter to the archbishop of Canterbury (1758), in "Letters of Anthony Benezet," *Journal of Negro History,* 2 (January, 1917), 83.

45. See Gregory Rigsby, "Form and Content in Phillis Wheatley's Elegies," *CLA Journal,* 30, No. 2 (December, 1975), 248–57. See *The Poems of Phillis Wheatley,* ed. Julian Mason (Chapel Hill: Univ. of North Carolina Press, 1966), pp. xxii–xxvi; hereafter cited as Mason.

46. Mason, pp. 3–4, 7.

47. See *Philip Vickers Fithian: Journal and Letters 1767–1774,* ed. John R. Williams, (Princeton: Princeton Univ. Press, 1900), p. 119; *Universal Magazine,* September, 1773, p. 153.

48. Bernard Romans, *A Concise Natural History of East and West Florida,* 2 vols. (New York, 1775), I, 105.

49. Wheatley, *Poems,* p. 7; *Universal Magazine,* September, 1773.

50. See the review of B. B. Thatcher's *Memoir of Phillis Wheatley, A Native African and a Slave* (Boston: Geo. W. Light, 1834), in *The Liberator,* March 22, 1834.

51. Indeed, perhaps the most sustained impulse in the history of the criticism of Afro-American creative writing has been the determination to dismiss Jefferson as a "racist." See Henry Louis Gates, Jr., "Preface to Blackness: Text and Pre-Text," in *The Reconstruction of Instruction,* ed. Robert Burns Stepto and Dexter Fisher (Urbana: Univ. of Illinois Press, 1978).

52. See, e.g., "Article VII," *Monthly Review,* 49 (July–December, 1773), 457–58;

Richard Nisbet, *The Capacity of Negroes*, p. 3; Thomas Jefferson, "Notes on the State of Virginia, Query XIV," in *Thomas Jefferson: Revolutionary Philosopher*, ed. John S. Pancake (Woodbury, N.Y.: Barron's Educational Series, 1976), pp. 308–14.

53. As I hope to demonstrate implicitly, the figure of metaphor and mentonym blur when utilized consistently to describe one phenomenon.

54. Except when indicated otherwise, the biographical details of Phillis's life come directly from the memoir written by Margaretta Matilda Odell for the 1834 reprinting of the 1773 edition of *Poems on Various Subjects, Religious and Moral;* see Margaretta Matilda Odell, "Memoir," in *Memoir and Poems of Phillis Wheatley* (Boston: Geo. W. Light, 1834), pp. 9–29. See also William H. Robinson, *Phillis Wheatley in the Black American Beginnings* (Detroit: Broadside Press, 1975), passim; Mason, pp. xi–xlviii; M. A. Richmond, *Bid The Vassal Soar* (Washington, D.C.: Howard Univ. Press, 1974), passim; Nathaniel B. Shurtleff, "Phillis Wheatley, the Negro Slave Poet," *Boston Daily Advertiser*, December 21, 1863, rpt. *Proceedings of the Massachusetts Historical Society*, 7 (1863–64), p. 9.

55. As Benjamin Brawley suggested in 1918, "the bibliography of the works of Phillis Wheatley is now a study in itself" (*The Negro in Literature and Art* [New York: Duffield, 1918], p. 161).

56. See William H. Robinson, "Phillis Wheatley in London," *CLA Journal*, 21, No. 2 (December, 1977), 187–202.

57. See Mason, pp. xv–xvi.

58. Dorothy Porter, "Early American Negro Writings: A Bibliographical Study," *PBSA*, 39 (3rd Quarter, 1945), 261–63.

59. Ebenezer Pemberton, *Heaven the Residence of Saints* (London: E. & C. Dilly, 1771), App.

60. Mason, p. 67.

61. See Seymour Gross and John E. Hardy, eds., *Images of the Negro in American Literature* (Chicago: Univ. of Chicago Press, 1966), pp. 3–4; LeRoi Jones, *Home: Social Essays* (New York: William Morrow, 1966), pp. 105–06; Addison Gayle, Jr., "The Function of Black Literature at the Present Time," in *Black Aesthetic* (New York: Doubleday, 1971), p. 409; Nathaniel Huggins, *The Harlem Renaissance* (New York: Oxford Univ. Press, 1971), p. 199.

62. I mean here "misinformed" reading and not the Bloomian sense of that term.

63. Robinson, *Phillis Wheatley*, p. 47.

64. Quoted in Robinson, *Phillis Wheatley*, pp. 40–41.

65. Phillis Wheatley to Arbour Tanner, Boston, May 19, 1772, in Nathaniel Shurtleff, "Phillis Wheatley, the Negro Slave Poet," *Proceedings of the Massachusetts Historical Society*, 7 (1863–64), 273–74.

66. First printed in Robert C. Kuncio, "Some Unpublished Poems of Phillis Wheatley," *New England Quarterly*, 43 (June, 1970), 288–90.

67. Kuncio.

68. *Royal American Magazine*, 1 (December, 1774), 473–74; 2 (January, 1775), 34–35.

69. *Royal American Magazine*, pp. 34–35.

70. See Harold Blodgett, *Samson Occum* (Hanover: Dartmouth College Publications, 1935), pp. 119, 148; and Kenneth Silverman, "Four New Letters by Phillis Wheatley," *Early American Literature*, 8 (Winter, 1974), 259.

71. *Connecticut Journal*, April 1, 1774, p. 1.

72. *Connecticut Journal*.

73. Cf. Phillis Wheatley to the Reverend Samuel Hopkins, Boston, February 9, 1774; in Benjamin Quarles "A Phillis Wheatley Letter," *Journal of Negro History*, 24 (1949), 463–64;

Boston, May 6, 1774, in Chamberlain Collection of Letters, A.6. 20, Boston Public Library; and Wheatley to Arbour Tanner, Boston, May 19, 1772, in *Proceedings*, 7 (1863–64), 273–74.

74. Rigsby, pp. 248–57.

75. Rigsby, p. 248.

76. Rigsby.

77. J. C. Bailey develops this distinction in *English Elegies* (London: John Lane, 1900), p. xxix.

78. Bailey.

79. Cf. A. L. Bennett, "The Principal Rhetorical Conventions in the Renaissance Personal Elegy," *Studies in Philology*, 51 (1954), 107–26.

80. Robert Henson, "Form and Content of the Puritan Funeral Elegy," *American Literature*, 32 (1960), 111.

81. Rigsby, 250.

82. Rigsby.

83. These five include "On Virtue," which she wrote in free verse but ended with an heroic couplet; "To the University of Cambridge in New England," written in blank verse; "Ode to Neptune," composed in three stanzas of six lines each, four of which are in iambic tetrameter couplets, followed consistently by an heroic couplet; "Hymn to Humanity," written in six stanzas of six lines each, and each stanza following a form of iambic tetrameter couplet, followed by a line of iambic trimeter, followed by an iambic tetrameter couplet, followed again by an iambic trimeter line which, invariably, rhymes with the third line of the stanza; and "A Farewell to America," in ballad stanza. Cf. Mason, p. xxix.

84. Loggins, *The Negro Author* (New York: Columbia Univ. Press, 1931), p. 24.

85. Loggins, p. 27.

86. Loggins, p. 373, n. 75; cf. Mason, p. xxxiii.

87. William B. Cairns, *A History of American Literature* (New York: Oxford Univ. Press, 1930), p. 136.

88. David Hume, quoted in Estwick, p. 78n.

INDEX